DISASTER
Major
American
Catastrophes

DISASTER

MAJOR
AMERICAN
CATASTROPHES

by A. A. Hoehling

HAWTHORN BOOKS, INC.
PUBLISHERS / *New York*

DISASTER: MAJOR AMERICAN CATASTROPHES

1 2 3 4 5 6 7 8 9 10

Contents

Introduction

One is never really prepared for disaster, whether in peacetime or in war. The United States armed forces, with all of their emergency plans, antiaircraft defenses, fighter planes, and the combined firepower of a major portion of the Pacific Fleet, were dealt a paralyzing surprise blow on December 7, 1941. Pearl Harbor would become a dreadful kind of "classic" in unpreparedness. Few people had really believed that the Japanese could or would do such a thing, but they did, and the United States was in World War II.

In October, 1871, no one thought that Chicago could be reduced to ashes, but it was. The fire department was considered adequate for the time. There was water to spare from the dual reservoirs of Lake Michigan and the Chicago River. The summer, however, had been exceptionally dry, a fact that seemed to have been overlooked. Whether, as legend would have it, Mrs. Catherine O'Leary's cow kicked over a lantern in a South Side barn or, as reporters then wrote, the fire had started in a wood-planing mill didn't matter. When the flames finally smoldered out, most of the midwestern hub of 300,000 inhabitants had been incinerated. One had to be thankful that no more than 250 had perished. The same week, as a matter of fact, some four times that number died in Wisconsin timberland fires.

In 1871 fireproof or even fire-retardant construction did not enliven a builder's lexicon, and some decades would pass before it did.

"Natural" disasters may take a populace even more by surprise. The Signal Service (forebear of the Weather Bureau) lacked the meteorological experience, precise instruments, and availability of rapid communications to predict the great blizzard of 1888 that congealed New

York City to an icy halt. No one then could have done much about the freak of nature, even if he had known it was coming, except perhaps to remain at home. The immense storm claimed nearly twice the number of lives as the Chicago fire.

The flood at Johnstown, Pennsylvania, a foundry and mining community seventy-eight miles east of Pittsburgh, on May 31, 1889, was spawned by an unfortunate coupling of rampaging nature and man's inadequacy. Incessant rains piled up the waters pressing on the dam at South Fork, eighteen miles upriver, until it gave way, resulting in the Conemaugh River's rising thirty-six feet in five minutes and washing most of Johnstown away. The waters with the resultant fire in the debris caused the deaths of 2,200, and possibly more, of the city's 30,000 residents.

Fire in the Iroquois Theater, Chicago, during a matinee of *Mr. Blue Beard*, a musical comedy, five days after Christmas, 1903, had been about the last possibility in the minds of the audience of two thousand, mostly women and children. The theater, the largest in Chicago, was new and sturdily built and had an asbestos curtain. All in all, the building seemed so safe that there wasn't any "crash" plan for emergencies.

When a short-circuited calcium footlight ignited the tassles of draperies, smoke combined with panic to take the lives of 602 persons. Many suffocated in a hopeless bottleneck at the common passageway for the second and third balconies. Although the theater had thirty exits, none was clearly marked, some were locked (at least one of them on both sides), others were jammed, and it was too late by the time all were found, opened, or battered down.

An exit problem was also responsible for the deaths of 491 persons when the Cocoanut Grove nightclub in Boston caught fire nearly forty years later, on a Saturday night in November, 1942. Again, the patrons couldn't get out. The owners of public places appeared to have learned nothing from the Iroquois Theater catastrophe.

In February, 1904, a bulging swath of Baltimore's business section —140 acres—representing 1,343 buildings was leveled by fire. At least 2,500 firms were put out of business, but there was, fortunately, no loss of life. The major East Coast port had fallen victim to carelessness— the dropping of a cigarette, it was theorized—and again there was disbelief that the conflagration could have gained such headway. Fire departments from as far away as Washington, D.C., and Wilmington,

Delaware, moved their teams in on railroad flatcars. Dynamite was employed. Still, the conflagration did not burn itself out until almost two days after the first flare.

Two years later, in April, 1906, fire again finished off a city—San Francisco—after an earthquake had triggered the process of destruction. Following earlier quakes, including an especially severe one in 1868, the city perched astride the San Andreas fault had gone on a construction boom, setting up all kinds of structures, especially tall brick buildings that could, and did, topple like card houses. The constructors had learned nothing. That no more than 452 were believed to have perished in the quake was in itself a miracle. In addition, the presence of many army troops from the Presidio, under command of Brigadier General Frederick Funston, hero of the Philippine Insurrection, helped to avert panic. In this case dynamiting proved effective. The story has become a sort of legend, and no child can pass through the elementary grades without hearing it.

If in these varied disasters any common linkage can be found or attributed, it would be in the abrupt shattering of routines and dreams of the future. For thousands of human beings, life could never again be picked up quite where it left off, but the survivors try. There is always a will, if not necessarily a way, as illustrated by this conversation after a recent southern flood between a Red Cross worker and a woman who asked only for a couple of mattresses:

"What are you going to put them on?" the worker asked.

"The floor."

"Isn't it covered with mud?"

"Yes," the woman replied.

"Can you cook there?"

"I could if I had a little hot plate. The stove's ruint."

"Do you have any electric power?"

"No."

"Do you have water?"

"No, the pump is out, and there's no water and no plumbing."

"Well, how will you eat if you stay there?"

"We could drive twelve miles over to my boy's house. He will feed us."

"Can you stay at your boy's house?"

"That's where we've been staying ever since the flood."

"Isn't it drier and more comfortable for you than trying to stay in a wet, muddy house with no power and no water?"

"Yes, but I want to get home. If I can just get home, I'll feel better."

The worker explained that the Red Cross could give her mattresses but didn't want to give her pneumonia. The woman left, saying she'd have the place cleaned right up and would be back for the mattresses.

In the decade ending in 1970 the American Red Cross paid out a record $146,000,000.

To attempt to define, much less codify, a "major disaster" is a challenge that no less an entity than the United States Government would likely accept. In 1970 a federal relief act established a "major disaster" as follows:

> . . . any hurricane, tornado, storm, flood, high water, wind-driven water, tidal wave, earthquake, drought, fire, or other catastrophe in any part of the United States, which, in the determination of the President, is or threatens to be of sufficient severity and magnitude to warrant disaster assistance by the Federal Government to supplement the efforts and available resources of States, local governments, and relief organizations in alleviating the damage, loss, hardship, or suffering caused thereby. . . .

Coordinating the help between the Federal Government and other governments and organizations is the Office of Emergency Preparedness (O.E.P.), a function of the executive branch of the United States Government. In fiscal 1971, according to O.E.P., there were nineteen major disasters, for which $164,000,000 was drawn from the President's relief fund. Here, however, the interpretation of "disaster" can be very broad indeed, in the determination of which political considerations cannot be wholly overlooked.

The purpose of this book is not to catalog all major disasters, nor to dwell upon horror for horror's sake, and surely not to reawaken hurt within living memory. Except for the draft riots of 1863, this study is a focus on certain disasters of the twentieth century—how they happened and how they were resolved. They are measured by varying yardsticks and not necessarily by the count in human lives.

The subjects of the thirteen chapters of this book, with one exception, were major newsmakers of the times. The coal-mine explosion in

Monongah, West Virginia, in 1907 was the exception, although it remains the worst such disaster of its kind. Although it loosened the pens
of some compassionate editorial writers, the populace as a whole at
the turn of the century thought of mining as the dangerous labor that it
was and was hardened to mass deaths.

This narrative, above all, is the story of people and their reactions
under types of challenge that are not apt to occur in the lifetime of the
average person.

From lightning and tempest; from earthquake, fire and flood; from plague, pestilence and famine; from battle and murder and from sudden death. . . . Good Lord deliver us.

—*The Litany*, The Book of Common Prayer, according to use of the Protestant Episcopal Church in the United States

DISASTER

*Major
American
Catastrophes*

1

The Draft
Riots, 1863

It has never been fully determined how the draft riot came to be organized—if it was—or who might have been the organizer. There was no doubt, however, that a mob numbering at its ultimate between five thousand and ten thousand men, women, and adolescents—stirred to "a perfect frenzy of rage"—held the greater portion of Manhattan captive for three days in July, 1863, smashing, burning, looting, and murdering.

With the pick of the reportorial staffs of the area's many dailies off with the armies, this major story of how the nation's largest city was brought to its knees was also among the most poorly covered of the Civil War. To this day, facts, figures, and motivating impulses remain clouded with blank spaces and contradictions.

The basic dissatisfaction, it was quite apparent, could have been inspired by the conscription act, aimed at furnishing an additional 300,000 men for the Federal armies, belatedly passed by Congress in March, 1863, a year after the Confederacy itself had reluctantly acknowledged the same necessity. This measure was less than perfect, filled with loopholes and inequities, and quite possibly, as the coup de grace, it was unconstitutional. Easily the most disastrous and questionable loophole provided that an unmarried man between the ages of twenty and forty-five or a married man between the ages of twenty and thirty-five could become legally exempt by furnishing someone to serve in his place or by paying three hundred dollars to the federal treasury.

The exemption hit the immigrant worker the hardest. Newly arrived, he existed on a quasi-poverty level and held scant hopes of ever raising the munificent sum of three hundred dollars in one lump at one time. New York, as a principal funnel port from Europe, maintained the greatest proportion of such new citizens or potential citizens, with the Irish predominating. Their young men, with no inherent interest in the War of the Rebellion or its causes, believed that conscription discriminated against them, just as though it had been intended that way.

This July of 1863 should have brought heart and hope to the North and all who lived there. The fighting at Gettysburg had ended on July 3, with General Robert E. Lee's army broken and routed. On July 4, far to the west, General Ulysses S. Grant accepted the surrender of Vicksburg, Mississippi, and the Mississippi River was opened to the Gulf of Mexico, or, as Abraham Lincoln saw it, "The Father of Waters again goes unvexed to the sea." Although the Confederacy's desperate northern invasion had been broken in the Pennsylvania hills, the President was less than pleased with Major General George Gordon Mead's failure to capture an army, as had the aggressive Grant.

In spite of the personal patriotisms within the volunteer regiments, which seemed finally to be winning the "War for the Union," there remained many Northerners who sympathized with secession and others who, at best, disagreed with the abolitionists. Horatio Seymour, the scholarly appearing Democratic governor of New York State, was not precisely in either category, but he was convinced of the illegality of the draft law as written. He had joined the New York City's Republican mayor, George Opdyke, a not particularly forceful leader, in asking Washington to suspend conscription until some more equitable procedure could be promulgated. Both men at least knew their constituents.

Seymour also evinced concern for the New York militia's ability to protect life and property, most of the effective members having been sent to Pennsylvania to hold Lee's powerful if futile thrust to the north. He had expressed the opinion that "one thousand men could have seized the forts" and other municipal strongpoints. In this belief he was seconded by Major General John E. Wool, commanding the Military Department of the East, who, in fact, had written the governor on June 30, as follows:

Allow me to call your attention to the defenseless condition
of this city. I have only 550 men to garrison eight forts.
One-half of these cannot be called artillerists, having been im-
perfectly instructed. . . . I have called the attention of the mayor
as well as others again and again.

For a teeming city of 900,000 souls, the protection at hand did seem
rudimentary.

Wool, in his eightieth year, could reflect upon a long career that
encompassed the War of 1812 as well as the Mexican War. He had held
Fortress Monroe after the Confederates seized Norfolk, the Federal
Naval Base, and much of the Hampton Roads area at the time of the
Monitor and *Merrimac* duel. The fact remained, however, that the old
soldier was well past retirement.

In spite of official concerns in New York, the draft was ordered to
commence, the final realization of which, according to *Leslie's Illustrated Weekly*, fell "like a thunderclap on the people."

One of the lottery places for the selection of draftees—this one for the
Ninth Congressional District—was in the Provost Marshal General's
offices, a common-enough three-story brownstone at 677 Third Avenue,
on the corner of Forty-sixth Street, not far from the present Tudor City.
Its quota was fifteen hundred men, and the drawing began on Saturday,
July 11, under the scrutiny of the provost, Captain Charles E. Jenkins.
The procedure involved a wheel and a drum, containing the names. By
evening the remarkable number of 1,236 names had been selected.
Reporters returned to their newspapers, and the board closed down for
the Sabbath.

This same Sunday, July 12, was not, however, observed in all areas
of Manhattan with uniformly humble spirit. It was quite noticeable to
the patrolmen of Police Superintendent John A. Kennedy's force that
there were "rumblings" among little groups of laborers who had been
forming, wandering off, and then re-forming along the East River all
day. Their fluctuating composition, according to Anna Dickinson, a
writer and lecturer on antislavery, temperance, and women's rights,
numbered "railroad employes, workers in machine shops, and a vast
crowd of those who lived by preying on others: thieves, pimps, professional ruffians, the scum of the city, jailbirds or those who were running
with swift feet to enter the prison doors."

Whether or not their morals were so debased, Superintendent Kennedy was convinced that something was in the wind. He alerted his thirty-two precincts, especially his lieutenants such as James Crowley, superintendent of the police telegraph bureau, as well as John Decker, chief engineer of the fire department. He advised Thomas Acton, president of the Board of Police Commissioners, Mayor Opdyke, and the governor's office. The governor, who usually spent more time in the city than in Albany, the capital, was visiting friends in New Brunswick, New Jersey. The police chief also contacted Major General Charles W. Sandford, head of the First New York State Militia.

Thus passed a sultry, portentous Sunday night. For the police superintendent it was a sleepless one as his subordinates scurried back and forth to his house with periodic reports, none of them comforting. A group of toughs that had swelled from no more than a cluster to three hundred, or even as many as five hundred, was going from machine shop to machine shop, store to store, and to the many small factories sprawling in all their squalor along the sooty banks of the East River. Anyone found at work during these unseemly hours of darkness was not urged but told to accompany the growing multitude. Those who refused or showed hesitance were beaten, dragged along forcibly, or both.

The situation was so ominous by morning that Kennedy, at 8:55 A.M., issued an order: "To all platoons, New York and Brooklyn—call in your reserve platoons and hold them at the station subject to further orders." The trouble was, there weren't enough patrolmen. In fact, the entire Metropolitan Force numbered only 1,620 men. They were good beat cops, husky and loyal, able to handle drunks, footpads, and, less frequently, homicidal cases, but their forte was not civil insurrection.

The police director might have saved himself the trouble of his alert, for it was too late. The mob was already assembling over a wide area commencing on a vacant lot at the southern extremity of Central Park and ranging down Fifth Avenue to the reservoir and Bryant Park (the future location of the New York Public Library), some seventeen city blocks. As an eleven-year-old resident of the district, Edward P. Mitchell,* would describe, "It was a crowd not merely of spectators but of participants, or candidates for participation in whatever evil might be done. They were there to burn, to plunder, to rob. . . ."

* The future well-known editor of the New York *Sun*.

Quite evident in the welling assemblage, numbered by 9:30 A.M. in the thousands, were women, easily matching the males in roughness, frowsiness, and general menace. The common cry was audible enough amid a rising discord of fulminations, epithets, and obscenities: "Kill the abolitionists!" One tousled giant in suspenders waved aloft a banner on which had been scrawled, "No draft!"

The throng, "a more wild, savage, and heterogeneous looking mass could not be imagined," in the words of another bystander, "started moving generally south along Fifth and Sixth Avenues, but shortly veered toward Third." Charles Chapin, a police telegraphist, noted: "It was a strangely weaponed, ragged, coatless army as it heaved tumultuously toward Third Avenue." At the same time splinter groups, like bees wandering off from their queen, detached noisily in a north and west direction.

Meanwhile the office at 677 Third Avenue had reopened on schedule. The wheel had already picked 100 names, leaving 164 more to go. "Shay, Z." had been drawn out of the barrel when a paving stone and then a brick slammed through a first-floor window, narrowly missing the provost himself, Captain Jenkins. Those inside—and the majority were women—rushed out through a rear door, followed by reporters who had been covering the drawing, and the mob surged in.

"Lists, records, books, the drafting wheel," wrote Anna Dickinson, "every article of furniture or work in the room was rent in pieces and strewn about the floor or flung into the streets." When the outraged intruders found that they could not open the safe that contained the "hated [draft] records," they beat at the unyielding iron sides and hinges "in a mad frenzy of senseless hate and fury" until their knuckles bled. Soon, the policemen assigned to the building were themselves compelled to retreat, followed closely by Captain Jenkins, "accelerated by the curses and blows of the assailants."

The mob's anger, rum-stimulated, according to onlookers, was still not sated. The house was fired before anyone checked the top floor where tenants lived but it was believed that the several women and their children there had escaped down a rear stairway. The blaze spread swiftly to neighborhood buildings. In an unbelievably short time "the whole block stood a mass of burning flames," Miss Dickinson concluded redundantly. One of these doomed houses, at the corner of Forty-seventh Street, had been fired specifically after someone shouted that

Horace Greeley, abolitionist or anti-slavery editor of the *Tribune*, lived there or happened to be on the premises. The notion was in error. The messianic-appearing Greeley, with the white muttonchop whiskers and sideburns, was actually fuming in his *Tribune* building on Printing House Square, just beyond City Hall Park. It did not help his frame of mind to believe that Governor Seymour himself was somehow responsible for the mob's getting out of hand.

Whether or not the word factories of the fourth estate on Printing House Square could be saved, surely nothing less than frontier blockhouses could have defended the buildings on Third Avenue that were already subsiding into glowing embers. With more courage than caution, nonetheless, Superintendent Kennedy made a final plea to the mob, dismayed as he was at the "bewildered attitude" of his scattering patrolmen.

Kennedy did not long make his stand. His exhortations to "disperse" choked in his throat as he was knocked to the pavement and beaten unmercifully—"bruised and mangled" in the words of Miss Dickinson. Then he was almost drowned in a small puddle of water by those who forcibly held his head under water. The sixty-year-old police chief likely would have paid with his life for devotion to duty—and early reports asserted he had been killed—had not unknown benefactors hustled him off the avenue and into a back street and ultimately to Bellevue Hospital in a feed wagon.

"At last," Anna Dickinson continued, "when there was nothing more here [677 Third Avenue] to accomplish, the mob, swollen to a frightful size, including myriads of wretched, drunken women and the half-grown vagabond boys of the pavements, rushed through the intervening streets, stopping cars and insulting peaceable citizens. . . ."

One of these numerous "peaceable citizens" was Crowley, of the police telegraph, who was hauled off an omnibus on his way to work.

"He's one of 'em!" shrieked a woman.

"Hang him!"

"Smash him!"

"Kill him!"

Crowley managed to escape, but the mob began destroying what he represented. Men armed with axes and sledgehammers chopped down telegraph poles and severed the wires. Repairmen sent to the downed poles realized the folly of their efforts. The mob hacked away.

All telegraph bureaus locked up. The post office, fearful that its offices would be next, closed down. The Associated Press wires went dead as staffers either raced out to cover this surging story or sat at windows, clutching knives, muskets, scissors—anything available for the defense of their own precincts.

The scene on Third Avenue was, by now, in the words of Chapin, "appalling . . . the hot July sun was obscured by heavy clouds which cast dark shadows over the city . . . giving a wild and terrifying aspect to the scene." It would in moments, as the noon hour approached, become yet more appalling. In response to earlier appeals for help, Lieutenant Abel Reade, still limping from a foot wound sustained the past December at Fredericksburg, arrived on Third Avenue with a detachment of seventy-five soldiers, themselves invalided back from the war.

Moving toward the mob, the soldiers had barely fixed bayonets when they were met by stones and bricks. They were ordered to fire over the heads of the throng. When this did not stop the oncoming mass, Reade commanded his men to shoot low. Six fell, mortally wounded. The bloodletting had the opposite effect intended. The counterattack by the troops surprised and infuriated the rioters who rushed through the gun smoke still in the air and wrenched the weapons from the Union Army veterans. The latter were then beaten over their heads with the butts by the mob.

The half-sick regulars were no match for the muscular foundry puddlers and railroad bruisers. The lieutenant's troops broke and fled, with the mob in pursuit. One soldier, unable because of his battle injuries to run any faster, was overtaken by a husky woman who then began stabbing him with his own bayonet. A second soldier was stripped of his uniform, beaten senseless, carried to a rise of ground, and hurled to a rock pile twenty feet below.

All in all, there seemed no immediate or expedient way of halting the rampage. The first objective appeared already to have been won, as Manhattan's provost marshal, Colonel Robert Nugent, of the 69th Regiment, ordered the Broadway conscription center closed, thus halting the draft for the time being.

It did not deter the mob, however, which was now descending upon the New York State Armory on Second Avenue at Twenty-first Street. By 2 P.M. thirty-two policemen were guarding the premises. The rioters rushed the building, led by a big man who wielded a sledgehammer. He was shot and killed as he smashed through the main door. Another man behind him also paid with his life. Nonetheless, the throngs piled inside, trampling the two bodies of their comrades. The police fled, but not permanently.

Weary, out of breath, most already bruised, the officers were reinforced. They regrouped and charged those still outside the armory, flailing at heads with their unyielding locust clubs.

At this stage, those who had seized the armory became their own worst enemies. They set the place, an old wooden building, ablaze. When they attempted to escape, the police brought their heavy sticks down on their heads. They either surrendered or scurried inside again. Some jumped from windows; others were trampled, suffocated, or burned to death in the greatest single carnage of the uprising. The guns the horde had captured now were no use to them.

This episode was quickly followed by a stand organized by Commissioner Acton, who was now serving as police chief, since Kennedy remained unconscious at Bellevue. A group of the rioters was bent on capturing police headquarters itself, at 300 Mulberry Street, in the Bowery, but Thomas Acton was in no mood to surrender, and neither was Sergeant Daniel Carpenter, a tough, veteran inspector. "I'll go, and I'll win that fight," Carpenter was quoted, in an impromptu speech reminiscent of the Alamo, "or Daniel Carpenter will never come back a live man!"

With two other inspectors at his side and cheered on from a more prudent distance by Acton, 125 patrolmen outside of headquarters repeatedly charged seemingly hopeless walls of men and women coming at them with swinging clubs until the spirit of the aggressors was broken. Daniel Carpenter and all his defenders lived to reminisce about this little-documented chapter in police valor.

The 18th Precinct, however, on Twenty-second Street, was not so fortunate. Overwhelmed by a mob of rioters, it had to be abandoned, with little or no fight. In other acts of violence, during daylight hours, rioters tore up a portion of the Harlem and New Haven railroad tracks on Third Avenue and roughed up the passengers aboard at least one train. The Weehawken Ferry was burned at its Forty-second Street slip on the Hudson River. Its captain, unlike others with similar commands, had failed to cast off in time. A black woman was hanged from a tree limb on Clarkson Street, her clothing set afire. Several houses on Roosevelt Street were burned. The telegraph office in the Bull's Head Hotel (or Allerton's Hotel) on Forty-second Street was burned, as was a small inn, Croton Cottage, on Fifth Avenue.

The more famous Fifth Avenue Hotel, meeting place of politicians, military leaders, and the literati, was threatened but spared. This was true also of the St. Nicholas, at Broadway and Spring Street, headquarters of the mayor and General Wool, which was ringed by both militia and police. The United States Sub-Treasury, on Lower Manhattan, was formidably garrisoned by soldiers and cannon that had been hurriedly ferried from the Brooklyn Navy Yard.

There remained much aimless wandering, window shattering, and firing or looting of stores on a haphazard basis. Stables for omnibuses were invaded. The grooms and drivers were warned not to move their vehicles out or—better still—were ordered to join the rebellion. Transportation had come to a standstill. Pedestrians, tired of being molested or robbed, remained inside, behind shuttered windows, nervously eyeing any object that suggested self-defense.

Scattered over a nine-square-mile area of the city, south from Central Park, the rioters were strangely leaderless. An elusive figure, John Andrews, "of Virginia," heavy-set, tall, and moustached, was said to be one of the rabble-rousers, but no others were so much as named.

The reporter for *Leslie's Illustrated Weekly*, after being fleeced of money but relieved to be unhurt, made his way home on foot to the east Eighties in Yorkville. "Two or three houses burning," he would write, "fires in Harlem, and fires around us. The fire bells continually ringing, the mob shouting, and the reign of terror established. No sleep."

In the early evening the mob returned to Fifth Avenue. The Negro Orphan Asylum, between Forty-third and Forty-fourth streets, had been overlooked. "Murder the damn monkeys!" lifted the cry.

The staff, worried all day, had removed the more than two hundred children to police stations and other edifices that appeared more secure or that might be overlooked by the rioters. In so doing they passed families of blacks pushing their possessions in carts after their tenements had been fired.

First, the orphanage was ransacked. "Beds, bedding, carpets, furniture, the very garments of the fleeing inmates," according to Anna Dickinson, were hauled outside by a human conveyor, hand to hand, the outer perimeters of the multitude then disappearing off into the city's Styx with the plunder. In the course of this pillage, by the testimony of one reporter, a little girl was discovered hiding under the bed. The writer believed she was killed. Soon the building was yellow-red with flames, and the whole neighborhood came alight.

"Some of the mob," recalled Edward Mitchell, "were struggling to get nearer the front of the asylum where the firemen were fighting like demons to do their duty, whatever their sympathies. . . . Now and then a geyser spurted at one of the unguarded hydrants. There would be a stampede to avoid a ducking, then cheers from the mob and jeers."

At one point Chief Fire Engineer John Decker was recognized. The now familiar cry went up, "Hang him!" He was able to slip into the anonymity of Hook and Ladder Company 15.

Downtown, in the Bowery, the night continued badly for those of African lineage. Four or five blacks fled to the roof of a building only to have it put to the torch beneath them. They clung to the gutters until their fingers were scorched, then fell to the streets to the hoots of a howling mob, which beat out whatever life flickered in their broken bodies.

Another group lurched into the *Tribune* building, still not properly defended. Chanting, "We'll hang old Greeley to a sour apple tree!" they knocked the first-floor furniture around and lit fires. A police charge, however, drove everyone out, the flames were extinguished, and the *Tribune* went to press as usual, only a couple of hours late.

In its editions and in those of other morning papers were pleas by General Wool for any veterans in the area to help save "the great emporium city from the threatened dangers of a ruthless mob"; from General Sandford for all state militiamen to report for duty, particularly those of the 7th Regiment, New York's "own"; and from Mayor Opdyke for "all loyal citizens" to present themselves for deputization by the police.

A thunderstorm at 11 P.M. combined with exhaustion to clear the streets, though a pall of smoke lingered over the ravished metropolis through most of the night. By dawn the smell of burned wood and masonry persisted. The city, nevertheless, was still there.

Through a continuing drizzle, remnants of the rioters reappeared, in clusters, like two-legged predators emerging from under rocks, stumps, and the forest slime. Here and there extruded crude barricades of the night before, reminiscent of the revetments of Cold Harbor or Vicksburg.

The reporter for *Leslie's*, aware that "all conveyances . . . stopped," sat home. At breakfast he observed a swarm of women, men, and boys setting fire to a neighbor's house. When it was charred, the mob chopped what remained into firewood and carried it all off, "the neatest thing we ever saw."

Mayor Opdyke's house on Fifth Avenue was charged by a medium-sized group of men who didn't know the occupant was at his head-quarters in the St. Nicholas. After they had broken a number of windows, the mayor's military aide, Colonel B. F. Manterez, rallied the neighbors who armed themselves with old hunting rifles, clubs, and even fire pokers to hold off the crowd until police arrived.

A drumfire of messages from Mulberry Street headquarters to be telegraphed to the precincts and messages tapped in from them attested to the frenetic quality of the day:

> 10:45. From 16th [precinct]. A mob has just attacked Jones' Soap Factory. Stores all closed.
>
> 10:55. To 20th. From General Brown [Brigadier General Harvey Brown commanded the garrison troops of the New York harbor area]. Send to arsenal and say a heavy battle is going on.
>
> 11:18. From 16th. Mob is coming down to station house. We have no men.
>
> 11:26. From 18th. The mob is very wild. . . .

The police dispatches continued as fast as the overworked operators could tap away at their keys, chronicling in the curious drama of under-statement peculiar to officialese.

On South Street, far downtown, a smartly marching contingent of marines fired over the heads of a scrubby group, which didn't linger for another round. The marines had been guarding a howitzer just ferried across from the Brooklyn Navy Yard for placement in the lobby of the *Tribune*, whether Greeley wanted it there or not.

Clearly, a major clash with the "regulars" was inevitable. It was mid-morning when Colonel H. J. O'Brien, of the 11th New York Volunteers, swung up Thirty-fifth Street, leading about 150 militiamen, hastily patched together from various regiments. Many, as in Reade's ragtag company of the previous day, were recuperating from wounds. Behind them they dragged two six-pounder cannons, far more formidable than anything possessed by the rioters. Not far from the East River, in front of Oliver's Livery Stable, O'Brien opened fire: several crashing broadsides from the muskets, then six rounds of canister and grape, point-blank from the cannons. A young lady* would write of the carnage:

> Women from the roofs threw stones and brickbats upon the soldiers. Then came the volleys. The balls leaped out, and the mob gave way at once and fled in every direction.
>
> A great crowd rushed through our street, hiding in every nook and corner. We closed doors and blinds but still peeped out of the windows. . . . A boy on the sidewalk opposite was struck. He fell in a pool of blood and was carried away to die.

No one—as in other similar encounters of mob against police or against the military—recorded the casualties, dead and wounded.

Following this bloody repulse, at least two hundred policemen swarmed inside the newly seized Union Steam Works on Twenty-second Street. This sturdily constructed five-story factory had previously turned out boilers and steam engines. Since Bull Run, it was manufacturing carbines and some ammunition as fast as the craftsmen could produce them for the army.

The street gang did not long hold the building. Floor by floor, the lawmen fought upward, flailing mercilessly with their nightsticks, employing service revolvers only as a last resort. Soon the last trespasser was under arrest or had tumbled out of a window. At least one of the occupants was shot to death; another, described as a pale youth with "sensitive" features, leaped from the roof, impaling himself on a spiked iron fence.

Governor Seymour arrived from New Brunswick that morning and registered at the St. Nicholas Hotel, where he could confer with both the mayor and General Wool. Shortly, he ordered such militiamen as were not in the Gettysburg area to start for Manhattan from every part of the state and then issued a proclamation that the city was "in a state of insurrection," a deliverance that came as a surprise to very few.

The Empire State's chief executive then appeared on the steps of

---

* Later identified by some as "Ellen Leonard," the lady anonymously recorded this vignette in *Harper's Monthly*, January, 1867.

City Hall, where he addressed those of the mob who were within hearing or shouting distance. Adopting a conciliatory note, he implored them to return "to your homes as peaceable citizens." However, his impromptu speech neither mollified the mob nor augmented his portfolio as a politician. The majority were not even American citizens yet, even to the point of having sought first papers.

In acknowledging Seymour's pleas, in their own way, the men and women moved off to set fire to what was left of the Bull's Head Hotel, this time finishing the job; burned a lumberyard and a grain elevator; the pier and shed of the already gutted Weehawken ferry; the City Cattle Market, thereby loosing a stampede of the maddened animals; fired a Negro church at Thirtieth Street and wrecked the firehouse of the unfortunate company that had responded to the alarm.

Brooks Brothers, the haberdasher on Catharine and Cherry streets, was cleaned of its stock, but the establishment itself was not badly harmed. The rough, burly male rioters cut a provocative contrast as they swaggered into the streets with top hats, lace cuffs, and swallowtails. They found their equal, nonetheless, in the frowsy women wandering down Fifth Avenue toting fine silver and cut glass from looted residences.

All over the city, the racial pursuit continued. At least three black men who had wandered across the mob's meandering route were hanged to trees and a lamppost. A fourth was hauled from his horse and cart and thrown into the East River. As he struggled toward shore, he was pelted with rocks and bricks until he disappeared beneath the dirty waters. "A strange spectacle," wrote one observer, "to see one hundred Irishmen pour along the streets after a poor Negro. If he could reach a police station, he felt safe. . . . Whenever the police could strike the track of a manhunt, they stopped it summarily, and the pursuers became the pursued."

Inspector Carpenter encored his qualities of boldness and improvisation as he was called upon to dislodge a group of rioters, believed armed, who had converted an outhouse into a strongpoint. His solution was to push off a heavy cornice from the overhanging roof of a building. With assistance he did, and the desired result was obtained.

Colonel O'Brien did not long survive his dubious victory over the mob. He rode home in midafternoon, dismounted, and was pounced upon before he could gain his parlor. By the testimony of witnesses, who did not, and probably dared not, come to the officer's aid, O'Brien was methodically beaten to death.

Wednesday was marked by the hanging of more blacks and desultory raids on a variety of stores, from tobacconists to the sellers of millinery and hoopskirts. This third day of rioting also saw the arrival of New York State artillery and cavalry units, as well as additional infantry. Colonel Gershom Mott, a regular army officer, in command of a mounted detail, ran his saber through one protester who had just participated in a lynching and was next trying to unhorse the cavalryman.

On Thursday the elite 7th Regiment arrived, followed by 150 troops of the 2d; contingents of the 8th Battery as well as Infantry; the 14th Cavalry; the 65th Infantry, fresh from Harrisburg; the 74th, 152d, 162d infantries; and the 26th Michigan Infantry; and still more battle-tested state volunteer regiments were en route. Secretary of War Edwin M. Stanton had freed these forces, since they were no longer needed in Maryland or Pennsylvania. This canny politician, however, unwilling to make decisions to use federalized troops in domestic or municipal strife, had simply allocated them for Governor Seymour's "discretion." Major General Judson "Little Kil" Kilpatrick, the cavalry leader who had played a signal role in turning the tide at Gettysburg, arrived in Manhattan to command all cavalry.

Now bivouacs marched their neat rows of tents over the parks and squares of Manhattan, soon spilling into Brooklyn and Staten Island. The rumble of boots and caisson wheels proved a reassuring fortissimo to the frightened and harassed population.

By Friday it was all over. The senseless and sadistic violence ended not in a crackling pitched battle, but in a fading whimper. Those responsible melted away into the oblivion of a sprawling city.

Sunday, the *Herald* could observe that New York had returned to "a state of profound tranquillity." This was true as well in other cities, including Boston; Troy, New York; and Portsmouth, New Hampshire, where incipient trouble had been quickly "squelched," as one reporter phrased it. It was time now to clean up Manhattan in the wake of property damage conservatively claimed to aggregate five million dollars. The companion figure of fifty-four structures leveled was also too low, possibly by as much as 100 percent.

The loss of life would remain the highest of any civil disturbance in the United States, not to be approximated by the combined casualties of the race riots in the 1940's or 1960's. Some measure of the price might have been gained by the police notation weeks later in 1863 that fifty barrels of human bones had been carted away from the rubble of the Second Avenue Armory, toward Potter's Field.

The police admitted to having lost three members from its force, with countless injured; the military, fifty dead. Of the blacks and rioters killed, there were no exact totals. Governor Seymour would employ the round figure of one thousand, or about twice the rough police estimate, without attribution or breakdown. Most reference works have since relied upon Seymour's approximate total, exaggerated or not.

Considering the intensity of the rioting, there was surprisingly little retribution. The few arrests included that of the shadowy John Andrews, "of Virginia," who vanished forever into a military prison. There were only twenty grand-jury indictments and nineteen convictions, with jail sentences averaging about five years apiece.

If legal and physical revenge was conspicuously mild, the same was not true forensically. Anna Dickinson and others of the extreme abolitionist fraternity blamed Governor Seymour for the whole internecine orgy. *The New York Times* failed to evince a great deal more restraint, editorializing, "he [Seymour] was proclaiming . . . that mob law ought under certain circumstances to override that of Congress." More philosophically, the *Times* then mused that "no civilized government could in decency maintain relations of amity with a community of cowards, bullied by cutthroats and governed in their greatest straits by hordes of thieves."

Even so, whether one tried to be fair toward him or not, Seymour was ruined. Manifestly, very few cared to be fair. The echoes of his fruitless talk to the rioters haunted him. He was voted out of office the next year, 1864, and was trounced by Grant in the presidential elections of 1868, thus becoming one of the nation's earliest victims on the political altar of "law and order."

The futility of violence and bloodletting was further underscored by the scant use to which conscription was ever put. By Appomattox only 52,000 men had actually been drafted into the army. Thus, the stupidity and brutality of the rioters that long-ago July was properly matched by their overflowing impatience.

2

Galveston Tidal
Wave, 1900

More than a quarter of a century—and a meaningful one—had passed.

Summertime lingered Friday night, September 7, 1900, at Galveston. In spite of freshening winds, lengthening swells, and the known presence of a "tropical disturbance" somewhere off the southeast Louisiana coast, vacationers were still present. They were undoubtedly attracted, as one writer described in his baroque prose, by the "glistening white sand packed as hard as asphalt, which fringed the saffron waters of the Gulf."

The population of this fourth largest city of Texas varied between 25,000 and 38,000, depending upon the number of visitors, businessmen, and ship's crews present. Huge warehouses and towering elevators stretching along the waterfront like a ragged mountain range of timber and masonry attested to the millions of dollars' worth of cotton and grain exported annually from the area.

Residents loved their city, which had been in existence barely half a century. It had survived a Civil War blockade, capture by the North, and then recapture. The city was perched precariously in mixed Victorian splendor upon an island of the same name—a twenty-five-mile-long sandbar, two miles wide and barely five feet above sea level—and was connected by four bridges, including the world's longest wagon span, to the mainland two miles distant. The citizens of Galveston had ridden out many storms and fought several bad fires to a standstill. They had learned to live by and with the sea, building no cellars and propping the first floors of their homes and businesses several feet above the ground.

Saturday morning, September 8, which began with a drizzle under fifteen-to-twenty-mile-an-hour winds and ominous skies, was also marked by an increasing surf. Townspeople and tourists wandered down to the beach to observe the waves that, as one reporter remarked, were "very high and boisterous." The barometer was dropping, registering barely more than 29 inches of mercury, at least an inch below normal. The Gulf continued to encroach inland, until in addition to being "boisterous," the brown waves were smashing against warehouses and grain elevators. The crests burst at telegraph-pole height into spectacular mushrooms of dirty foam. The spectators little by little started to draw back from the Gulf. Although they were nonprofessionals in weather science, they knew something was very wrong this time. No ordinary storm was building.

The eight ships in port doubled up their anchor lines, or moorings if warped alongside Galveston's many wharves. They furled awnings and lashed tarpaulins over hatch covers. Those on bridge watch noted with mounting concern that the barometer was continuing to drop until by midmorning it stood at a shaky 28.5 inches.

The tide rose, then rose some more. Street gutters were awash with rivulets of water. The two-mile channel to the east, between Bolivar Peninsula and Galveston Island, foamed with Atlantic-like whitecaps as the Gulf fought toward Galveston Bay. Nonetheless, a familiar "norther," a strong northwest wind, continued to be the islanders' salvation, holding back the easterly storm.

Weather-bureau employees Joseph Cline and his similarly tall, spare older brother, Isaac, needed none of their meteorological instruments or training to be filled with presentiments of far worse to come. For one omen, there was water over the backyard of their sturdy two-story frame house, on ground as high as could be found on the long Gulf sandbar. The brothers phrased a warning to the bureau's central office in Washington, D.C., via Houston: "Unusually heavy swells from the southeast, intervals one to five minutes, overflowing low places south portion of city three to four blocks from beach. Such high water with opposing winds never observed previously."

Then, with a word of caution to his wife and three daughters, Isaac Cline harnessed up his horse and sulky and rode toward the waterfront where he advised lingering groups to return home or hasten to any available higher ground. A few accused him, in effect, of being a Jeremiah, a prophet of doom, but Isaac persisted, repeating, "A hurricane is bearing down on the city and the water is rising rapidly . . . almost any shelter is better than nothing at all," or variations of this urgency.

Shortly after 10:00, the Houston office ordered the Clines to change the storm hoist atop the Levy Building, visible to all ships in port, from a northwest flag signal to northeast. In a few minutes the flag itself was being ripped. Before noon the "rubberneckers" on the beach had all left, not entirely inspired by Cline's entreaties but because the light rain had become heavy, and the wind had now increased to thirty miles per hour. The tide, too, was building up, as—true to the weather warning—the protecting "norther" was losing its power to hold back the angry Gulf. In fact, the ugly brown waters were beginning to flood the rim of the island. The Deep Water Saloon, near the piers, for example, was rapidly becoming just that.

The few inhabitants of Bolivar Peninsula had gathered bedding and loaves of bread, then hurried over to the lighthouse. It looked like one structure that could not possibly come awash. People in the entire area were following suit, with a curiously deliberate, determined quality rather than headlong flight. An old man was hobbling on his cane, moving toward the center of Galveston; a woman shooed her brood of children before her; a large family group hurried along, carrying various items of furniture, a lamp with a mosaic cut-glass shade, wicker baskets, and a suitcase; one lone individual struggled with the weight of a sewing machine.

The Gulf had now stretched its dirty fingers to Twelfth Street, a dozen blocks from the eastern limits of the city. Like sheep, the crowd came on, many of them making for the ample Victorian lobby of the Tremont Hotel at Twenty-third Street, on ground as high as could be gained. Adjoining St. Mary's Cathedral, the grand old hostelry was once the finest south of St. Louis and a favorite of General Grant's.

By now, all beach or near-beach dwellings had been abandoned, except for some last stragglers carrying a few prized belongings atop their heads and wading desperately into the city. The word had been passed that all houses on higher ground or sand were being opened to anyone—rich or poor, white, black, or yellow (the Chinese crews caught ashore)—who wished to come in. The Beach Hotel itself, the Bathing Pavilion, and the Olympia Pavilion were already chewed up by the twenty-foot waves, with every likelihood that soon nothing would remain to mark the locations where they had stood.

The wind kept picking up, to thirty-five and even forty miles per hour by 2 P.M., and that was very odd to veteran "hurricaners" who seemed to remember the gusting more than this constant, weird, and implacable gale. Joseph Cline, at this hour, struggled up to the roof of the Levy Building. He could barely insure his footing. The rain gauge had been swept away, he discovered, and the anemometer, the wind recorder, threatened to go at any moment. Before he descended, he was able to note that "half the city is under water."

Cline decided that he had better convey this intelligence to Houston. Wading through water up to his knees, swirling with debris that included wooden paving blocks, he arrived in the Western Union office to learn that the wires had been down for two hours. In fact, the last message had been to a Jerry Gierrad in San Antonio advising of the drowning of his brother in Galveston.

It was the same story at Postal. However, Cline managed a telephone call to the Western Union office in Houston, just finishing his message when the instrument went dead. In fact, the entire electric generating plant of Galveston flickered, then expired, its generators submerged.

As midafternoon approached, events accelerated with such speed and chaos that no one—not even the Clines—would ever be able to swear to a reasonably exact sequence. All at once the anemometer raced up to eighty-four miles an hour, hung there for a few minutes, then blew off to join the rain gauge in a hurricane's oblivion. One could only speculate whether the winds attained, then exceeded, one hundred miles per hour. Instead of a chance drowning or the isolated crumbling of the side of a building, wholesale destruction tore loose. The trigger was the letup of the "norther." Now the Gulf could rampage unfettered.

"To go upon the streets was to court death," wrote Richard Spillane, the fiercely moustached editor of the Galveston *Tribune*. Its presses, as a matter of fact, were already under water. "Cisterns, portions of buildings, telegraph poles, walls were falling, and the noise of the wind and the crashing of buildings were terrifying in the extreme. The people were like rats in a trap."

There was meager choice—to drown out-of-doors or risk being caught in a collapsing house. In some cases there was no alternative, such as with the Old Women's Home on Rosenberg Avenue. All perished when the wooden structure fell apart. The occupants could not be moved in time, and they were too enfeebled to save themselves.

With a wind shift to the southeast, the Gulf and bay waters met, leaving not one dry inch in the entire city. There were very few residents who had not abandoned all hope of survival.

As evening added its own gloom to the storm, Bishop Nicholas Gallagher, of the diocese of Galveston, turned to Father James M. Kirwin, pastor of St. Mary's Cathedral, where both clerics officiated, with a strangely matter-of-fact admonition that he help "prepare" the other priests "for death." As if to underscore the prelate's words, the two-ton bell that was still echoing to the Angelus crashed from its fastenings, and its tower, one of three, shook as though to announce imminent departure from the sacred precincts.

At the Ursuline Convent, a substantial brick building five blocks from the beach, the sisters proved their strength by hauling people out of the raging waters as they floated past upper windows. Using poles or ropes when necessary, the nuns soon had saved several hundred. Their most remarkable rescue was that of Mrs. William Henry Heidemann, who bumped alongside the convent walls while afloat in an open trunk. After gasping that her house and husband were gone, she told the sisters that she was in labor. Within the hour she had given birth to a boy. As though this were not in itself sufficiently out of the ordinary, her brother, perched in a tree on the convent grounds, reached out an arm and caught a small boy drifting past. He turned out to be the older child of Mrs. Heidemann.

Trees, uncertain a refuge as they were, figured in other survivals. The Reverend L. P. Davis, of Bolivar Peninsula, lashed his five children and wife to high branches in a nearby grove of cottonwoods. Drenched and terrified, they would weather the blow. The family of Ralph Klaes, like so many others, had kept inching upward in their house as the waters rose—chairs to tables, onto shelves, finally to the attic beams and out the skylight to the roof. Then they struggled over to a clump of salt cedars and successfully entwined themselves among the branches.

Others, not so fortunate as the Davis or Klaes families, drowned in the trees, unable to escape the entanglements when the water surged past their elevations.

Everywhere, houses were disintegrating like so much cardboard. Clarence Howth, an attorney, had just finished moving his family, which included a newborn baby and father-in-law, to the attic when the entire place collapsed. Thrown out into the surging waters, Howth reflexively grabbed at the first object he encountered: a window frame. On it he was carried southward into the Gulf, then back again. His house and his family were gone, however.

The Clines fared no better. Isaac had waded home under the greatest of difficulty to find some fifty neighbors inside, including the builder, along with his family and his younger brother. The house, constructed with storms in mind, conceivably would have weathered this one had not a two-hundred-foot length of streetcar trestle, complete with tracks, smashed against it. Presumably, it had already knocked into other structures and bumped people off their rafts, or "drifts," as they were dubbed.

The Clines' home floated free. Then, top-heavy and caught by a gust of wind, it capsized, leaving some people on its side and others adrift in the roaring darkness. Joseph and Isaac managed to keep together, although they changed from drift to drift, until they "could see no lights anywhere" and believed they were far out to sea.

A flash of lightning revealed, at one time, a child floating by. With great effort the Clines pulled in a girl whose name she was finally able to reveal as Cora Goldbeck, aged seven. At another time Joseph had to draw his knife to scare away a man who threatened to push him off the raft.

The whole city was going, or so it seemed, under a record storm tide that crested at fifteen feet above normal. Inside St. Mary's Orphanage, at Twenty-first Street and Avenue M, Mother Superior Camillus watched helplessly from a second-story window as the boys' wing collapsed. She told the sisters to hurry and tie themselves to little groups of the girls. Soon, as reporter Spillane would write, the orphanage "fell like a house of cards." All but two of the boys and one girl drowned, the victims still securely fastened to the ten nuns who perished with them. Many others—a father and a son, a mother and a daughter—would expire through this ill-conceived notion of linkage.

On the same orphanage grounds those who sought the second-floor rooms of St. Mary's University had chosen wisely, or fortuitously. The walls resisted every surge and blow from flotsam. At some juncture the assemblage was joined by a cow, which stood her ground and in turn was undisturbed by the other occupants.

Families such as that of Clarence Ousley, editor of the *Evening Tribune*, survived the collapse of their homes without any special plan or chance help.

The quick and the dead intermingled this howling night. Since there was no such repository in Galveston as a deep grave, the city's six cemeteries were being scoured out by the waves as thoroughly as though by steam shovels. Corpses swirled in the rushing waters with the living or the newly drowned. Heavy, waterproof bronze caskets were picked up and started along the coast, capable of floating great distances.

Two miles down the beach, the soldiers of Battery O at Fort Crockett were drowning both inside and outside of their barracks. Almost thirty had been lost. It was a case of every man for himself. Captain W. C. Rafferty, commanding this unit of the First Artillery, had won a heroic gamble to reach his own living quarters, which were about to be swept into the Gulf. Rafferty lashed doors and chairs together into some semblance of a raft, put his wife, small children, and a servant on it, then navigated the rapids frothing over the fortifications to one of the ten-inch coastal defense guns. The captain had been seized with the idea that a small steel vault beneath the gun carriage would serve as a shelter. There was little ventilation, but Rafferty was right. The cramped room withstood the seas and wind.

John Kirwin, a butcher, had his own ideas about how to protect children. On a raft after losing his wife, he placed two of his sister's family upon the hay of a floating stable. It would prove a sure refuge.

Rafts or drifts, however, were vulnerable to other, larger objects and also could shrink back to their component small bits of wreckage, leaving those atop to struggle in the water. If the drift kept more or less together, there was still the constant peril of the exhaustion of those aboard. Many fell off simply out of terror and sheer fatigue.

Fathers, such as S. W. Clinton, an engineer at the stockyards, watched his whole family, including his wife and five children, drop or be knocked from their drifts, one by one, in spite of all his efforts to save them. Only he survived, after being carried forty miles north and deposited on the mainland.

Some of those who were certain of death were surprised. R. L. Johnson said a hasty if solemn good-bye to his wife and three children, then kissed them, even as one of the latter protested, "Father, it is *not* our time to die!" As it turned out, the youngster was correct.

The tremendous storm was too much even for those who made their living by and on the seas. The entire crew of the Fort Point lifesaving station, opposite Bolivar Point, was lost. The Galveston Bar lightship was blown hard aground on Bolivar Point, but this crew was far luckier in the hurricane's caprice. Huddling aboard as the vessel banged around the beach, every man survived.

All but two of the oceangoing ships caught in harbor were unable to defy the wind and tide. The English freighter *Roma* snapped all lines, mooring her to Pier 15, and lurched off on a crazy voyage that carried her through all three railroad bridges before finally grounding. Another British vessel, the *Kendall Castle*, came to rest in a shallow estuary off Texas City. The *Taunton*, also of English registry, careened on the longest, unwitting journey of those in Galveston—thirty miles up the coast, after drifting all the way across flooded Pelican Island, no more than a big, sandy blob due north of Galveston.

Steamships, in their wild, unguided voyages, were joined by hundreds of railroad boxcars, being tossed willy-nilly around the bay, like so many oversize toys.

By late evening all who could reach such relatively secure structures as the Tremont, St. Mary's Infirmary, or the Ursuline Convent were inside—approximately one thousand in each of the former two and two thousand in the big convent. Many, in spite of the deep, rushing waters, would have made it had it not been for flying debris, which included roof slates. Those not killed from the blows were knocked unconscious and drowned.

The lobby of the Tremont, in spite of the hotel's eminence, was awash, four and a half feet deep, with furniture floating around like images out of a nightmare or a Dali painting. Three persons sprawled, legs outstretched, upon the grand piano. Others fended off bobbing palms in their pots. Upper floors, corridors and bedrooms alike, were jammed to overflowing. Sparkling white sheets, blankets, and pillowcases had been torn and muddied by people's feet.

Then, before midnight, people began to notice that the lobby furnishings were not afloat anymore. One could sit, for example, in a straight chair without treading water. Outside, the roar of the wind had lessened. The tide was flowing out.

Hesitantly, the refugees began to peer out of windows or try doors. Soon, one could walk in water that reached only to the ankles. And there was no more wind.

Before dawn the water had gone.

It was an incredible sight that the unscarred Victory Monument, commemorating Texas heroes at the Battle of San Jacinto, 1836, surveyed. The warrior woman, with hand outstretched, looked down upon the ruins of fifteen hundred acres, one third of the city almost obliterated. Much of the remaining area was shattered, splintered wood. Every vestige of the beach resorts and cottages was, as one person observed, "effaced."

Isaac Cline, whose wife had died beneath the house atop which others had been saved, prepared a report for Washington to be delivered to Houston when someone could get away: "Sunday, September 9, 1900, revealed one of the most horrible sights that ever a civilized people looked upon."

Everywhere amid the debris was a thick slime, as a dazed, half-naked, bruised populace picked its way in search of loved ones. Death rested upon the whole sandbar, singly, in groups, in long windrows: corpses of horses, cows, pigs, and mules interspersed with those of men, women, and children. Some protruded from the broken timber of buildings; others lay stark and cold under the unkind glare of daylight. Still others were found on beaches as distant as fifty miles up and down the coast.

One lady, a Miss Sarah Summers, had perished not far from her home on Tremont Street. When a curious passerby had pried open her hand, closed by rigor mortis, something that apparently had represented her greatest and most meaningful treasure dropped out—diamonds.

A very few, pulled out of rubble for dead, proved to possess a feline's tenacity for life. One such was William Nisbett, a cotton man, exhumed from the heap of masonry that had been the Cotton Exchange Saloon. Nursing merely a few bruised fingers, he retained the heart to quip: "Say, *what* was in that last drink?"

As burial or disposal parties began their tasks, hampered by a lack of carbolic and camphor, horses, wagons, and shovels, several men set out for the mainland. Among them was James G. Timmins, a Houston businessman, who chartered a schooner that had survived the storm. Another, Spillane, the newsman, carried telegrams for Governor Joseph D. Sayers, in Austin, and President William McKinley, advising them of the plight of Galveston.

Spillane's varied journey commenced in a small boat, continued on a railroad handcar, and finally ended in League City, where the reporter met a train sent down from Houston, three miles north. Timmins preceded Spillane by a couple of hours. Both men had somewhat different versions of the disaster, although little doubt remained of its severity.

The world beyond the Gulf had, as a matter of fact, already suspected the worst. When the telegraph wires went silent, *The New York Times'* editors felt justified in preparing this headline for the Sunday editions: "Galveston May Be Wiped Out by Storm." They hadn't missed the mark by much. More than six thousand, by best approximations, had died. In terms of human fatalities it was the worst catastrophe the United States had ever experienced, and it has yet to be equaled. Added to this sobering figure were two thousand dead elsewhere. At Texas City, across Galveston Bay, sufficient wreckage had accumulated, Spillane would write, "to rebuild a city."

Whole families had ceased to exist. Scarcely a person survived in Galveston who had not been touched in some way by the immensity of the cataclysm. There were children who had lost a father, a mother, or both. The orphans presented an especially vexing problem for those who strove to prepare some recapitulation of the vast waste in human life. Many of the children were too young to know their own names, much less where they lived or even the size of their family.

In addition, there were vacationists from other communities. It could be a long time before they were missed by their neighbors, and even if their absence were speedily noted, why should one jump to the conclusion that they had gone to Galveston? As Isaac Cline faithfully chronicled, "Where twenty thousand people lived on the eighth not a house remained on the ninth—and who occupied the houses may in many instances never be known." More dramatically, Clarence Howth, the attorney who had lost his entire family, postscripted, "It seemed as a dream of a thing that had never been."

On the opposite and possibly more pragmatic perimeter of emotion, a store clerk, wearily making inventory of his losses, asserted, "I'm sick and tired of the whole business!" He spoke for many. Damage estimates, tallied laboriously even while the debris was being swept or hauled away, ran like this:

Galveston Dry Goods	$25,000
Jake Davis, Wholesale Grocers	$75,000
Pabst and Limbach, Produce	$40,000
Southern Coffee Company	Total
Galveston Shoe and Hat Company	Total
Galveston Gas Company	All four reservoirs gone
E. Dulitz, Furniture	$30,000
Thomas Goggan and Brothers, Music	Total
St. Mary's Infirmary	$130,000

The list ran on and on, into the multimillions of dollars.

The looters, as had been expected, slunk in, and martial law was declared. With the scavengers, however, there also arrived help—boatloads of food, clothing, medical supplies, and rescue teams of every size, type, and degree of skill, from heavy laborers to nurses and doctors. Among the latter was Clara Barton, in her eightieth year, "angel of the battlefields" of the Civil War, who also had served in the Franco-Prussian and Spanish-American wars. Emergency hospitals were set up in buildings less harmed than others.

The plight of Galveston had captured a nation's imagination and touched its heart. William Randolph Hearst, the publisher, dispatched a relief train, complete with doctors, nurses, food, and medicine— together with reporters and photographers. Virtually every city and hamlet in the United States assembled its own Galveston fund. Small boys and girls for days brought nickels and pennies to school in empty cream bottles.

All week long, the grisly job of cleaning up went forward. The interment of the dead posed as monumental a challenge as any. At first it was planned to bury the corpses at sea. An experimental barge loaded with seven hundred was towed eighteen miles out into the Gulf. When bodies began to float back ashore, however, the method was abandoned, and the deceased were cremated in mountains of rubble. For days a pall of smoke from these many funeral pyres hung over the shambles of the "city on a sandbar."

There were some unexpected reunions. Joseph Cline, unwell after his experience (and doomed to a life of frail health), was in a drugstore when a man from New Orleans entered inquiring for a Cora Goldbeck. In disbelief Cline replied that he had rescued her and she was at a friend's home. The child and her mother had been visiting a grandmother. Both ladies had perished. Now Cora was reunited with her father.

Under the speedily adopted if obvious slogan "Galveston Shall Rise Again!" the sound of hammer and saw rang its cheerier lentissimo against the dirge from the shovel and spade. Banks reopened. Partial telephone service was reestablished. The lights weren't yet ready to flash back on, but one lack—electric trolleys—was temporarily made up by mule power. The several railroads serving Galveston had joined in a massive push to repair one bridge. Within twelve days trains once more were whistling in from the mainland. The fresh-water supply, a curious mixing of cisterns and water towers flowing by gravity into central mains, would not be back to normal for a while.

"This great wild throe of loss, grief, and anguish has come and gone," Clara Barton wrote to a friend on September 28. "The sun shines over Galveston's placid bay, and the people go about as before. . . ." She was, at the same time, appealing for a national effort to rehouse some eight thousand homeless.

All in all, it looked as though Galveston would indeed rise again. But what of the future? Could such devastation be prevented?

Engineers advised the city fathers. A seawall should be built, high enough so that a storm tide, comparable even to the monstrous one just passed, could not prevail, and the whole level of the city should be shored up. Anything so ambitious, however, demanded time. It was two years before the creaking axles of battalions of mule carts and the raucous calls of the "skinners" echoed along the Gulf front, against a background of steam trip-hammers driving down creosote pilings. Tens of thousands of tons of concrete would be consumed, but the residents of Galveston knew that before too long they could sleep secure in any weather.

3

Disaster at
Monongah, 1907

By 1907 Galveston's seawall was virtually complete. Seven and one-half miles long—to be extended gradually to ten—the barrier was seventeen feet above mean low tide, with a sidewalk on top believed to be the longest in the world. The wall proved to be such an attraction that a roadway—Seawall Boulevard—and hotels, restaurants, and curio stores sprouted behind much of its length. Best of all, this more modest descendant of China's Great Wall worked. Sightseers could stand to leeward during Gulf blows and thrill in complete safety to the spectacular foam and spray pluming at the wall's crest.

Safety, or the lack of it, was a factor dominating other vistas of living in the swaddling years of the new century. In 1905, so soon after the Iroquois Theater conflagration, fifty workers perished in a Brockton, Massachusetts, shoe-factory explosion and fire. Why, the public had reason to inquire, was the loss of life *always* so high? Exits or not, this structure, unlike the Iroquois, burned with the speed of dry tinder. Many stables, comparatively, were more sturdy.

Nowhere, however, was there more attention needed for even minimal safety conditions than in coal mines. The record, a horror, was worsening with the cold inevitability of an arithmetic progression. During the decade ending in 1900, about 150 miners were killed each year through explosions. Looking at it another way, the United States mortality rate for coal miners had risen to 3.4 percent per thousand, which compared with 1 percent in Belgium and .91 percent in France.

The nemesis of the miner was an old but deadly one—methane gas, odorless and readily ignitable when present in air in concentrations of from 5 to 15 percent. The combustion, by a spark or flash, then would set off a chain reaction of ever-present coal dust, to explode throughout all the interconnecting tunnels of the mine until the gasses were consumed. "Blackdamp," or carbon dioxide, involving a lack of oxygen, and cave-ins, although killers, could not compare with methane—"firedamp"—in collaboration with coal dust as a mass murderer of miners.

The natural process of subterranean gas production cannot be readily stopped. Coal dust, however, can be rendered less explosive through the introduction of inert rock dust, and in high proportions—at least 65 percent. Some years would pass before this procedure was introduced. It was known, however, as early as Revolutionary times that the coal dust itself should be wet down.

The miner faced these perils for little reward: one to two dollars per day for ten hours' work, six days a week, grossing about five hundred dollars a year if he was fortunate. He lived in company houses and shopped in company stores.

It was not surprising that established families in Appalachia and other coal regions of the East came to be increasingly disenchanted with this occupation. But there was no shortage of the muscle supply. The coal companies recruited strong young immigrants as they disembarked in New York, Boston, Baltimore, or Norfolk. In West Virginia signs in the mines and at the markets were printed in six languages in addition to English: Italian, Hungarian, Polish, Greek, Turkish, and Russian. If the newly arrived worker did not pay attention, at least it was a sop to the owner, who could say, "I did my best to tell him!"

The year 1907 had already been an exceptionally bad one. Thirty-four had been killed on December 1 at the Naomi mine in Fayette City, Pennsylvania. However, there seemed some reason to hope that one mine complex—at Monongah, on the West Fork of the Monongahela River, six miles southwest of Fairmont, West Virginia—might prove the exception to the nation's almost unblemished record of disaster beneath the surface of the earth. Lying in a slight hollow, Monongah, a company town, had grown from literally nothing in twenty years to a noisy, thriving community of three thousand. It represented the largest mine workings in a thirty-three-mile stretch south to Clarksburg and beyond.

Owned by the all-powerful Fairmont Coal Company, capitalized at twenty million dollars and producing four million tons a year, Monongah seemed to be leading the way in safety. Mines Nos. 6 and 8, for example, one and a half miles apart but interconnected by the same "bank," or passageway, boasted the largest ventilating fans in use. The larger was twenty-two feet in diameter, powered by an electric motor that could kick up a fifty-mile-an-hour gale, moving 179,000 cubic feet of air a minute.

This was not all. The mines—"slope" types of relatively shallow depth—were fully electrified for pumping out water, cutting seams, and hauling the coal. West Virginia state mine inspectors had repeatedly pronounced Nos. 6 and 8 among the "best" they had ever been in. In fact, the two had been inspected early in this first week of December, 1907.

Despite all the modernization, the mines could not be maintained especially dry. The pumps expelled the significant quantity of one million gallons of water daily from the complex labyrinth, honeycombed for several miles underground. Still, it seemed as though the men were always wet. "My sister used to tell me to quit the mines," recalled Clay Fullen, then eighteen. "She said I'd sure catch pneumonia and die. I'd come home dripping every day, no matter what time of year." But he persisted, as did all the other mine people of Monongah.

Nor could the chasms under the surface of the earth be properly lighted. In spite of electrification for power purposes, it was impractical to string light globes in the constantly changing banks. The miners depended on their cap lamps, burning either a lardlike tallow solution or kerosene. The flickering flames, not the brightest, did serve a secondary purpose of consuming methane before it could attain dangerous concentrations.

Friday, December 6, was a raw, windy morning. The day commenced, as usual, at 3 A.M. when the "fire bosses" entered the mines down the footpaths, or "manways," to check on gas and ascertain if excessive coal dust in the haulways, or main corridors, had been watered. So-called safety lamps were employed to "sniff" for gas—that is, the color of the flame altered depending on the amount of methane in suspension.

Anywhere from two to three hours after the predawn visit—which had found everything normal—the day shift started entering the mines. The miners carried their wide shovels, lunch pails, and, many of them, the regulation five-pound tins of black blasting powder. Others accompanied them: foremen, motormen, drivers, trackmen, timbermen, slatemen, boys as young as twelve years, who opened compartment doors for the mule carts, as well as friends who might be visiting from elsewhere in the United States or from the old country. This morning there was even a life-insurance agent below. It was not uncommon for hustling salesmen to enter the mines, aware as they were that potential customers would be too tired immediately after they emerged and shortly after that, possibly too full of beer or whiskey to be sensibly receptive.

About 60 percent of the day shift was composed of recent immigrants, the remainder about evenly divided between white and black Americans of at least a few generations' standing. Neither Fairmont Coal nor the pit bosses had any exact idea of how many miners or their camp followers entered mines Nos. 6 and 8 that morning. This was customary: No roll was called, no check-off made. The official guess, however, put the day shift at somewhere between 350 and 367 men. Since apprenticeship was a miner's own affair—and he might have as many as two with him—the approximation could have been 100 or even 300 too low.

Completing this considerable and heterogeneous congregation were forty horses and mules for hauling the carts until they were hooked up to the electric engines and drawn out.

Soon, as a recent visitor had penned of a typical scene, "the lights of their caps flitted about in the darkness like fireflies." The morning wore on.

A few minutes before 10:30, Pat McDonnell, eighteen, was working on a loaded "trip" of coal cars emerging from the entrance of No. 6, headed for the trestle and tipple, or processing plant. A coupling pin sheared off at the engine, permitting the entire trip of eighteen cars to roll back into the mine. Realizing that the heavy train might seriously damage the mine or even produce a short circuit, Pat raced in panic for the switchboard beside the entrance. He was too late. The next thing he knew he was flying through the air, propelled by a monstrous force.

It was worse at No. 8. From its mouth a long tongue of flame licked out, followed by a thick cloud of purplish-black coal dust and gas that billowed skyward. Heavy 12 by 12 timbers and stone supports at the entrance were disgorged as from a volcano, followed by the twenty-two-foot-high fan itself. A total wreck, it fell to earth nearly one hundred feet from its base. One of its vanes, along with bricks and mortar, was projected more than five hundred feet across the West Fork River, on which the entrance faced. This shrapnel-like matter came to rest all around the tipple itself.

With a "sullen roar," as witnesses would describe, the whole earth shook. Windows were broken. The noise was fully audible in Fairmont, six miles away, and at least one resident thought his house was "rocked as if by an earthquake."

Clay Fullen, by a quirk of luck, was not in the mines that day but loading hearth coal on a truck for a friend. He heard the blast, thought a minute, then decided he'd better go on over to No. 6, nearest to him, and try to find out what had happened.

Everyone in Monongah was on the move. The townsfolk saw the huge plumes of smoke rising from the mines' coal entrances and the "manways" alongside. As the smoke dissipated, each caved-in opening was like "a reeking cannon, recently fired." The people, by one appraisal, were "an excited group, their pallid faces betraying their fears, their nervous actions indicating anxiety to know the full truth . . . their hopes gradually giving way to despair." Another appraisal appeared in the Wheeling *Register*:

> The scenes about the mine opening were agonizing in the extreme. The anguish of wives and mothers who wrung their hands and cried hysterically out of their solicitude for breadwinners who were locked up in their underground sepulcher were painful. Women fainted, strong men gave way. Little children, only faintly realizing what had happened, cried pitifully, not for absent fathers and brothers, but because of the distress round about them and their intuitive knowledge that it was an occasion that called for tears.
>
> The first effect was to daze everybody. Then came a realization that something must be done to aid the men in the mines.

What could be done? Clay Fullen's reaction was typical. He waited and looked about, and his only answer was the mute wreckage at the mine mouths. No one was emerging. Nearly four hundred men and boys, conceivably many more, had entered on the day shift. No one was walking or even groping his way out. There was the singed and blackened figure of Pat McDonnell, not knowing what had hit him, but he had not been inside at the time. Neither had another, Joe Newton, fifty feet from No. 8, who nonetheless had lost his right eye and a finger.

Without having any real facts on which to base a judgment, it was evident to all present that a disaster of staggering proportions had just occurred.

With all the pit bosses and others trapped below or already dead, the higher directing echelon remained intact. Management, instantly aware of the challenge, reacted coolly and efficiently. Phone and telegraph lines were monopolized. Calls were placed to Clarence W. Watson, forty-three-year-old president of the Fairmont Coal Company, in Baltimore, to neighboring communities for physicians and ambulances, to the state mine inspector's office in Charleston, and to other mines for physical assistance. Watson ordered his private railroad car readied and two locomotives were pulled out of the smoky Baltimore roundhouse, their engineers instructed to "highball it for West Virginny!"

Robert Brooks, a teen-ager at the Despard Mines in Clarksburg, was among those who received word that mines were being shut down so that the workers might assist in Monongah. He hailed his brother Frank and caught the next eastbound trolley.

A silence crept over the women of Monongah, shivering in the cold atop the ridge dominating the mines. They waited.

By noon the fan to No. 6, not seriously damaged, was whirring again. Volunteers began inching their way in, the first group led by a railroad man, Peter McGraw. Clay Fullen was in the next party. The rescuers were equipped with hatchets, saws, canvas, and other materials to erect brattices, which were temporary partitions. These served to cover polluted galleries of "crosscuts" leading from the main haulways or passageways as the rescue parties cleared away debris impeding the flow of fresh air.

At the same time watchmen patrolled the hills around "toad" or "crop" holes—emergency exits—fearful that relatives would hysterically crawl down without appreciating any of the problems involved. On the next hill, above the hill of No. 8 entrance, one of the guards thought he heard a cry. He placed his ear to the nearest aperture and heard a low moan. A miner was immediately lowered by rope. About a hundred feet beneath the surface, the wavering flames from his small cap light silhouetted the figure of a miner crouched over the body of another. Pete Urban, of Poland, thus became the only man to survive the explosion.

It was now midafternoon, and the little town on the West Fork was already jammed with people and wagons, from mine inspectors and hospital staffs to undertakers and those from neighboring communities who had no reason to be there other than morbid curiosity.

Robert Brooks, the miner from Clarksburg, stepped from the street-car to venture a short distance into No. 6, but he decided he had no stomach for this sort of work. His brother Frank, on the other hand, did, and he settled in for a long stay. There was every reason to be repulsed and almost no hope for finding even a second man alive. The search parties had already shoved, pushed, and battered their way several hundred feet into the twin mines. They had sent half a dozen bodies back.

The miners had met varying intensities of violent death. Some had been blown to pieces. Others were not burned and, in fact, continued in stop-motion postures held at the instant of the blast. One man, propped against the mine wall, with dinner bucket in his hands, was in the act of eating lunch. A fourteen-year-old trapper boy who opened the doors was discovered in much the same stance.

Procedures had already been determined. The dead were, on discovery, saturated with carbolic acid, protected with sheeting, and borne out on stretchers, carried by men wearing rubber gloves. Animal carcasses were disinfected, covered, and temporarily bypassed.

Something about those first stretchers—the motionless forms beneath the sheets, the penetrating, oppressive odor of carbolic, or the expressions of the bearers—underscored the futility of hoping and pronounced a final amen, in advance of burial. Dusk and the increased damp of evening was at hand. "Dismal" was understatement enough.

Even as the bodies were being taken into the new First National Bank building—commandeered as a morgue—Clarence Watson's magnificent private car was grinding to a stop on the siding just down the street. The engineers had opened their throttles full steam for a record run over the mountains and around the many curves leading in from Baltimore.

Newspaper reporters, now assembled in constantly growing numbers, swarmed about the car's rear platform. "It is too bad," the coal company's president commented, then repeated, for once at a loss for words, "It is too bad." None present cared to dispute Watson, a shrewd and daring young executive. As head, also, of Consolidation Coal Company, he was beyond question among the most powerful figures in the industry, of a stature comparable even with Andrew Carnegie.

By midnight twenty-five miners had been recovered. A sleepless night passed. By Saturday morning "headings" had been cleared and ventilated as far as three thousand feet down. Portable "stein" fans had been hooked up to keep the air flowing. The dead miners were now being sent up six, eight, and a dozen at a time.

In the wait for embalming and identification, the morgue in the bank building overflowed into the town's theater, then upon the sidewalks, and finally into tents near the mine entrances. "The tents were soon filled with the lifeless bodies of ghastly men," wrote the captain of a National Guard detail, thirty-three-year-old Matthew Neely. "On every hand there were weeping fathers and mothers, wailing wives, and sobbing little children, and scenes of horror and outbursts of agony so heartrending that earth has no language adequate to describe them."

Some of the dead were well known. One such was John M. McGraw, member and leader of the First Regiment Band of Fairmont, whose father had been killed in the mines ten years earlier. Many more were little known, such as José Abatta, fourteen, a trapper boy who had not lived long enough to cut much of a figure around Monongah.

Five Greeks had shared one house. It echoed now only to the footsteps of the vandals who thoroughly ransacked it before the National Guard's patrol and shoot-to-kill orders had proved effective.

Some families had been rocked so many times by violence that they were numb: that, for example, of Fred Rogers, the fourth member to perish in an accident. Many miners, men in their late thirties or forties, left large families, five or six children, in ages descending to the crib. On one street not a husband, father, or son of legal age had been left alive. By one count, there were 250 new widows and 1,000 children denied the support of a father, older brother, or other breadwinner.

Considering the magnitude of the tragedy, it was not wholly surprising that some of the bereaved would shield themselves behind a cloak of fantasy. One woman, for example, kept the table set for her husband and the bed sheets turned back, explaining, "I know he is injured, and nobody can take care of him like I can." Another waited two days at the mouth of No. 6 with white carnations in hand. Her vigil was rewarded on Sunday. That same day, Mrs. John Hinerman, whose husband was a victim, died in childbirth, with perhaps little will to live and the doctors all busy at the morgues.

A fire in No. 8 retarded operations as a crowd of more than ten thousand persons shoved and pushed their way into Monongah to render snarled communication within the cramped area immeasurably worse. Rawboned mountain folk, carrying infants on their backs, gawking schoolchildren, and store clerks from Fairmont, Morgantown, and Clarksburg jostled past the grimed rescue crews and hearse drivers. At one point there wasn't a scrap of bread left in all of Monongah and no coffee other than already reused grounds. The town's outhouses, barely sufficient anyhow, became so overworked by those who did not bother so much as to ask permission that a new sanitary peril compounded the many and obvious existing ones in the wake of the catastrophe.

Families that had already identified their dead were packing up to live with relatives elsewhere. Some talked of returning to the old country as soon as they could acquire the passage. Their numbers would mount. They could not endure to remain in these surroundings, and it was small wonder. As R. L. Goshorn wrote in the Pittsburgh *Dispatch* of the mine itself, "Dante's Inferno could not surpass it for horrors." Another reporter scribbled out much the same threnody: "Think of hell as a hollow hill."

Like Bob Brooks, who had taken the trolley back to Clarksburg, there were others who couldn't go below into "hell."

Edgar Forbes, rushed to Monongah by *World's Work* magazine, asked of someone leaning against a coal car, "What's the matter with foreign miners?"

"They can't stand it," was the reply. "They can handle a pick all right, but when something happens, they lose their heads."

Whether "they" did or not, a sufficient work force had been recruited, including Baltimore and Ohio Railroad gangs brought in by the coal company for a variety of heavy chores, from the shoring up of the mines to digging graves. With so great a proportion of a population suddenly deceased and awaiting burial, the physical problem of disposal was "almost beyond comprehension," according to the official report of Frank Hass, the coal company's chief engineer. It continued:

At the time of the explosion both the Italian and Polish Catholic churches had cemeteries immediately adjoining, separated by a wire fence. At the very start, the men at work in these cemeteries were admonished by the representatives of these two churches to be very careful not to allow any member of the Italian church to be buried in the Polish side, or vice versa, and again, later, not to allow a Protestant to be buried in either of these cemeteries.

For this reason, a new cemetery was located, adjoining the Polish, to be used as a burying ground for Protestants and unknown. This fact made it necessary to have representatives of the Catholic churches present who had lists of the members of their congregations and whose advice was followed in determining the cemetery in which each body was interred.

The men in charge of the work of digging graves thought it advisable to dig trenches in which to place the bodies, but it was finally decided that each casket should have a separate grave.

An acre of land was purchased by Fairmont Coal to be used in great part for those of the Muhammadan faith.

There were other problems, arising, as Hass added, from "the ignorance of some of the bereaved." To save funeral expenses, a relative supposedly identified was allowed to be buried by the company as an "unknown." Then, after dark, one of the family would place a stick or distinctive rock by the grave or even notch a nearby fence post, with the intention later of erecting a small headstone.

Some bodies were found with as much as one hundred dollars in the trouser pockets. These, too, were sometimes claimed by persons who well knew they bore no relationship to the deceased.

Everything seemed to work against those who were seeking to restore a semblance of normalcy to little Monongah. Rain, sleet, and snow set in the first of the week, producing several inches of brown-gray muck everywhere, which was churned into a soupy consistency by the great numbers of horse-drawn wagons coming and going around the clock. A grave completed one night might be half filled with water by morning. A worker, alternately sweating and shivering, would have to lower himself until he stood waist-deep in the chilly mess to bail it out. The road up the hill to the cemeteries was so rutted and muddy that coffins slid off the wagons and had to be reloaded. Clay Fullen himself, assisting in several burial parties, was jounced off along with the pine boxes. Runaway hearses several times terrified the packed streets of the town.

On Tuesday seventy-eight bodies were recovered. Since there was now a three-hour burial law in effect, the strain imposed on everyone was incalculable.

Several volunteer committees hastily formed by Mayor W. H. Moore went to work to keep the mothers and children fed even if they could not do much about alleviating grief or, in some cases, hysteria. A ladies'-aid group distributed coffee and sandwiches at all hours. Other committees canvassed homes, accompanied by interpreters, to ascertain immediate needs. The use of chits at Fairmont Coal stores was suspended. The company during the emergency was supplying all the food and fuel needed.

A Mines Relief Fund was established in Fairmont. Its nationwide pleas in the press started dollars flowing in almost overnight. Cities in states as distant as Wisconsin and Texas sponsored benefit performances. Galveston wired in $127, including $1 from the Deep Water Saloon. The Fairmont Coal Company's contribution of $20,000 was the largest, with the Pittsburgh Chamber of Commerce second, raising $9,135. The Cleveland *Press* was third, with $2,960. President Theodore Roosevelt dug into his pockets for $100. Before the fund closed its books, it would have disbursed $147,000.

The coal corporation also settled $150 upon each widow, plus $75 additional for each child, including those unborn. If a mother, say, was left with three children, she was thus presented with the equivalent of about eight months of her late husband's earnings in the mines. Although something less than munificent, it seemed adequate in 1907.

On December 12, six days after the disaster, Watson announced, "We can positively say that the death list does not exceed 338." But, one by one, the bodies kept coming up on the white-sheeted litters until on December 22 the count was 347. In addition, three engaged in the rescue operations died from what was described as "exposure."

Meanwhile, there had been two more mine disasters; At Yolande, Alabama, upward of 91 were lost, and three days later at Fayette City, Pennsylvania, 239 died.

On Christmas Eve relief committees and charities from Fairmont and Clarksburg left little presents on Monongah's doorsteps. There were no candles in the windows or wreaths on the doors. None of the mothers, surely, had the heart for a tree.

Christmas Day came and passed. Right up until New Year's Day, the announced toll at Monongah continued to rise until, finally, the count stopped at 362, of which 284 were listed as having been buried in Monongah. The remainder were removed to other areas for interment.

The surviving miners—Clay Fullen, for example—would always insist that many more had actually perished that December 6. As they continued to work the reopened mines, they found grisly enough evidence for many months to support their belief.

The dead—or at least the identifiable dead—had been buried. The widows had received their small recompense. The coal cars were rattling up once more from No. 8 and No. 6. New immigrants had been trained in from eastern ports to fill the depleted ranks. The disaster would live on, however, and not only in the broken hearts of those who had known and loved the men who died.

"The explosion," observed Colonel Joseph McDermott, president of the West Virginia Senate and the representative of Governor William O. Dawson at the disaster site, "is just one of those things which happen in coal mining. No possible change in state mining laws could have prevented it."

Others tended not to agree with the legislator. More than 700 miners had perished in this bloodiest month in American coal-mining history, making a total of 3,242 in eighteen mines in the dark year of 1907!* This was more than three times the number of combat deaths suffered by the United States in the Spanish-American War of 1898.

The nation's press evinced editorial horror. The Pittsburgh *Dispatch*, for one, thumped: "If human life has been sacrificed to negligence or stupidity, the manslaughter cannot be stopped unless those responsible for it are made to suffer an adequate penalty."

Little voices began to be heard, among them those of Clarence Hall, an explosives expert with the United States Geological Survey, and George Harrison, chief mine inspector for the state of Ohio. They took the view that death and ruin, far from inevitable or "one of those things," could be substantially reduced if not ultimately eliminated. In

---

* U.S. Bureau of Mines figures.

addition, they asserted that the United States Government alone had the power and prestige to promote, if not *order*, safety in coal mines.

The inquest conducted by the coroner of Marion County, begun in Monongah and concluded at Fairmont, during the second week in January, 1908, came to no definitive conclusion. Mine inspectors from other districts of West Virginia, from adjacent states, and even from foreign countries at President Roosevelt's invitation disagreed, except on one manifest aspect: the violence of the blast. According to the joint Ohio mine inspectors' report:

> Our observations revealed to us evidence of the awful power of the explosion. We noticed the iron and concrete work of the tunnel leading into the powerful fan and the massive timbers adjacent thereto, at the entrance to No. 8 mine, forced hundreds of feet from their position. Inside of this mine we saw overcasts of concrete, strengthened with steel rails and wire ropes, blown to fragments and some pieces of them nearly two thousand pounds in weight moved many feet from their proper locations; concrete and wood stoppings practically all destroyed; mine cars, loaded and unloaded, torn to shreds and forced into every conceivable position and in every direction; electric wires blown down and motors disabled; timbers displaced and general debris scattered hither and thither about the mine.
>
> Intense heat was manifest in rooms and headings in many locations—posts charred; coked dust on roof and coal walls and cones of soot adhering thereto; solid coal pillars spalled or blistered and actually on fire. We saw evidence of coal having been shot out of the solid wall face by the miners; bad judgment used by them in placing of the holes in the coal seam and shots had been fired without doing the work they intended to do and much dust everywhere in the rise workings.

In summation, however, the coroner accepted the view of James W. Paul, chief mine inspector of West Virginia, as being the "most probable cause." Paul attributed a "blown-out shot" as igniter of the explosion. That is, a blasting charge of powder tamped into the coal wall exploded backward instead of into the coal deposits it was intended to break up, thereby igniting gas and coal dust. On the other hand, it was noted that such shots were fired at the rate of about one a minute in a large mine and that blowouts were a "comparatively common occurrence."

The other possibility recorded by the jury was that powder containers in No. 8 had been ignited through one cause or another, conceivably by a miner's lamp. The theory expressed by one or two inspectors that the runaway coal cars had started an explosive chain commencing with a short circuit proved unconvincing to the coroner.

The Ohio state inspectors would, however, conclude their joint statement with a blunt warning: ". . . if the general conditions of operating mines in the various states is not soon covered by adequate Federal laws . . . the sacrifice of human life in the mines has merely just begun."

To this the coroner's report postscripted, ". . . we recommend that Congress make an appropriation for the establishment of a Bureau of Investigation and Information to aid in the study of the various conditions under which explosions occur, and as to how they may be prevented."

Congress, historically slothful to act, finally was made aware of the public's disgust at the ever-increasing waste of both life and resources in the mining industry. After several preliminary steps in the ensuing months, an act of Congress—36 Statute 369—effective July 1, 1910, established the U.S. Bureau of Mines. This twentieth-century Magna Charta, as it were, of coal workers' safety, set forth as part of its guiding purpose:

> That it shall be the province and duty of the bureau . . . to make diligent investigation of the methods of mining, especially in relation to the safety of miners and the appliances best adapted to prevent accidents, the possible improvement of conditions under which mining operations are carried on . . . the use of explosives and electricity, the prevention of accidents and . . . to make such public reports . . . as the secretary may direct with the recommendations of such bureau.

This milestone act did not and could not insure against any more miners losing their lives beneath the surface of the earth. It has not made these subterranean pits either a fully safe or a pleasant place of toil, but it has helped. The horror of Monongah, therefore, had been somewhat less than total, meaningless waste.

4

The *Eastland* Rolls
Over, 1915

The twentieth century began on a disastrous note for steamships. In June, 1904, the excursion vessel *General Slocum* burned in the East River, New York City, with the loss of life of nearly one thousand persons, mostly women and children, on a church picnic.

By mid-1915 more than seven thousand passengers had died in seven major ship disasters, including the losses of the *Titanic* and the *Lusitania*. It was a highly unenviable record, especially in view of the fact that only one, the torpedoing of the Cunarder *Lusitania*, in May, 1915, had represented an act of war.

After the pitiable tragedy of the *Slocum*, however, which was seared with a deeply personal meaning for families all over the United States, one conclusion seemed justified: Never again would "the authorities" allow any kind of excursion craft to venture from dock without the most rigid inspection. Boating of this comfortable and often even plush sort upon lakes, inland waterways, or along the coast remained popular, if only because the auto age was still in the diaper stage. Companies vied with one another for the largest and finest vessels. Some were side-wheelers; others were equipped with propellers astern.

The two-thousand-ton steel-hulled *Eastland*, for the Lake Michigan traffic, was in the conventional propeller category. She was 265 feet long, built with a thirty-eight-foot beam and a maximum draft of not quite twenty-three feet, depending upon how much water ballast was aboard and the shallow nature of channels in which she steamed.

Her owners wished for her to be the "fastest" as well as the "largest and finest" on the Great Lakes. Thus, when she came off the ways in 1902, *Eastland* was equipped with twin screws, driven by two triple-expansion engines, in turn powered by four boilers. However, *Eastland* did not at first perform up to the advance expectations. Sporting four decks, she appeared a bit top-heavy, like the ancient galleys. Furthermore, her construction in the last months had been hurried, it was said, to place her into competitive service at the earliest possible date. Her detractors alleged that there had been "shoddy workmanship." Although the steamer's hull was light, the superstructure was too heavy seemingly even for two engines working under a full head of steam, and the ballast was not quite right.

Entering the excursion trade from Chicago to St. Joseph, Michigan, seventy-six miles across the lake from Illinois's largest city, the *Eastland* offered early indications that her stability left something to be desired. On one crossing she suddenly listed to starboard. The passengers were quickly ordered to the opposite side. The *Eastland* then creaked over to a port list. Officers, stewards, and concessionaires quickly hauled down her life preservers and ordered the passengers to don them. Then, hurriedly, the engine crew opened the ballast-tank flood valves to "full."

The steamer settled down on even keel. Her equilibrium had been restored. When she was moved to Cleveland, on Lake Erie, in 1907, someone must have remembered this experience, which revealed beyond any chance of refutation that the *Eastland* was a "tender," or unstable, vessel. The top, or "hurricane," deck was modified and barred to passenger use, which made her less top-heavy. At the same time her boilers were rebuilt to increase steam pressure.

With all this face-lifting and internal surgery, *Eastland* persisted as a cranky, unpredictable ship. One weekend she ran hard onto the Cleveland breakwater, leaving her fast for the night. The passengers, with minimum assistance, made their way back to shore along the rocks and concrete. Twice after that, the steamer was beached, unquestionably the result of bad navigation.

The temperamental craft by 1910 had accumulated such an unfelicitous reputation that her owners ran an ad in the Cleveland *Plain Dealer* offering five thousand dollars to anyone who could "prove that the *Eastland* is not the staunchest, fastest on the Lake!" Apparently, there were no challengers.

She was returned to Chicago where, by 1914, her former vagaries had been wholly forgotten and her latest pirouettes not yet known. At least among the "fastest" by this time, she became reasonably popular on her old run to "St. Joe" as well as the shorter round trip to Michigan City, Indiana. She could plow along at twenty-two miles per hour, which was a smart clip, even measured against such oceangoing queens as the *Mauretania*.

The dream of her original owners and builders had at long last been realized. Her encore upon Lake Michigan was thereby a source of pride to her master, Captain Harry Pedersen, her chief engineer, Joseph M. Ericksen, and her owners, the St. Joseph–Chicago Steamship Company. As an item of mixed responsibility, however, *Eastland* ran for most of the time under charter to the Indiana Transportation Company.

Perhaps the only sour note that first year of this prodigal's return was struck by the Chicago Federation of Labor which, after some investigation, decided it didn't like *any* such craft plying the Great Lakes. "We believe," a formal statement directed at Illinois and Michigan commerce officials began, "the condition of the excursion steamers are altogether too unsafe to be permitted to continue without a most vigorous protest." The labor group noted that one vessel, the *Christopher Columbus*, when overcrowded was unsafe "even if she were tied to the docks." This attitude, however, was deemed hysterical and, at best, somehow political in nature, as were most union pronouncements. The warning went unheeded.

July, 1915—which also represented the ending of the first year of the war in Europe—was sunny in Chicago, but not too hot. It was not surprising that when the Hawthorn Club of employees of Western Electric (a Bell Telephone Company subsidiary) debated on the form an outing should take that its members overwhelmingly chose a cruise to Michigan City. Nearly five thousand signed up for the excursion-picnic. Some would say they were pressured into buying a ticket, so determined were the club's officers.

The *Eastland* was one of five steamers made ready for the outing, scheduled for Saturday, July 24.

The families and secretaries started arriving at the Clark Street pier, on the Chicago River, as early as 6:30 that morning. The skies were leaden, with a presentiment of rain, but it didn't worry any of the Hawthorn Clubbers.

"We planned to have a nice time," observed one officer of the group, Mildred Anderson, and thereby spoke for many. Like the other girls, she was dressed in a long skirt and wide floppy summer bonnet. Most people carried picnic baskets, not relying on the fare of the steamers. Family groups predominated, some of them comprising as many as seven or eight individuals. Since the main Western Electric plant was in Cicero, a historically "immigrant" neighborhood, the mothers and fathers were of Polish, Czechoslovakian, and Hungarian extraction.

On the *Eastland*'s hurricane deck a steam calliope wheezed "The Good Old Summer Time" alternating with "Bedelia." These nostalgic piping notes blended into discord with more raucous selections issuing from bands on the decks of two adjacent steamers, the *Theodore Roosevelt* and the *Petoskey*.

Somehow, the people kept funneling onto the *Eastland* as though it were the only "ark" in the face of rising flood waters. By 7:15 there were nearly two thousand already on board her while only a few hundred had gone on the adjacent two. It didn't much matter to the excursionists. Some were on the decks, the men absently studying the structure of the steamer, the women swinging their parasols in anticipation of sunshine, the children tugging to be let loose. All the cabins were filled. Mildred Anderson and her sister Lottie were two of ten girls in one such below-decks state-room, "having a little party of our own. We were just laughing and talking about the excursion. . . ."

Meanwhile, the picnickers were still jamming into the pier toward the *Eastland*. No one seemed to know why they chose the *Eastland*, with four other largely empty steamers waiting. The men, women, and childdren kept coming, and like the girls in the cabin social, all were "laughing."

About that time, too, several deckhands, both on board and at the dock bollards waiting to cast off lines, noticed a port list, away from her berth. Yet if there had been an order to stop the oncoming horde, no one would remember it. A seaman glanced at a hawser and saw that it was taut, even though the propellers hadn't begun to turn over. He started to lug the gangplank back onto the pier.

Possibly in response to some word passed by the crew, but more likely as a reflex, since there was a noticeable tilt to the decks, many of the excursionists started toward the starboard, or dock, side. The *Eastland* shuddered, then leveled almost to an even keel. This seemed to satisfy the crewman at the gangway. Acting seemingly on his own, he pushed the walkway back across the scuppers, and loading continued.

It was anyone's guess how many were aboard the vessel—anywhere between 2,000 and 2,500—when at last even the attendant at the gangplank could perceive that hardly one more human being, adult or child, could possibly be squeezed on, even if pushed. This time he closed off the entrance and announced, "No more aboard!" The *Eastland*, however, remained a Lorelei, squat, weatherbeaten, and ugly as the steamer was, only a few strakes upward in the scales of nautical pulchritude from a scow.

However, people continued to jump the foot or two distance from the dock above the filthy Chicago River (used as a sanitary canal) along the length of the steamer to her decks. One was E. W. Sladkey, head of the Western Electric printing department. At least he had an excuse for not walking onto the next vessel loading: All of his department was on the *Eastland*. Sladkey was probably the last. He saw a tug moving at the *Eastland*'s bow and figured she was already on her way.

He took a few steps back, clutched his straw hat, and then ran for it. He cleared the gap between ship and pier, landing feet first. Even as he was congratulating himself, he could not help but notice a list, and "the thought flashed through my mind that there might be trouble before we got far." Then he saw a group of some thirty young men and women from the print shop waving at him from the bow on an upper deck. He waved back and started through the jam of picnickers toward them.

There was a slight strain on the lines from the tug *Kenosha*, although at least some of the ropes still held the *Eastland* to her dock. Those who might have known something about maneuvering weren't altogether surprised or even dismayed at this seeming clumsiness. Leaving a hawser or two temporarily secured was, for example, a proper way to swing a larger ship around in a tight area such as a river or a slip.

The calliope on the *Eastland* paused, as if for breath—or steam— and there were those who would remember a few bars from the band on the *Theodore Roosevelt* blaring, "I'm on My Way to Dear Old Dublin Bay."

The time was 7:20 A.M., and something was distinctly wrong. Crewmen began jumping from the already moving steamer to the dock. A woman screamed, either jostled or having lost her footing on the slanting deck. She couldn't fall, however, since there wasn't any room in the swarm of people. She screamed again. All on that deck, at least, turned toward the sound. Some believed there was a blast on the whistle, followed by the cry from the captain: "Open the inside doors. Let the people off!"

The passengers looked at each other and at those still on the pier, as if for reassurance. Then an icebox on the deck broke loose, plunged through the crowd, knocking women and children aside like tenpins, and went crashing through the rail and into the river with a dull splash.

Mildred Anderson and her friends stopped their talking as well as their fun "when all of sudden we felt the boat going over. We all fell in a heap. Then I began to hear the screams and the shrieks of the other people."

Sladkey, who hadn't progressed close to his friends in the bow, thought the steamer was listing as much as forty-five degrees, but like everyone else, he could do nothing about it. He heard "a shout of warning from sailors and officers." It was too late. The cranky *Eastland*, like a weary old monster of the deep plunging down to die, just kept rolling. People screamed, fought, and clawed up the starboard decks and railings, up the stairways inside and the walls, or "bulkheads," of the saloons and cabins.

Bollards, with splinters of pilings hanging from them, were torn from the dock with the crack of cannon shots as the steamer flopped over, still tied to her pier. In a washroom Lillian Heideman "went down and down. Water rushed into my nose and mouth." Those on the port side didn't have a chance, unless they jumped with a sprinter's speed and swam like fury. It was at least possible on the starboard to save oneself.

"In an instant," Sladkey continued, "passengers who were not, like myself, gripping the starboard rail or leaning against the starboard side of the deckhouses were slipping down the deck. In another instant it was all over with the *Eastland*!"

He climbed onto the now horizontal starboard side, still glistening with slimy river water, calling and beckoning others to follow. He jumped and landed on the deck of the tug *Kenosha*. His straw hat, if slightly askew, clung to his head. His shoes weren't even wet.

From the *Theodore Roosevelt* deckhands were throwing life pre-servers. Her passengers, momentarily, were too stunned to do that much. They simply stared. The spectacle of a ship, laden with people, sinking at her very dock challenged even the most lethargic imaginations.

Men, women, and a few children-in-hand were walking up the star-board side of the capsized steamer, much as Sladkey had. Others were struggling in the water. One man balanced himself on the starboard propeller, which was out of water. If they did not at once panic and go under, they would be saved. Their rescuers for the most part were crewmen from the tugs nearby and the four other excursion vessels who went into action with unusual speed, considering the trauma of the moment.

The *Kenosha* held her bow hard against the keel of the capsized *Eastland*, while stokers shoveled ashes onto the slippery side and bot-tom plates. The sailors also tossed lines and life preservers down to the struggling, flailing mass. The swimmers dived right in and went after the nearest survivors.

Another tug had the oxygen resuscitator operating within the minute. Fortuitously, a Coast Guard patrol vessel and the city fireboat *Graeme Stewart* were moored just a few slips away. They cut their hawsers and steamed hurriedly to the *Eastland*, whose keel remained jammed with people. Air hissed and bubbled up from the hull.

Inside the murky wreck many still lived. Some, like picnic-dressed divers, were surfacing. "I went into the water," Mildred Anderson would continue, "and I didn't see my sister Lottie or any of the girls after that." A tug crewman pulled Mildred out and gave her oxygen. Of the ten girls at the party, she alone lived to tell of her experience. Lillian Heideman, who had been caught in a washroom, also floated clear.

In some cabins and compartments the water leveled off with a foot or so of air space, leaving occupants to wait in horror for rescue. Some were surprisingly calm; others were hysterical. Their cries could be heard through the bulkheads.

The majority who would survive were hauled to safety within min-utes. A few, like Anna Golnick, floated phlegmatically on life pre-servers or in life jackets. "I thought they were crowding the boat too much," Anna observed in understatement to a tugboat sailor, who rescued her.

Almost none had a chance to don an *Eastland* life jacket. Most of these were padlocked securely in their lockers. Mrs. H. A. Thayer held her three children above water until her arms went numb, and one by one they "slid off" and disappeared. What had happened to her husband she would never know. Joe Brozak's coat caught on a nail not quite under water and held him until he was saved. Louis Martin grabbed a chicken coop and floated ashore some distance downriver.

Helen Repa, a Western Electric nurse, who had missed the *Eastland*, jumped into the river and pulled two victims out. She restored their breathing with artificial respiration before racing off for blankets. She obtained five hundred from the Marshall Field's department store and then established a morgue in the Second Regiment Armory on Washington Boulevard. The steamer *Roosevelt*, too, was rapidly being converted into a morgue.

William Sisson, a steamship claim agent who happened to be on Clark Street, helped throw lines and haul people, dead and alive, out of the river until finally, pale and sick, he had to stop. "I hope I never see anything like it again in my life," he would assert.

The old and socially prominent Plamondon family had again been struck by tragedy. Mr. and Mrs. Charles Plamondon had drowned that May when the *Lusitania* went down. A daughter, Charlotte, had barely escaped from the Iroquois Theater in 1903. E. K. Plamondon, a cousin of the late Charles Plamondon, had taken his wife, Susie, and four children on the *Eastland*. All but the mother were saved.

News of the tragedy spread swiftly throughout the city. Fire equipment, police vans, ambulances, and hearses were clanging down streets and boulevards to converge at the Clark Street dock. Steel workers with eye shields and acetylene torches were soon astride the hull, cutting the plates through. The river became impassable with all manner of craft, including yachts. Every pulmotor or oxygen tank and mask that could be located was on the pier or being rushed to it. For the most part the equipment had arrived too late, with seconds spelling the fine demarcation between life and death.

Someone on the dock spied Captain Pedersen, who had easily walked off the only half-awash pilothouse. "Drown him! Drown him!" arose the spontaneous cry. He might well have been drowned had not guards and police surrounded the unhappy master, then hurried him away.

Men with megaphones were being placed at intersections up to four blocks distant, repeating for the information of Hawthorn Clubbers still arriving: "Picnic called off! Picnic called off!" A reporter for the Chicago *Tribune* listened in wonder as a group of girls, baskets swinging, exclaimed: "Oh, *what* will we do now? Isn't it a shame!"

There really wasn't a great deal more to do, except to retrieve the dead. By 2 P.M., as a drizzle fell steadily, 679 bodies had been placed in the makeshift morgues.

At 3 P.M. a baby, about a year old, was brought up through a hole cut in the side. She smiled and kicked her feet to show white stockings and blue booties. As her rescuers held her over their heads, cheers arose from the multitudes that had refused to quit the Clark Street Bridge.

No more would be found alive.

The newspapers had already thrown extras out onto the bleak Saturday afternoon streets, announcing death totals of two thousand or more. Fortunately, the figure was exaggerated by more than double, but even the more than eight hundred who perished—the figure would remain in dispute—represented far too many on the ill-starred July picnic to Michigan City.

Night came. Searchlights cast their odd shadows over an unreal, drenched scene. Relatives filed past long rows of still figures on blankets, even as their counterparts had once done in Monongah. Pulleys and masts were already being affixed to the steamer's side to raise her. A grapple caught onto a bulky but yielding object. As it broke surface, rivulets of water gushing from every aperture, its identity became unmistakable—the steam calliope.

The press lost no time in venting its outrage. ". . . No thrilling midocean fight against raging winds and mountainous seas," editorialized the *Tribune*. "No hidden iceberg on a lonely course, no crash of midnight collision, no thunder of big guns in a clash of rival fleets. . . . Literally in the heart of a great city." One Chicago paper, the *Day Book*, laid the blame on the Hawthorn Club with the singular charge that its officers "should have known" the *Eastland* "was unsafe."

Now, after the fact, waterfront "authorities" came forward to chorus a requiem of the steamer's unseaworthiness. Only two days prior to the foundering, exclaimed one "Captain" John Morrison, the *Eastland* had "snapped" her hawsers at dock and nearly rolled over. Others disputed whether her stability line was twenty inches or four inches without ballast, or if she was licensed for 600 or 2,600 passengers, and similar quibbles. Yet all that really mattered now was that the steamer had capsized, taking hundreds with her.

Chicago receded into mourning. The mayor ordered all places of amusement closed for two days as he authorized an emergency fund of $500,000 for the survivors. Free typhoid vaccinations were given anyone who had been in or near the polluted Chicago River. Telegrams of condolence tapped in from every city and town in the nation, including the White House. They were matched by cables from overseas. King George and Kaiser Wilhelm, joined by officials of Austria-Hungary and some other leaders of the warring sides—the Allies against the Central Powers—paused in their fratricide to express their own sympathy. After all, they knew a thing or two about sudden death.

Sunday afternoon, a horse and wagon, bearing two newly sealed coffins, stopped at a row house on the near South Side. Two Western Electric families, comprising seven persons, had dwelt there. The driver, in need of burial instructions, knocked on the weathered door and knocked again. No one answered, and no one ever would. Every soul there had perished on the *Eastland*.

Burials continued for a week. At St. Mary's Roman Catholic Church twenty-nine coffins were carried in for a single funeral Mass.

Many of the victims went unidentified for a long while. The public's imagination was especially drawn to coroner's No. 396, described only as "a boy." Finally a grandmother claimed the remains which turned out to be those of Willie Novotny. She had already buried her daughter, son-in-law, and Willie's sister, dead in the same tragedy.

So upset was the whole Midwest that newsreels of the capsizing—and the story had been as well covered as the last sailing of the *Lusitania* —were forbidden to be shown in cities as far west as Omaha and as far east as Pittsburgh.

Someone would have to "pay" for *this* disaster, thumped the city prosecutors. Captain Pedersen, Chief Engineer Ericksen, and officials of the excursion line were held for grand-jury action, then indicted for manslaughter and negligence. A distinguished lawyer and jurist, Judge Kenesaw Mountain Landis, was appointed to a special investigative panel. An equally illustrious attorney, Clarence Darrow, would defend the master of the *Eastland*. Under direct orders from President Woodrow Wilson, the U.S. Department of Commerce entered the inquiry.

In Federal District Court, Michigan, in February, 1916, Darrow pursued tactics that would consolidate his fame in subsequent and far more prominent trials. Hour after hour, day after day, the lawyer interrogated an expert witness on ship construction, a university professor and designer who immodestly conceded that only one other man in the world, a Swede, knew as much about marine architecture as he did.

When Darrow at last informed a weary and exasperated court that he was finished, he summed up his case succinctly: How, he asked, could one captain be expected to know much about the characteristics of his vessel when only *two* men on the whole earth really understood these complexities?

The court was impelled to a decision. "The dead cannot be restored to life," ruled the bench. "The evidence . . . wholly fails to establish probable cause." Pedersen was a free man, although the other defendants were not per se absolved or the liability claims adjudicated. The *Eastland* had, in the meanwhile, been raised and sold to the navy for $45,000, which was scarcely sufficient to settle one suit.

July, 1916, came and passed. On the first anniversary of the tragedy the magazine *Survey* mused in print, what was happening? The Commerce Department, which had promised unequivocally to dig down to the crux of the affair and inform the public, remained silent. The following April the United States marched enthusiastically into the World War. The *Eastland* was largely forgotten in the overriding preoccupation of the moment. The exceptions were those naval recruits who trained on the Great Lakes upon the gunboat U.S.S. *Wilmette*, which was the rechristened and modified *Eastland*. The 1920's came and passed. The 1930's moved on. The *Eastland* and those who had served or died upon her became a shadow out of another incarnation. But in the tortoiselike inching of the judicial system the legacies of the disaster lived on.

Lawyers and prosecutors alike who had initiated the various proceedings retired or passed on. They were succeeded by others to whom the steamer was only a name, the connotations of which were merely a part of their day's docket. Then in 1935, exactly two decades after the sinking, the courts suddenly were ready. A new generation of reporters had to scurry to their "morgues," or newspaper libraries, and drag out yellowing clips to discover what the *Eastland* was all about.

At long last a ruling was handed down: The steamer had been "seaworthy," a pronouncement with an astounding ring to the still surviving kin of those who had been lost. She obviously, however, had not been sufficiently "seaworthy" to guarantee the lives of the 835 men, women, and children whom the jurists found to have perished on the ship.

The effect was to absolve owners—if still around—officers, and their heirs of further liability. However, the brief, as rather an afterthought, while conceding that the *Eastland* did indeed sink, expressed the opinion that some unnamed careless member of the engine gang had forgotten to fill the water-ballast tanks properly, if at all.

The old excursion boat and her black memories weren't, however, quite put to rest. She taught a new crop of sailors how to shoot for World War II. In 1946, now forty-four years old, the *Wilmette*, decommissioned, was hauled from her dock at the Great Lakes Naval Training Station. She was towed south along the shore, into the Chicago River toward a scrap yard, progressing under the Clark Street Bridge, past a still-used dock where early on a July morning in 1915. . . .

5

The Spanish Flu
Epidemic, 1918

In March, 1918, even before the American Expeditionary Forces had a chance to go into battle, Fort Riley, Kansas, was seized with an epidemic of what first appeared to be head colds, coughs, and, at the very worst, pneumonia. The old military post that sprawled over twenty thousand flat prairie acres baked in the summer and congealed under sleet and ice in the winter—a historic cavalryman's nightmare.

The outbreak then zeroed in upon one cantonment within the huge reservation, Camp Funston. Before it burned itself out in April, more than eleven hundred had been bedded, with fevers up to 104° or higher, and forty-six soldiers had succumbed. Doctors wrote as cause of death, "pneumonia."

At the same time similar flulike epidemics had incapacitated other military camps on the east and west coasts and on several navy ships at Norfolk and Boston. Five hundred of the nineteen hundred inmates at San Quentin prison, California, were taken sick. Three died.

At Brest and St. Nazaire, France, two major debarkation points for the doughboys, what was now positively diagnosed as an influenza epidemic erupted. French *poilus* began to sniffle, sneeze, and ache in their wet, cold, and drafty trenches with what their surgeons pronounced *la grippe*.

56

Next, the British Tommies were knocked down for a long count— "Flanders grippe," doctors dubbed it. All at once the Royal Navy was impeded with 10,313 cases of "something or other" in the respiratory department. Scotland, overnight, was suddenly recording nearly 110 deaths a week.

The disease hit with stealth and ferocity. "In the midst of perfect health," read a report of the British Ministry of Health, "the patient would be seized rapidly . . . with a sense of such prostration as to be utterly unable to carry on what he might be doing."

In Germany it was the *Blitz Katarrh*. Some 160,000 residents of Berlin were ill. Across the North Sea, by early summer, Londoners were expiring at the rate of nearly 300 a week.

Rumor had it that people were dying by the thousands in China and India, as if from "a tidal wave." Certain it was that the fever had hopped the Pacific to Hawaii, where Schofield Barracks had virtually been knocked out of action. There were eleven deaths one week.

Norway, Iceland, Alaska, Puerto Rico, Sierra Leone, Zanzibar, the Falkland Islands—the epidemic was raging around the world with the reckless abandon of a homicidal maniac. Spain was hard hit, but not proportionately worse than other countries. Even so, and for reasons about as capricious as the course of the plague itself, physicians began to label it the Spanish influenza, and nothing else. By late summer, by any name one might choose to call it, the flu was running amuck in the United States: 250,000 residents of Pennsylvania were seriously ill, 75,000 of them in Philadelphia, enough almost to shut down the important Hog Island shipyard complex in the Delaware River. The shoe and other defense-oriented industries of Brockton, Massachusetts, a city now of 50,000, were all but paralyzed, and Dr. Carl Holmberg, chairman of the board of health, admitted in despair that he was "fighting with a ghost."

Ships, such as the *Bergensfjord*, from Norway, docked at American ports with half their crew and passenger lists stricken, masters reporting multiple burials at sea. Within a few days of the transport *Olympic*'s docking at Southampton, 2,300 of the American troops that had been aboard her were bedded with flu. At least 119 died. Another troopship, the huge *Leviathan* (former German *Vaterland* seized by the United States), dropped anchor in Lower New York Bay September 19. Among the influenza cases removed was a distinguished one: Franklin D. Roosevelt, thirty-six-year-old Assistant Secretary of the Navy. He was taken to the Manhattan residence of his mother, Mrs. James Roosevelt, to recover.

The *Leviathan* fared worse yet on her outbound passage, carrying the more than 3,100 members of the 57th Pioneer Infantry Regiment, a Vermont outfit, of the 31st Division, together with other smaller units. Not only did 100 of the soldiers collapse as they marched to the liner's Hoboken pier, but in the several-hour interval before departure with all aboard, 100 additional men were carried ashore.

The transport never should have sailed. The voyage was a nightmare, as Colonel E. W. Gibson, of Brattleboro, commanding a battalion, attested. "The sick bay became overcrowded," he would recall. "It became necessary to evacuate the greater portion of Deck E and turn that into sick quarters. Doctors and nurses were stricken . . . the conditions during the night cannot be visualized . . . groans and cries of the terrified added to the confusion of the applicants clamoring for treatment, and altogether a true inferno reigned supreme." Nearly two hundred were buried soon after debarkation, in French soil. Many more undoubtedly died later, en route to their base camps.

The whole trouble, even as the public health doctor in Brockton had lamented, was that no one could come to grips with the plague. What was it? How was it transmitted? How did you go about treating the infection? It was, announced public health officials of Virginia, "a tiny living poisonous plant called the germ of influenza." To confuse readers further, the authors postscripted their amen: "It will mean a blessing in disguise."

In somewhat more scientific key Surgeon General Rupert Blue, of the U.S. Public Health Service, commented on the illness's sudden onset, with fevers of 102° or higher. Then he added, "One is struck by the fact that the patient looks sick." It seemed a reasonable diagnosis.

A Seattle physician, Dr. Louis Dechmann, decided that the Spanish flu was definitely "a negative disease." The treatment to him was wholly obvious: an abdomen pack of towels soaked in hot vinegar.

Lieutenant Colonel Philip S. Doane, head of the health and sanitation section of the Emergency Fleet Corporation, wasn't at all sure about a cure, but he was relatively convinced of the germ's origin: through saboteurs landed from U-boats. "It would be quite easy," asserted Colonel Doane, "for one of these German agents to turn loose Spanish influenza germs in a theater or some place where large numbers of persons are assembled."

Others subscribed to the theory that flu could be disseminated with the relative ease and abandon of sowing wheat or passing out cookies at a large carnival. In fact, there was a persistent rumor that Kaiser Wilhelm's spies pumped germs into the air from a laboratory in Chevy Chase, a suburb of the nation's capital.

The Stock Exchange in Boston went on a half-day regime, along with other businesses, Liberty Loan parades were canceled, churchless Sundays were proclaimed, and the large shipyard at Quincy was all but shut down. In fact, on one September afternoon, three men died on Quincy's sidewalks before they could be taken to a hospital. To the west, at Camp Devens, a nurse and 50 soldiers died in one day, as 1,543 cases were reported in a twenty-four-hour period.

Still the cures kept being promulgated. A Boston firm rushed a preparation—"Cetolates Tablets"—on the market, advertising, "One tablet three or four times daily may prevent serious attack." It was a ripe area for quackery.

"Cut up two large onions," wrote Mrs. Katerina Poskocil, of Cleveland, to Secretary of War Newton D. Baker, "and add to them rye flour until there is formed a thick paste . . . wrap it in a thin white cloth and apply it to the chest. . . ." From Leavenworth, Kansas, Joseph Peloquin telegraphed the War Department, "Rinse the mouth with lime water . . . and go to bed." A Boston physician, Dr. Charles E. Page, penned to the New York *Herald* that "influenza is caused chiefly by excessive clothing." A nonprofessional person, Mrs. Julia Gibson, of Pasadena, California, believed that a "whacking" wad of chloroform and alcohol stuffed in the patient's mouth might do the trick.

Secretary of the Interior Franklin K. Lane opened a letter from an Amarillo, Texas, man who suggested "inhaling smoke from wood or wet or damp straw or hay." Pull out all the teeth, chimed in Dr. Alexander B. Leeds, of Chickasha, Oklahoma. Drench yourself in sulfur, urged an elderly Georgia physician to the editor of the Atlanta *Constitution*. Philip Lynch, a New York broker, thought the dust of old books carried the disease as he recommended a good shelf-cleaning, if not book-burning. Libraries, led by the New York Public Library, actually closed their doors for varying periods. "Fruit-a-Tives" was advertised in the Rochester *Times-Union* as a likely cure. In Chicago an unscrupulous patent-medicine salesman hired a snake charmer, complete with snake and flute, to help him hawk his "influenza cures."

So it went, the babble of a twentieth-century Alice in Wonderland's tea party. Some even found heart to joke: "I had a little bird, and its name was Enza. I opened the window, and in flew Enza."

The epidemic, obviously, was no laughing matter. No one, especially not the doctors, knew what to do.

Children joined adults in wearing worthless gauze face masks. Schools were locked in many towns and cities as September turned into October, with hundreds of thousands of Americans desperately ill.

Theaters joined the schools in sealing doors, leaving actors and actresses stranded in one-night stands all over the country. They were followed by department and lesser stores, including barber shops, which were deemed an exceptionally fertile source of germ propagation. In fact, beards sprouted from the chins of the beardless from coast to coast as hysteria pointed accusingly to the very act of shaving.

By the first Sunday of October, the 6th, a totally invisible scourge had effectively terrorized a nation and backed its people to the wall, something which the German army and all the U-boats had been wholly unable to accomplish. That day the shocking total of 289 men and women in Philadelphia had died of the disease. They were mostly young adults, including pregnant women. Children and the middle-aged were not so hard hit.

At Philadelphia Hospital alone, where four patients were dying each hour, there were scarcely enough hearses, ambulances, or other public wagons to bring in the sick, much less carry off the dead. The clanging of patrol wagons' bells throughout the city's almost deserted thoroughfares intoned a strident, disquieting dirge.

Crime had almost disappeared. It was fortunate, since policemen themselves were collapsing as they walked their beats. One could hardly make a phone call in this City of Brotherly Love since nearly one thousand operators were bedded. By Sunday night 5,561 additional cases had been reported since early morning. Obviously, the life and industry of Philadelphia had just about ground to a halt.

Providence, Rhode Island, was recording about the same incidence of illness. There, the ban on public gatherings collided with Billy Sunday, the evangelist, who was fighting Satan from a temporary tabernacle. It came as a surprise to none of the believers when Sunday blamed the Germans fully for the epidemic, "a part of their propaganda . . . darn their hides!" The curbing of this ardent prohibitionist's revivals at first brought immeasurable joy to the saloon-keepers. Their jubilation, however, quickly sputtered out when their doors, too, were shut.

Little towns were assaulted in the same proportion as urban centers of population, thereby fragmenting theories that city dust, smoke, dirt, and crowding were disseminators of infection. Canaan, Connecticut; Berlin, New Hampshire; Silverton, Colorado; and Belen, New Mexico, were among such communities where more than half the population was stricken. However, these "whistle-stops" were forced to take care of themselves as best they could, with or without medical assistance.

Dr. H. S. Mustard, a Public Health Service epidemiologist, was more concerned about keeping the nation's capital in operation, or else, he said rather theatrically, "there won't be any France!" First, he had Washington declared "a sanitary zone," then promulgated lists of procedures and prohibitions. For example, "No person shall knowingly expose himself or any other persons . . . to infection of epidemic influenza." In other words, it was now against the law to get sick, and, further, a person could be fined fifty dollars or more if he appeared sneezing in public.

Civil servants, whose ranks were thinned by at least 50 percent absenteeism, were marched several times daily from their desks. They wheezed and panted through calisthenics, then, like docile farm animals, were herded back inside the federal barns.

The House and Senate closed all visitors galleries, and the courts went into recess. So many of the District of Columbia's firemen were ill that the marshal in charge warned, "The whole city'd burn to the ground if [a fire] ever got started."

Hospital wards overflowed into corridors, then onto porches. There was already a shortage of doctors and nurses, with so many in Europe with the A.E.F. Many left at home had succumbed to the disease or were facing a long period of recuperation after having fought through it. "The only way we could find room for the sick," observed Dr. James P. Leake, like Dr. Mustard an epidemiologist with the Public Health Service, "was to have undertakers waiting at the door, ready to remove bodies as fast as the victims died. The living came in one door, and the dead went out the other."

Soldiers were brought in from the many camps ringing Washington to dig undesignated graves, in anticipation of deaths. Although there was some indication that the fever at posts such as Forts Devens and Riley was burning itself out, most camps remained raging pestilence holes. Five thousand recruits and draftees had already succumbed in their muddy, chill precincts.

Things were so bad along the East Coast that health-department doctors were literally stealing coffins from railroad yards and warehouses, consigned elsewhere. For example, on October 10, 528 died in Philadelphia. No city was prepared for so many burials. And the death rate, already 700 percent above normal, was still rising.

Hoping to solve the interment if not necessarily the casket challenge, the Reverend Dr. Joseph Corrigan, director of Philadelphia's Catholic charities, organized a convoy of six horse-drawn wagons and one truck. With volunteers that included parishioners and seminarians, he prowled the city day and night seeking the many abandoned dead, in houses, in tenements, beside buildings, and in alleys. By lantern light Father Corrigan's crews swung picks and shovels to bury the corpses—in blankets if coffins were not at hand. Their next of kin could tend to these matters later if they desired.

Only the most determined among medical workers could check on the country's remote areas—such as Luce County, in Michigan's wooded Upper Peninsula. Accompanied by a doctor, Annie L. Colon, a public-health nurse, used a handcar on a narrow-gauge lumber railroad to reach isolated settlements. The pair left a bottle of whiskey and a blanket for a sick logger, hoped for the best, and slogged on to the next cabin. Other times they brought out the desperately ill. "We hitched a flatcar to a handcar with wire," Nurse Colon recalled, "put a board floor on, mattresses over that, plenty of covers and a canvas to cover the top and break the wind, and we carried the patients fifteen or more miles to a decent bed and a chance to live. We rode twenty and thirty miles at night through the deepest woods and over the roughest roads to camps, and many times we would find thirty or forty cases, sometimes ten people all huddled together fully dressed in a tiny log cabin, probably all in two beds and all with fevers over 104°."

As October wore on, pathologists were gradually reducing the gap between ignorance or bafflement and understanding, even though they might never arrive at a vaccine or serum in time. Dedicated researchers, for example, such as Dr. Simon Flexner and Dr. Martha Wollstein, of the Rockefeller Institute in New York, were pretty certain that the enemy they were tracking was no relatively sizable bacillus but a virus, a filterable microbe. They also were coming to the conclusion that the cyanotic, or blue-black discoloration of the patient, was not necessarily indicative of pneumonia, as generally associated. This vicious strain of influenza appeared quite capable in itself of inflaming the lung cavities until they filled with fluid and suffocated the patient.

Nonetheless, if a hint of medical progress was noted, the country's war effort remained disrupted. All draft calls were suspended: Too many men were unable even to answer, and no reception centers were fit for the selectees. General John J. Pershing, Commander in Chief of the A.E.F., cabled the War Department in vain for more replacements as the great Meuse-Argonne drive ground on toward heartland Germany. Nearly 100,000 army cases had been reported in early October, with more than 7,000 deaths since the start of the epidemic. This loss came within 2,500 of the battle dead thus far. Two weeks later, combat deaths were exceeded by the flu: Nearly 11,000 succumbed. One day in mid-October there had been 889 army fatalities from influenza-pneumonia. The doctors were not, nor ever would be, certain in their own minds just where to attribute the guilt.

The navy, meanwhile, was not spared. The epidemic struck on far-away stations—for example, the cruiser *Pittsburgh*, on South Atlantic patrol off Rio de Janeiro. At one time her complement of twelve hundred officers and men was more than 50 percent depleted through "sick call," and fifty-eight officers and men had expired. The situation was no better in Rio itself—a quarter of a million ill and two thousand deaths a week. The imagination was staggered.

Navy and Coast Guard vessels limped into ports around the world with sickness rates exceeding even the *Pittsburgh*'s. For example, the cutter U.S.C.G. *Seneca* dropped anchor off Gibraltar with only one officer able to stand watch. The navy patrol ship *Yacona* steamed into Boston harbor with more than 75 percent of her crew in bunks, some dying. The captain had to request aid in tying up her lines. Few aboard possessed the strength.

At Camp Custer, Michigan, one soldier was dying every fifty minutes, with twelve thousand fighting for their lives. Driven to the limits of human endurance and responsibility, the camp's commandant, although not ill physically, threatened with court-martial anyone who was "lax" in allowing the monstrous thing to spread. Surely, he did not himself know just what he meant.

The fever or even the anticipation of it maddened minds. Peter Marrazo, a laborer on Chicago's South Side, slashed the throats of his wife and four children before cutting his own and screaming, "I'll cure them my own way!" He alone survived. None had been especially sick.

In France the reaction of Private John Lewis Barkley, of Holden, Missouri, was typical of those doughboys coming down with the flu: "I was so miserable that I hoped I would die!" John, who was in Company G, of the 356th Infantry Regiment, was lucky. He lapsed into semi-consciousness in a cow barn while bivouacked at Cunel. The farmer's family found him and nursed him along until ambulance drivers picked him up.

Deaths in Great Britain were averaging two thousand a week. Omnibus service in London was greatly curtailed. The Metropolitan Police were hit particularly hard. Odessa, in the Ukraine, reported seventy thousand cases and "many deaths." Soldiers in German and Austrian cities were ordered back from the crumbling fronts to dig graves. Capetown, South Africa, counted at least two thousand children fatherless or motherless, some having lost both parents to the influenza. All public buildings were closed, tramways, postal and telegraph systems paralyzed.

Trappers returned from the jungles to reveal that baboon corpses were "all over the place, by the thousands." The apes apparently possessed no resistance to the infection.

In India, with accurate counts out of the question, it was obvious the people were dying by the hundreds of thousands—ultimately, 12,500,-000, it would be estimated. Dr. M. C. Nanjunda Rau, of Madras, did not consider his own theorizing especially radical when he announced, "This pandemic . . . operating on the vitality of all living things, reducing their power of resistance against disease . . . must have been the result of some cosmic influence."

Other men of medicine linked the germs with the battlefield, specifically the total effect of so many high explosives on the mutation of organisms.

Whatever had spawned this exceptionally virulent strain, it continued to leapfrog around the world, from coast to coast in the United States, and back again. As far as could be ascertained, among places of habitation, only tiny Tristan da Cunha Island, in the South Atlantic midway between Brazil and Capetown, escaped wholly unscathed. That it was isolated could not of itself have been the reason for immunity, since remote Eskimo villages, claiming little or no communication with the world's greater amplitude, were found to have been wiped out to the last child—nothing but frozen corpses, as found by special Coast Guard search teams. Could sea gulls have carried the disease? the question was asked.

As the last full week of October ended, on Saturday, the twenty-sixth, 21,000 Americans—a seven-day peak—had succumbed to influenza or a combination of that, pneumonia, and, perhaps, debility. New York City's mortality rate was 800 a day. Manifestly, the nation could not continue to function under such attrition and demoralization to its people.

The "lonesome October," as some pondered it, ended. November arrived. Then, one day soon, the Philadelphia *Inquirer* wrote: "From every street and highway, from every quarter and purlieu, from the stately mansions of the rich, from the modest homes and lodgings of the workers, from the alleys and courts of the lowly and the poor, its multitude poured forth. . . ."

Although the writer referred to the signing of the Armistice—on November 11—ending the Great War, he could as well have described the thanksgiving over the passing of the great plague. Coincidentally, perhaps, the worst of the Spanish influenza halted with the fighting in France. There was no brilliantly logical explanation for this phenomenon, but that's the way it was.

At all events, it had been the worst epidemic in the recorded history of mankind. More than twenty million the world over had died. This was some two million more than *twice* the total battle dead of the war. In the United States there were a total of 548,000 deaths out of 20,000,000 who had contracted the flu.

Not until fifteen years later was influenza's principal secret unlocked: its channel of transmission. This was almost happenstance in the course of experiments at the National Institute for Medical Research, London, upon the heels of discovering that flu could be transmitted artificially to ferrets. A repetition of ferrets sneezing at one another and into laboratory technicians' faces demonstrated beyond possibility of refutation that the nasal passages were the sole source of the microbe's entry. All the flimsy gauze face masks and the infinite variety of nostrums of 1918 now seemed like the witchcraft that indeed they were.

At about the same time in the 1930's the new electron microscope "mugged" this virus for the first time. The strain proved to resemble fluffy, cottonlike balls, so minute that twenty or thirty million of them could fit on the head of a pin without crowding. How they multiplied with virtually the speed of light none could say. It was established, however, that their first targets were the epithelial cells, themselves almost as invisible as the virus. Once these cells were broken down, all bodily functions ground to a halt, comparable to immersing a fine watch or other piece of moving machinery in water.

But *where* had the Spanish influenza gone? In 1951 a medical research team from the State University of Iowa journeyed to Alaska and the graves of known victims of the 1918 pandemic. There they exhumed the bodies perfectly preserved within the permafrost line of the icy earth. Lung sections were excised and removed in frozen packs to laboratories in Iowa City for culture. Why shouldn't a culture and transmittal to ferrets, mice, monkeys, or guinea pigs be possible?

The highly imaginative undertaking came to nothing. The mass murderer of 1918 had fled, elusive killer that it was. It has not returned to earth since, in its very same lethal form. Its exact, peculiar, and deadly characteristics will never be fully known to man.

6

LZ-129 *Hindenburg*—
Last Flight, 1937

The spring of 1937 began on a tragic note. At 3 P.M. Thursday, March 18, in New London, Texas, some seven hundred students and forty teachers of the Consolidated School were awaiting the day's final bell. With the dismissed primary grades already swinging their books and empty lunch boxes as they moved homeward, there were only fifteen more minutes to go.

Consol, as it was called, was a new school serving a thirty-square-mile area and had been built at a cost estimated from $125,000 to an even $1,000,000. What some said was the largest "country" school in the nation could seat and instruct fifteen hundred pupils.

At 3:05 P.M.—by the stoppage of many wall clocks and wrist and pocket watches—the monstrous thing occurred: The roof of the big structure lifted up, and the walls split and tumbled in. In the rubble were 455 bodies, including those of 14 teachers. Of the senior class, only 50 survived to graduate in late May. The victims, noted the sixty-one-year-old superintendent, W. C. Shaw, were like "rag dolls with their clothes torn off."

The cause was soon determined: leaking natural gas used for heating that had accumulated in the hollow tile walls, then been ignited possibly from the small spark of a wall switch. No one was really to blame. The appalling waste of young lives proved very little; natural gas, for economy and other reasons, would still be used widely for fuel, as would hollow tiles and cinder blocks for general construction.

Less than two months later a light drizzle was falling on the New Jersey coast. Fewer than one thousand spectators were on the expansive field of the Naval Air Station in Lakehurst, New Jersey, to watch the luxury dirigible *Hindenburg*'s first arrival of her second season of transatlantic passenger and freight service.

Three days out of Frankfurt, Germany, the 803-foot-long zeppelin, LZ-129 (or the 129th to be designed), had battled headwinds over the Atlantic, finally arriving ten hours late over Lakehurst at 4 P.M., Thursday, May 7. Since a thunderstorm was then crackling over the field, Kapitan Max Pruss had decided to cruise up and down the coast for a few hours until conditions improved. There seemed to be no urgency. The thirty-six passengers could wait, and for the sixty-one officers and men of the crew, their job was to fly, not to be grounded, especially this trip, which was for the training of some twenty of the unusually large complement.

Shortly after 6 P.M. Commander Charles E. Rosendahl, skipper of this home cote of the navy's lighter-than-air fleet, radioed the *Hindenburg*: "Conditions now considered suitable for landing."

Pruss conferred with Captain Ernst Lehmann, veteran of World War zeppelin bombings of England, who happened to be aboard. The two senior dirigible pilots decided to take their friend "Rosy's" advice. They ordered the helmsman to swing the nose of the sixth-of-a-mile-long airship around.

A few hundred feet below, the residents of the clamming community of Tuckerton, north of Atlantic City, watched the great shape droning up the coast toward Manahawkin, Barnegat, and Toms River.

Line parties were ordered to their stations in the bow and stern of the dirigible. All was in readiness for debarkation. Baggage was stacked in the main passenger lounge, a large luxurious compartment, complete with an aluminum grand piano. State-rooms had been cleaned, the berths already remade in preparation for the turn-around trip that night for Germany.

Those passengers who were not watching the changing panorama of Jersey seacoast, pinewoods, and towns below were seated in the lounge or the special smoking room, sealed by double doors against the ever-present danger of introducing fire to an area of gas. There was reason for concern. The airship's sixteen fabric cells carried seven million cubic feet of hydrogen, among the most inflammable of gases. However, it was a superb lifting gas, imbuing the *Hindenburg* with the unique payload (for an airship) of twenty tons.

She was, for all her splendid construction—a Gothic-like framework of aluminum rings, struts, and catwalks—"sensitive." Just before "sailing," the Deutsche Zeppelin–Reederei (the operating transport company) had received threats that the *Hindenburg* would be destroyed. It was enough to inspire Gestapo and Sicherheitsdienst men to make a microscopic inspection of all baggage in the assembly hall, which happened to be the baroque lobby of the old Frankfurter Hof hotel.

The travelers all felt that they, too, were under unusual scrutiny as they boarded the airship swinging lightly from her mooring mast under the floodlights of the beautiful Rhein-Main World Airport. It was nearly 8:30 P.M. before the familiar command *Auf Schiff!*—up ship!— sent the waiting, uniformed band blaring "Deutschland über Alles" and the Nazi marching song, the "Horst Wessel Lied," as the huge zeppelin soared into night skies.

By 7:10, May 7, *Hindenburg* was no more than two hundred feet over the Naval Air Station's landing apron. Spectators, including those waiting to welcome friends and relatives and a few early arrivals of her next passenger list and 230 navy and civilian line-handlers, looked up at the lights gleaming through the dusk from the control cabin, from the promenade deck, and from the hatches in the bow where crewmen were preparing the ropes and heavier mooring cable. The silhouettes of passengers were clearly visible behind the many windows. The airship then circled the field, her four twelve-hundred-horsepower Mercedes-Benz diesel engines throttled back.

"Here it comes, ladies and gentlemen," spoke Herb Morrison, an announcer for radio station WLS in Chicago, who was cutting a disk for later broadcast, "and what a sight it is. . . . Now and then the propellers are caught in the rays of sun, their highly polished surfaces reflect. . . . The ship is riding majestically toward us like some great feather. She's standing still now, they've dropped ropes out of the nose of the ship, and they've been taken hold of down on the field by a number of men. It has started to rain again. The rain had slackened up a little bit."

About 7:24, Rosendahl, who possessed a gift for words as well as airmanship, observed, "The vast silvery hulk of the *Hindenburg* hung motionless like a framed populated cloud."

Time had run out on LZ-129. Francis Hyland, one of the Lakehurst hired linesmen, was startled by what he thought was an engine backfire, flames spurting out. W. W. Groves, Yale & Towne Company engineer, on hand to check some copper tubing and pumping machinery, noticed a small spark, "like static electricity," dancing somewhere overhead and underneath the hovering airship, not far from the tail. Two of the four crewmen inside the massive lower fin saw a red, mushrooming glow deep within Gas Cell No. 4. Rosendahl observed "a small burst of flame" just forward of the upper vertical fin.

Mrs. Madeline Lupton, of Asbury Park, who was at Lakehurst just because she liked to watch such arrivals, detected "a faint pink glow in the lower center of the ship . . . like some thick silvery fish with a rosy glow in the abdomen. It began small and pale and spread redder and larger." Mrs. W. R. van Meter, of Upper Darby, Pennsylvania, thought the stern had "lighted up sort of like a Japanese lantern . . . then flames inside swirling around. . . ." A "pufflike flame about fifty feet forward of the vertical fin . . . the size of a house door" impressed Albert E. Reitzel, Department of Commerce official present on immigration matters.

"It's burst into flames!" screamed Herb Morrison into his recording "mike," continuing, "Oh, my . . . it is burning, bursting into flames. . . . Oh, the humanity and all the passengers!"

To Murray Becker, photographer for the Associated Press, this was "a moment of spectacular madness." He could hardly switch film in his speed Graphic fast enough to record the split-second changing scene. The newsreelmen, perched atop their cars, impeded by the heavy equipment, held their ground even though the airship was exploding with dull booms right over their heads.

Passengers, at first hearing nothing, were made aware of something catastrophic-looking below them. Leonhard Adelt, on the *Hindenburg*'s promenade deck, noticed "a remarkable stillness." Adelt, a Dresden author who was working on a biography of Captain Lehmann, obtained a hint of tragedy by observing that the spectators and linesmen on the ground had "visibly stiffened." Then there came to his hearing "a light dull detonation, no louder than the sound of a beer bottle being opened . . . followed by a delicate rose glow as though the sun were about to rise."

As passengers began to be thrown one against the other in a struggling heap, Margaret Mather, of Morristown, New Jersey, heard a guttural male cry, "*Mein Gott—es ist das Ende!*" Colonel Nelson Morris, multimillionaire Chicago meat-packing executive, heard a report like "a regular service rifle would sound." Then Joseph Spah, an American acrobat returning from European performances, was dazzled by "a blinding light" and deafened by a much louder explosion.

Far forward in the control gondola, the noise was so slight that Captain Anton Wittemann, one of the five of his rank on this semi-training flight, at first thought only a line or a light girder had snapped. Then the automatic emergency bell commenced its clangor, and a voice broke the momentary silence on this the airship's bridge: "Fire!"

Once started, the flames raced from hydrogen cell to hydrogen cell, popping them like distant thunder. Rosendahl, "spellbound," watched fire "greedily devouring the illustrious name *Hindenburg* letter by letter."

Herb Morrison was too overcome to continue his recording as he half-sobbed into his microphone, "I can't talk, ladies and gentlemen. . . . It's the worst thing I have ever witnessed . . . !"

Alice Rogers Hager, syndicated aviation writer, observed "fire everywhere, rushing, sweeping its way through the pitiful crumpling wreckage. It was not possible that anything should be alive in that inferno. Yet men leaped out." Crewmen and passengers alike were jumping as the "inferno" sank toward the ground. Joe Spah, using every ounce of his acrobat's skill, forced his way through a window, hung momentarily to a metal bar, then dropped nearly fifty feet into a sandpit, hitting so hard that he bounced once. Then, like others already out of the airship, he raced away from that tremendous, incandescent bulk, now almost on the ground. Before her tail hit, she cracked in the middle, her bow tilting skyward, allowing flames to pour from her nose like fire out of a volcano—a monstrous torch in the fading twilight.

Of the twelve riggers and other crewmen positioned in the nose to handle the lines, only one, Joseph Leibrecht, an electrician, survived. As the bow tilted upward at a ninety-degree angle, the men, one by one, lost their grips and tumbled back into the raging crucible that had been the interior of the *Hindenburg*. With the strength of terror, Leibrecht, frightfully burned, rode the structure down as the nose section, still aflame, straightened out.

"We all seemed to get the message at the same instant," thought Vincent Sheridan, among the navy ground crew, "for we all started to evacuate en masse." Heavy with their wet clothing and hampered by the sodden, sandy terrain, they nonetheless clomped off, barely in time to escape the falling, crackling debris.

Corpulent Detective Arthur C. Johnson, of the New York Police Department's alien squad, fell down three times as he attempted to flee, then was knocked over by an automobile. Undaunted, Johnson reached a telephone to flash to the New Jersey State Police what was in likelihood the first bulletin of the tragedy: "Ambulances, doctors, nurses. . . !"

Although Johnson's lifelong assignment had been to watch debarking passengers from ocean liners for known "unwanted" aliens, he did not have any particular alert today. There were, however, two Luftwaffe pilots, one of whom was an intelligence officer, on board.

Spectators now watched a further unbelievable sight: Navy and civilian ground crewmen halted, turned, and started toward the eight-hundred-foot-long wall of fire stretched across the air-station apron. "They dove into the flames like dogs after rabbits," it looked to Gill Robb Wilson, New Jersey State Aviation Commissioner. They were in time to catch the two small boys thrown out of a window by Mrs. Matilda Doehner, whose husband, Hermann, owned a wholesale drug firm in Mexico City. She, too, would escape, although Herr Doehner and his sixteen-year-old daughter were lost.

Nelson Morris, breaking fire-rimmed metal rods that obstructed his path, walked to safety, although his hands were seared. Even at the time it occurred to the phlegmatic Chicagoan and former member of the A.E.F. that his act was a "most remarkable thing."

Margaret Mather, dazed, waited in the shambles of the promenade deck until she heard someone shout, "Come out, lady!" She would recall: "Two or three men were peering in, beckoning and calling to us. I got up incredulous and instinctively groped with my feet for my handbag, which had been jerked from me when I fell." Of a poetic nature Miss Mather, a sensitive, sparrowlike little person, was impressed with the utterly wild, netherworld beauty of the scene, flames "flying all around, like birds lighting on my arms so I would have to brush them off."

Mrs. Marie Kleeman, sixty-one, of Hamburg, en route to visit her daughter and son-in-law in Andover, Massachusetts, found salvation both unexpected and easy. The debarkation stairs, burned from their latches, fell almost perfectly into place, and she walked down them. Older yet, Elsa Ernst, wife of a Hamburg cotton broker, slid down a rope. Her husband, Otto, in his seventies, would succumb to his injuries.

Caught almost amidships with seemingly no hope for escape, Werner Franz, a fourteen-year-old cabin boy, came under the drenching of a waterballast tank. The liquid not only rendered him relatively "fireproof" but extinguished the flames around him and offered narrow but clear egress.

At first it appeared that all of the officers and their staff had made good an exit. Then Captain Lehmann, his clothes scorched and smoking, was spotted staggering away from his "beautiful" airship. To his friend Rosendahl he muttered, in German: "I cannot understand it. I cannot understand it."

Lehmann, although it was not generally known, was aboard this flight only because of his mounting concern for the safety of the *Hindenburg*. There had been too many threats to destroy her, of which those that delayed her departure were only the most recent. He had made a last-minute decision, packing only a few toiletries.

As Lehmann was carried off to the station infirmary, the *Hindenburg* lay a twisted, hotly smoldering skeleton, 4,381 miles from her base, Frankfurt, seventy-seven hours in time. Here in tortured death reposed the alpha and omega of the super-airship—the evanescently fulfilled dream of luxury liners of the sky. The era of the zeppelin had passed in thirty-two seconds in the wet New Jersey dusk. All at once the rigid, hydrogen-filled airship, like the dinosaur, was extinct.

The explosion had taken thirty-six lives, including twelve passengers and one line-handler.

Adolf Hitler received the news at 1 A.M., Friday, in his mountain eyrie, Berchtesgaden. Obviously stunned at the loss of so prestigious a vehicle, he ordered a state funeral for those crewmen who lost their lives. Along with the smaller, older *Graf Zeppelin*, the *Hindenburg* had been a familiar and effective propaganda attraction over Nazi party rallies.

In fact, the *Graf Zeppelin*, droning back from South America, was nearing the Canary Islands when the radioman brought Captain Hans von Schiller a bulletin copied from the French Havas news agency. It was all the more unbelievable since only a few minutes earlier the radio shack had picked up a terse announcement from DNB, the official German Reich news service, that the dirigible had landed in Lakehurst.

Dr. Hugo Eckner, protégé of Count Ferdinand von Zeppelin, was awakened at about the same time Chancellor Hitler was. Visiting in Graz, Austria, the celebrated airship designer made hasty preparations to fly to Berlin.

The headline in a number of German newspapers told the story: *Das Luftschiff Hindenburg Ist Nicht Mehr.*

Indeed it was "no more." But what had happened?

Captain Lehmann, who succumbed on Friday, whispered to Rosendahl that the destruction "must have been caused by an infernal machine." These were among his last words. He was unable to amplify. Rumors of sabotage arose almost before the last glowing girder had cooled into black, twisted junk. If this were true, how had it been accomplished? A marksman in the pinewoods firing an incendiary bullet? Commander Rosendahl himself was at first inclined to this theory, which was plausible enough considering the fact that Nazi Germany had cultivated passionate enmity within and without the Third Reich. Mysterious fires had been breaking out on her merchant-marine vessels. Why shouldn't this hate extend to airborne carriers of the swastika?

In 1937 there was still an anti-Nazi resistance movement, although an individual put himself in mortal peril even to hint at such sympathies. The state executioner had not known many idle hours since Herr Hitler came to power early in 1933. Not only the German Jews, an especial target of Nazi wrath, but all freedom-loving peoples had come to loathe and detest what the swastika—the "crooked cross"— symbolized.

If not a long-range rifle, perhaps a time bomb had been the cause of destruction. Rosendahl would be drawn secondarily to this hypothesis. How about a low-flying airplane that dropped "something" on the ample topside of the dirigible? A letter to a newspaper editor suggested this. The flaw was: No one had seen an airplane anywhere near the Lakehurst field at the time. Or a camera equipped with a fiendish shooting device where the lens should be?

The navy commenced a brief inquiry, but it was ordered to halt at once, since the Bureau of Air Commerce of the U.S. Department of Commerce claimed full jurisdiction over this commercial aircraft "accident." Survivors were interrogated in a portion of the air-station hangar that had been used as a passenger waiting room.

For the most part, their testimony, even allowing for the sterility of a translator, had obviously been constrained through orders from Berlin. All seemingly were in agreement that nothing out of the ordinary had occurred, the dirigible had been operating at peak performance, and no one had any personal theory whatsoever as to what had caused the catastrophe. Two witnesses in particular, however, provided especially graphic pictures of the origin of the fire. They were Helmut Lau, a helmsman, and Chief Engineer Rudolf Sauter, both of whom had been very close to Cell No. 4 where it was generally agreed the explosion started. To the burly Sauter, standing fifty feet below the cell, it was like "a flashbulb" going off inside. It looked much the same to Lau, before the "flash" spread throughout the fabric cell, and sounded like the gas burner of a stove being lit—"a low pop."

Nonetheless, with this and other testimony before them, endeavoring to pinpoint the core of the explosion and ignoring the fact that the thunderstorm had already moved out of Lakehurst, the Bureau of Air Commerce resolved officially that "a small amount of explosive mixture in the upper part of the ship could have been ignited by St. Elmo's fire or a similar electric phenomenon like ball lightning. . . ." This theorizing was compounded by two additional suppositions, unsupported by evidence, that there had been a "leak in a gas cell" in turn caused "by a torn wire."

What, then, if this were too gossamer except for the naïve, really *did* precipitate the end of LZ-129 *Hindenburg*—and the commercial, rigid airship?

The author of this book served for several months as a blimp student at Lakehurst before the squadrons were reduced, and he was ordered to sea as a gunnery officer on merchant ships. While at the air station, home cote of the navy's visionary and daring but doomed flirtation with lighter-than-air, he often pondered that May twilight, 1937.

The evening the *Hindenburg* blew up, he was a copy boy of a few weeks' standing on the Washington *Post*—his first job. He also obtained brief material for his first news story, interviewing an acquaintance, Peter Belin, a Washingtonian who was one of the survivors. He jumped and was not so much as ruffled by the experience.

Ever since, this writer harbored the mental image of that great clumsy zeppelin hovering low over the damp landing apron at Lakehurst and then, with no warning, blowing to bits. It was as compelling to the author as his own subsequent experiences in the war culminated by his going over the side of an exploding Liberty ship in the North Sea.

He made it his postwar business after hours to meet and talk with people who were in any way conversant with the *Hindenburg* or the *Graf Zeppelin* or had flown on either one. This file-for-future reference dossier ultimately led to a contract with a book publisher for the first definitive study of the disaster at Lakehurst. The book was published by Little, Brown in 1962 under the title *Who Destroyed the* Hindenburg?

The author had taken a leave of absence from his full-time job the previous year to hunt up crew survivors the length and breadth of West Germany, from Friedrichshafen to Hamburg. In the course of his research he talked with some twenty-five who served on the ill-fated airship that long-ago night in May. Several of them, major witnesses, including Chief Engineer Sauter, are since deceased.

On the basis of information supplied the author, some of it necessarily confidential or not to be attributed, he came to the conclusion that the destruction of the dirigible was no accident but well-planned sabotage— on the part of the Gegen-Nazi Wiederstand, the anti-Nazi resistance.

The trail then led to a prime suspect: tall, blond Eric Spehl, twenty-six-year-old rigger from the High Black Forest region of southwest Germany. Of the entire crew, on record as at least paying lip service to the Nazis, Eric was the only one even vaguely suspected of "not being one" of them. In fact, on this voyage he had been under surveillance by the several crew members with additional secret-police duties.

Eric, a camera bug, in likelihood would not have had the nerve by himself to accomplish carnage on the grand scale without inspiration. This was, in turn, supplied by a known Communist, a woman his senior whose lover had died in Spain fighting with the International Brigade. The author has had communication with this woman, whose name must necessarily be camouflaged under the random pseudonym Hilda Schmidt.

Although book-length treatment was and is necessary to weave the full texture of a case of circumstantial guilt, here in brief is the reconstruction:

Spehl was talked into placing a bomb next to a gas cell before landing but timed to detonate *after* landing. Neither Eric nor Hilda had any demonstrable desire to hurt people—just to eradicate the whole hated symbol of Nazi Germany, the airship itself with the big red, taunting swastikas on the tail fins. But the ship was unexpectedly delayed after it had come over the field the first time. The hours lost in cruising up and down the coast would prove fatal.

By the author's reconstruction, again based on his interviews, Spehl had fashioned an ingenious "bomb" that was in reality a photo flashbulb. Its surface coating was or could have been weakened to facilitate its explosion and to release split-second heat as high as 6,400° F.—six times that necessary to ignite hydrogen, twice that to melt steel. This could have been attached to a small battery and a timer such as commonly used in a photographic darkroom.

This combination of bulb, battery, and timer could have been placed in the rigging next to Cell No. 4. However, Spehl, ordered into the nose with the rest of the landing detail, had no chance to leave his post and to delay the setting of the timer.

Spehl perished with the others in the bow.

This young rigger was a loner, given to nightmares, a latter-day Wagnerian type seeking, through his own impatience perhaps, to hasten the Götterdämmerung of the Third Reich. He was the last man of only three to be in the immediate vicinity of the explosion—in the catwalks and rigging adjacent to Cell No. 4.

With the utmost difficulty investigators exhumed "clues" in the wreckage that might lead to positive conclusions. The incandescent heat of the destruction had taken care of that. There was, in fact, almost nothing that helped . . . almost.

A notation was tossed into the voluminous files of the Bureau of Air Commerce investigation, to be entombed with apparently no attention paid to it. This pertained to the finding of a one-and-a-half-volt dry-cell battery, or its burned remains, which were identified by the Bureau of Explosives of the Association of American Railroads, in New York. Commonplace? No. Passengers and crewmen alike were forbidden to have conventional-type flashlights because of minute sparks caused in switching on or off. Only special safety wet-cell batteries were used in lights and in the wireless shack of the *Hindenburg*.

There are other points of suspicion woven into a highly complex tapestry of possible guilt. Yet, in sum, do all these pieces of tattletale add up to coincidence? Perhaps. Perhaps not. At least, they are as possible as the Bureau of Air Commerce's theoretical chain of events and no less circumstantial than the evidence that sent Sacco and Vanzetti to the electric chair in 1927.

The human factor, for one, must remain an imponderable as well as a variable. Was Spehl indeed capable of such an act? And what about spite on the part of those survivors who directed a finger of suspicion at the young, withdrawn rigger, who was unpopular among fellow crewmen?

Who destroyed the *Hindenburg*, or *what* destroyed the *Hindenburg*? Something as simple perhaps as someone smoking illegally near a leaking cell? This regulation was violated regularly. The answer lay in the cold ashes of Lakehurst, long since skirled by the winds into the depths of the surrounding pinewoods.

Draft Riots, New York, 1863. Colonel H. J. O'Brien, of the 11th
New York Volunteers, rallies 150 militiamen for a stand against
the rioters in front of Oliver's Livery Stable, near the East River.
The colonel later paid with his life for his stand.
(*Leslie's Illustrated Weekly*)

Sacred Heart Church, Galveston, was ruined by the tidal wave
in 1900. (*Rosenberg Library*)

Wreckage of Galveston after the 1900 tidal wave, looking
toward the bay (*Rosenberg Library*)

Sailing vessels littered the Gulf Coast after the tidal wave. (*Rosenberg Library*)

Impromptu corps of stretcher-bearers after the Galveston tidal wave (*Rosenberg Library*)

Waiting, following a mine explosion after the turn of the century. This was not Monongah, but the situation, the surroundings, and the grief were all the same and repeated far too often. (*Bureau of Mines, U.S. Department of the Interior*)

LEFT
Polish-born Pete Urban was the only worker inside the mines to survive the Monongah blast. He tried his luck too far. He died in 1926 during a cave-in within the same mine complex. This photograph was taken several years after the 1907 explosion, as the improved lamp shows.
(*Bureau of Mines, U.S. Department of the Interior*)

One of the great photographs of "immediacy" of this century—
taken just after the *Eastland* capsized in the Chicago River, July 24,
1915—made by a news photographer on a routine assignment to
cover the Western Electric picnic. Those who survived brought
everything, as note the ladies with their handbags and the men with
their straw hats. For the most part, the life belts—many floating in
the dirty water—were totally useless. (*Chicago Historical Society*)

The old *Eastland*, now the *U.S.S. Wilmette*, during the 1920's
(*U.S. Bureau of Ships*)

The *Eastland,* read the ad, was "the Largest, Finest and Fastest" on the Lakes. Fortuitously, it did not claim that the steamer was the safest. The ad appeared within two weeks of the *Eastland*'s capsizing.

Lawrence, Massachusetts, was badly infected by the 1918 Spanish influenza epidemic. Tent hospitals were spread to shelter the accumulating hundreds of new cases. (*American National Red Cross*)

The conductor on this Seattle, Washington, trolley seems to be saying that the man without a face mask can't board—the Spanish influenza epidemic of 1918 was at its height. The Red Cross alone distributed more than a quarter million gauze and linen nose-mouth coverers. They were about as effective barriers against the deadly virus as voodoo symbols. (*American National Red Cross*)

Almost at the mooring mast, the beautiful *Hindenburg* is stricken over the Naval Air Station in Lakehurst, New Jersey. Gus Pasquarella, Philadelphia news and commercial photographer, snapped his shutter split seconds after the initial explosion. (*Photo courtesy of his widow, Elizabeth Pasquarella*)

The LZ-129 *Hindenburg*, 803 feet (nearly one sixth of a mile) long, with a capacity of seven million cubic feet of hydrogen gas, furnished with staterooms for seventy passengers, lounges, a bar, piano, and sun deck, was the largest, most imposing and luxurious creation of the skies in 1936. She could cross the Atlantic in three days or slightly less. (*Author's collection*)

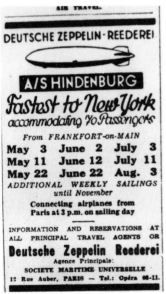

What was the role of Rigger Erich Spehl in the destruction of the *Hindenburg?*

Misquamicut Cove, along the Rhode Island–Connecticut border following the 1938 hurricane (*Lewis R. Greene, the Westerly* Sun)

Wreckage at Stonington, Connecticut, in the wake of the 1938
Hurricane (*Lewis R. Greene, the Westerly* Sun)

The flag still flies over the burning "big top" in Hartford, Connecticut, July 6, 1944, as the lucky ones make good their escape.
An obvious artist's touch-up somewhere along the line nonetheless does not obscure the drama etched on the faces. (*American National Red Cross*)

A scene of carnage and destruction at Texas City, April, 1947, following ammonium nitrate blasts on two freighters. Taken two days after the initial explosions, the photograph shows oil tanks and refineries burning in the background, against a foreground of broken cars and trucks, tree stumps, and rubble that defies identification. (*American National Red Cross*)

One of the great "just before" pictures of the mid-twentieth century—the *Grand Camp* minutes before the Liberty ship blew up in Texas City. All the firemen shown were dead moments later. The photographer is not listed. (*National Board of Fire Underwriters*)

Texas City burning fiercely into the second day after the ship explosions, 1947. The Monsanto plant, in ruins, is in the left foreground. (*American National Red Cross*)

It sounded like "an atom bomb" to one Richmond Hill resident that Thanksgiving Eve, 1950, when a Long Island Rail Road express telescoped the rear of another train ahead of it. (*United Press International*)

Death on Sterling Place, Brooklyn, December 16, 1960 (*National Transportation Safety Board*)

". . . a picture out of a fairy book," the scene on the ground had appeared to eleven-year-old Stevie Baltz before the midair collision that wintry December morning, 1960. The only one to survive the immediate crash of either plane, the little boy from Chicago rests on a snowdrift while passersby endeavor to comfort him. He lived only a day. (*United Press International*)

Journey's end for Flight 266 from Dayton, Ohio, on a small army helicopter field in Staten Island (*National Transportation Safety Board*)

View of Fourth Street area in Anchorage, Alaska, in wake of "Good Friday" Alaska Earthquake, March 27, 1964. The devastating quake, with a Richter magnitude of 8.5, dealt a massive blow to the south-central portion of the state. (*U.S. Department of the Interior Geological Survey*)

The earth shook violently, and buildings crumbled like matchsticks in a matter of minutes during the Alaska quake. (*American National Red Cross*)

The scene is Portage, Alaska, where American Red Cross disaster worker J. Wil Gaiser, of St. Louis, Missouri, peers into one of the many crevices opened up by the quake. (*American National Red Cross*)

After Buffalo Creek in West Virginia ran amuck (*American National Red Cross*)

Servicemen from Ellsworth Air Force Base digging through the rubble of Rapid City, South Dakota, hit by the June flood (*U.S. Air Force*)

Automobiles and trailers piled up in helter-skelter fashion after flood waters recede in Rapid City, South Dakota (*American National Red Cross*)

Rescue helicopter over Wilkes-Barre, Pennsylvania, during the onslaught of Hurricane Agnes (*American National Red Cross*)

A view of the smoke pouring from buildings in Wilkes-Barre, Pennsylvania, during the height of the flood waters caused by the rains of Hurricane Agnes (*U.S. Navy*)

Aerial view of a flooded airport in the Wyoming Valley area of Pennsylvania after the hurricane (*U.S. Navy*)

A U.S. Coast Guard rescue boat stops in the watery yard of a resident in Harrisburg to pick up stranded flood victims of Hurricane Agnes. In the background a private boatman pitches in to help at a neighbor's home. (*U.S. Coast Guard*)

7

Hurricane over
New England, 1938

About September 4, 1938, a "weak low" was recorded in the Bilma Oasis, South Central Sahara. Three days later it had moved on to the West African coast, bringing wind and rain. Assuming more positive configuration, the "weak low" became a "circular disturbance," so called on the tenth in the vicinity of the Cape Verde Islands, off Dakar. Since it pushed on westward, it seemed of no immediate consequence to any landmasses.

The empty wastes of the Atlantic it traversed, some six hundred miles north of the equator, have always been hurricane breeders during the summer and into the autumn, especially so at the equinoctial season. These storms, according to the Environmental Science Services Administration, are "tropical children, the offspring of ocean and atmosphere, powered by heat from the sea, driven by the easterly trades and temperate westerlies, the high planetary winds, and their own fierce energy." With reason, in Central America and the West Indies they have been known as *hurakans*, or evil spirits.

This particular "evil spirit" was lost sight of until the evening of September 16, when the Brazilian *Alegrete* reported a storm with winds in excess of sixty-four miles an hour. The next morning the Netherlands freighter *Socrates* wallowed in the same blow. Both ships were slightly

79

more than five hundred miles northeast of the Leeward Islands in the Caribbean. This meant that the mounting "disturbance" had traversed some three thousand miles of ocean at eighteen miles an hour, an average speed for a hurricane, although not all maintain so direct and uninterrupted a course.

At 7:30 that evening—the seventeenth—the storm was logged by the S.S. *Corales*, a British merchantman, well at sea off the tiny Dutch possession of St. Martin, in the Leeward group. Her captain recorded a barometer of 27.9 inches of mercury, a significant—and alarming—two inches below fair-weather readings in North America. Yet the master neglected to transmit wind velocities.

Forecasters were of the opinion that the storm was still of "no immediate threat to the mainland." Its forward progress remained somewhat less than twenty miles per hour; velocity, however, was picking up.

At 7:30 A.M. Sunday, the eighteenth, this "circular" development was whirling northeast of San Juan, Puerto Rico, but now curving toward the northwest and—if she held her new course—the Florida coast. At 7 P.M. the same day she was nine hundred miles east-southeast of Miami. Winds as clocked by other ships or estimated by outer island stations on the fringes were between sixty-five and seventy-five miles per hour. This kept the disturbance varyingly just below or barely within the official hurricane rating of seventy-four miles per hour, or sixty-four knots.

Monday morning, the nineteenth, at 7:30, it was howling to seaward of Mayaguana, giving the small Bahama possession of the British a sturdy shaking. Miami, remembering especially the hurricanes of 1926, 1928, and 1935, dug in. On Labor Day, 1935, nearly five thousand persons lost their lives. The majority were World War veterans working on the Key West highway, formerly the track and trestle bed of the old Flagler Railroad. The barometer reading of 26.35 inches set a record low for the United States.

From those same open-ocean keys—again menaced if the mounting storm did not continue its northward curve to Palm Beach, at least—residents were called in from the beaches, and shopkeepers boarded windows. The latter was no great chore, since any smart merchant had saved the plywood shutters he used in the last blow. Public buildings were readied as shelters. One hundred prisoners were moved inland from Belle Glade correction farm at Okeechobee.

Two Coast Guard radio trucks rumbled toward Lake Worth where they would serve as emergency replacements for any telephone centers that might be knocked out of operation. East and West Coast through trains provisioned their diners with extra food and beverage in the event of long delays.

The National Red Cross in Washington hurried five disaster team leaders onto Florida-bound airplanes. A man from Stockbridge, in the Berkshires, finishing business in Miami, telephoned his wife that he'd delay his return a couple of days. He wanted to see what a hurricane was like.

By 9:00 Monday night it appeared, however, that the curiosity-seeker was going to be disappointed. The Weather Bureau had already committed its own general assessment to the ticker that the storm "will probably recurve north-northwestward or northward during the next twenty-four hours."

Even as city-room teletypes were tapping out this calculated guess, the storm had completed a ninety-degree turn to the north. It was now paralleling the Florida east coast, 420 miles at sea, with a dangerous if typical diameter of 240 miles. At 10 P.M. it was 360 miles east of Palm Beach. The boards could come off the Miami store windows. The inmates could be returned to Belle Glade, and the radio trucks could be swung around. The Miami *Herald* set a headline for Tuesday's edition: "Storm Threat to the Florida East Coast Greatly Diminished."

Nonetheless, nothing was diminished about the storm itself. Approximately 450 miles northeast of Miami, the Cunard cruise liner *Carinthia* radioed that she was riding out gales of seventy-five miles per hour. The barometer read a low 27.85. In other words, the big storm was holding a very straight northward course, moving along at the slightly reduced speed of fifteen miles per hour.

Tuesday passed, and the hurricane was somewhat lost sight of. The likely assumption was that, as in the case of so many gales and "nor'easters," she would swipe at Hatteras and then follow the attracting currents of the Gulf Stream back out into the ocean.

There was, for that matter, much to think and worry about. The clocks in Europe seemingly were turned back to 1914. On Saturday, even as the storm was bowling into the Caribbean, President Eduard Beneš, of Czechoslovakia, declared a state of emergency. Chancellor

Adolf Hitler, demanding a parcel of Czech soil—the Sudetenland—had massed his German tanks, troops, and planes on the neighbor's border, by way of underscoring his ultimatum. The peace of Europe and quite probably of the world teetered in the balance. Only in March Austria had fallen to the Nazis, who suddenly seemed invincible. Charles Lindbergh himself said as much of the Luftwaffe.

If the Czechs were apprehensive and dismayed, the spokesmen for Great Britain and France were terrified. On Tuesday, Prime Minister Neville Chamberlain and Premier Edouard Daladier joined in an ultimatum of their own: that Czechoslovakia cede the Sudetenland "within twenty-four hours." Shocked beyond belief, President Franklin Roosevelt canceled three speeches and summoned Secretary of State Cordell Hull and other foreign advisers for conferences.

Throughout the same fateful Tuesday the storm continued northward, accelerating as it did so. While the ocean rose in large, angry white swells off the Carolina capes, the aircraft carrier *Enterprise* put to sea from the Norfolk Naval Base to ride out the high winds. Navy and army aircraft were flown to inland fields. Farther up the coast, the navy's bulbous blimps were herded into their two huge hangars at Lakehurst. Their chances of flying out a hurricane were less than poor.

Weather reports for Wednesday, the twenty-first, for most of the eastern seaboard, north of the Carolinas, read much the same: "Cloudy, continued cool, possibly rain." Forecasts for New York City, Long Island, and Connecticut contained an additional bon mot, after the word "rain": "probably heavy."

Actually, much of the East Coast, from the capes north, was already completing a fourth day of drenching. Norfolk's streets were awash. Manhattan's subways were, at least, very damp, drains backed up, rivers rising, smaller bridges impassable. Several major highways in Connecticut, including #9 and #15, were closed. New Haven had accumulated a total of eight and a half inches of rain. Trains were stalling. Underpasses lay deep under water. Commuters from northern New Jersey, Staten Island, Westchester County, and nearby Connecticut found schedules delayed or disrupted. Trolley cars were short-circuited. Many motorists abandoned cars to slosh toward relatively higher elevations.

Withal, the citizenry, with more patience than instinct for self-preservation, shrugged off the super-abundance of water. It rained like this every year at the autumnal equinox, didn't it?

Wednesday dawned over the Middle Atlantic coastal states. Above New England hung a curious patchwork of low, opaque clouds. There was rain interlaced with bright spots here and there. In Westerly, Rhode Island, for example, there was "a slight breeze and pleasant sunshine." At nearby Fisher's Island, just off the Connecticut coast, September 21 had commenced "queerly warm." At Westport Harbor, Massachusetts, near the Rhode Island border, overlooking Buzzard's Bay, Richard Hawes heard, as he dressed, something on WJAR about "strong winds" 150 miles east of Hatteras—or so he thought the Providence announcer had mentioned. Then, remembering a luncheon date at Fall River with his father, he realized he had more urgent matters at hand than listening to the radio.

In New Haven and all along the commuter railroad lines east and north from Manhattan the rain continued—heavy, without remission, implacable. The citizenry could not have been expected to know that all of this watery accumulation was to a hurricane like liquor to the town drunk.

Farther down the coast, in fact 75 miles, rather than 150, off Hatteras, the winds were indeed strong. The hurricane that was in the process of picking up an unheard-of forward speed in excess of fifty miles an hour—three times that of most hurricanes—tore past the famous cape of storms, continuing north to ignore the Gulf Stream. It smacked into the Diamond Shoals Lightship, knocking her far off station. Her grim and silent crewmen were thankful to be still afloat, if slightly awash.

Since the winds did not veer west, the Virginia, Maryland, Delaware, and much of the New Jersey coasts, recessed westward in a shallow curve from Hatteras, were spared. The storm, with ever-mounting fury, was aiming at the heart of Long Island with an assassin's singleness of purpose.

At 10 A.M. the blow was well at sea, no less than two hundred miles off Cape Henry, a little later pummeling Cape May and the southern New Jersey resorts. The latter, however, were treated to fringe winds only, between fifty and sixty miles per hour, still adequate to knock out the bridge connecting Atlantic City to Brigantine and marooning six hundred families.

In twelve hours the massive storm had progressed more than six hundred miles, and all the while the barometer was dropping at an alarming half inch an hour.

No one along the East's "gold coast"—of industry and abiding opulence—was wholly certain at just what hour or with what initial manifestations the full force of the blow arrived. Certainly, the storm had passed to seaward of the Delaware capes well before noon, while its almost casual destruction of the bridge to Brigantine, north of Atlantic City, indicated it was hauling landward.

In New York it was just another rainy early afternoon. Those who left their offices for lunch were careful to go equipped with umbrellas and raincoats. Others visited sandwich shops in building lobbies or ate at their desks.

The fact that the Hutchinson River and Sawmill River parkways leading north from New York City were becoming increasingly deep under water seemed to have been an overlooked harbinger, apparent as it was.

The storm had already arrived over the New York City–Long Island area before a much-belated tocsin was sounded, and only those who happened to be listening to their radios benefited. Announcers broke into Wednesday afternoon's lachrymose spate of soap operas with a familiar prelude: "We interrupt this program for a bulletin!" Many, thinking it "just another" report on the Sudetenland crisis, either did not listen or switched off their radios altogether.

"The tropical hurricane," commenced the Weather Bureau's warning, "is now in the vicinity of New York. The storm is attended by winds of whole gale force around its center and by winds of gale force over a wide area. Precautions should be taken against high winds and high tides and heavy rain." But it was already too late.

Subways and packways of Manhattan were badly flooded. Shipping scurried to the relative safety of piers or doubled up moorings. The *Queen Mary*, due to sail at 4:30 P.M., moved up the time to 5 A.M., the next high tide. Inbound, the *Ile de France*, with a disquieting port list, called for more and more tugs until twelve were assisting her up the Hudson River to a berth near the *Queen*. The Staten Island ferry *Knickerbocker* smashed into her slip at the Battery, then hung at a precarious angle. Her two hundred frightened passengers were compelled to remain aboard until two tugs hauled the craft loose. More than half of the pleasure boats tied up in Eastchester Bay, off City Island, were sunk or cast adrift. Those caught out in the blow came ashore with

Herculean efforts. A Darien, Connecticut, family thanked the Lord that they finally brought their yacht to dock—only to find their home awash. By 2:30 pieces of signs and roofing were hurtling like shrapnel onto Manhattan sidewalks. Workers left their offices at their own peril. Under gusts of 120 miles per hour, the Empire State Building swayed four inches. It blew so hard in Central Park that no one could stand up against the gales or the nearly horizontal sheets of rain.

As lights flickered in the five boroughs of New York, the eye of the augmenting storm was coming ashore with the fixation of a maniac sixty miles east of Manhattan, between Patchogue and Babylon, Long Island. At Quogue, a mile inland, breakers two feet high foamed over lawns, streets, and sidewalks.

At Bridgehampton, Long Island, well on the way to Montauk, at the tip, Olga L. Lafrentz, who had been whiling away a rainy morning, had been conscious of an increasing banging of the shutters and finally "that awful weird shrill singing of the metal weather stripping."

Luncheon at 1:00 became one continual interruption as Olga, her parents, or the maids tried alternately to keep the shutters closed. "Just a little storm from New England," Mr. Lafrentz said, trying to soothe his family. He said he had heard something about it over the radio. From the look on his face, however, it was apparent that he did not put much faith in his own efforts at reassurance.

At nearby Westhampton Beach the afternoon proceeded much as the one the day before and the day before that. Within the home of Mrs. William Ottman, Jr., the Norwegian butler, Arni Benedictson, was straightening up after lunch. Nearby, the George Burkhardts were watching the sea, but with a mounting uneasiness. Burkhardt, a New York broker, had the feeling earlier in the day that he should not go into the office—all that rain and the low, scud clouds.

There weren't many up the coast, however, who shared Burkhardt's vague presentiment. At Westerly, Rhode Island, for example, a women's church guild proceeded with its picnic meeting at the Watch Hill cottage of one of the members.

Benedict Thielen, a novelist, living at Chilmark, Martha's Vineyard, commented that the wind this Wednesday was "stronger than yesterday; the sand blew against your face like sharp bits of glass." Until now, to his poet's sensitivity, it had been "a summer of wind and quiet days, of mornings of fog and afternoons when not a shred of cloud hung in the round blue sky." He stood by the window of his cottage, much as the Burkhardts down at Westhampton Beach, while the waves appeared to build up.

Another author, Van Wyck Mason, had left his Nantucket Island home on the early ferry to New Bedford. From there he hoped to catch a bus to Providence and then a train to New York. He had just finished correcting the galleys of his Revolutionary War novel, *Three Harbours*, and wished to deliver them in person to his publisher. The thirty-seven-year-old former Second Lieutenant—an interpreter—with the A.E.F. noticed that the sea was rougher than usual and that curiously, some small yachts were already adrift. Still, he entertained no doubts at all that he would complete his day's mission as scheduled.

The summer people had all abandoned Fisher's Island, leaving the picturesque bit of offshore Connecticut to its year-round residents, such as Frances Woodward. All were engaged in the annual expiation of readying for winter. Miss Woodward heard someone observe, after looking at a peculiarly low, heavy sky, that there should be "a real southeaster by afternoon." It did not seem to deter those such as handyman Jim Hale, who was astride the ridge pole of the Malvina Parton house, trying to point up the cracks in the brick chimney. However, when a rising wind began to rattle the ladder, the wiry, capable Jim decided that the weather was becoming "a damned nuisance." While Malvina Parton, inside, tightened the window catches, Hale slowly made his way down to the yard. Late-blooming tiger lilies were bending in the garden.

At I P.M. the whistle blew in the old Kinney Machine Company, and it seemed to Frances Woodward as if this "had been a signal to the wind," which started to blow more heavily, bringing with it sudden rain. A crate of tomatoes toppled in front of the grocery while waves slapped over garden walls at the end of Race Street by the point. Large trees began to bend.

Miss Woodward watched Jim Hale tightening a "tree cover" in the yard, muttering as he did so, "Damn this wind—pushing up the high September tide. Apt to lose planks off the dock, or shingles off the guest house." Then she mused to herself, "Lucky the studio skylight was north. That wouldn't catch it anyway." As the wind "heaved" itself "farther forward," she saw and heard a jar of nasturtiums sweep across a table and crash onto the flagging. Frances would later write:

The Seymours looked up to see Charlotte Adams coming from her house down the street, her slicker yellow in the gray wind, laughing, as excited as the cocker. "Look, tell Aunt Malvina I couldn't get there this afternoon. They'll have to improve the village without me. I have to meet George in Westerly on the five o'clock, so I'm going to Watch Hill beach to see the storm. Be swell from there."

The brass cock of the weather vane jerked at a sudden angle, and the wind made a high humming against the metal.

The wind picked up still more. It had a strange quality of pushing. No gusts—just a great weight, like a wall, like a wall moving. The salt rain ran before it in horizontal streaks.

From his southeast window Tom Seymour watched a larger wave than the rest rear and break directly over the garden wall, dumping itself into the enclosure. Water—not spray. Even the heaviest winter storm had never managed that. . . .

The afternoon's routine continued more or less in pattern in spite of the rising wind and rain along the northeast coast. The 150-foot-long ferry *Park City* left its slip at Port Jefferson, Long Island, on schedule at 2 P.M. for Bridgeport across the Sound, where it was due at 3:45. There was a crew of nine on the forty-year-old craft plus six passengers, one of whom was a four-month-old girl.

Train No. 14, the *Bostonian*, rattled out of Grand Central Station, also on time. It paused at 125th Street, added more passengers for a total of 275, then picked up speed for its next stop, New Haven. A veteran engineer, H. W. Eaton, was at the throttle.

The Coast Guard buoy tender *Tulip* started on its tedium of checking moorings, then as abruptly put back. The O.D.—officer of the deck —who had been meticulously watching the barometer discovered it was falling at the rate of half an inch an hour, and that could only spell a stiff blow, perhaps a hurricane.

At Middletown, Connecticut, parents filed into the old chapel on the campus of Wesleyan University. The service was part of the ceremonies attendant to the opening of the new semester.

At Bridgehampton, thirty miles east of Patchogue, Mr. Lafrentz had decided it was time to get out of the house. He couldn't explain to his family just what had brought him to this conclusion. He had never been evacuated from anything anywhere before. Abruptly packing his suitcase with overnight items, he called for Olga to give him a nightdress for her mother. Olga, too excited to obey, just repeated, "Hurry, please, hurry!" Then she put on her coat, tied a bandanna around her head, grabbed a coat and scarf, and again implored her parents to hurry.

"Better bring a dry pair of stockings for Mother," her father called to Olga, who hurried to her bureau and "jammed" a bunch of stockings into her pocket—nine in all!

For some reason George, the chauffeur, did not answer his employer's summons. Since the family could not see out because of the closed shutters, Olga went to the kitchen and called the maids. "As I stepped out of the kitchen on the back porch," she would write, "I stepped in water—warm water—almost to my knees. I was terrified. Mother stepped right after me. We got onto the porch. I tried to open the door, but the force of the wind and water was so strong I had to give it up."

Then they tried another door. They both pushed, and it slowly opened. Olga continued:

> Dad and I held Mother tight. Off went our hats in a jiffy. I looked once. What is that awful black thing by the tool shed, trying to come through a passage by an arbor?
>
> I never looked again. We stumbled on and into the garage. The chauffeur all the time had been trying to open the garage doors. The water was up to the running board of the cars. We three got into the back seat of the car; two maids and chauffeur in front. We started. As the car went down a slight incline to the driveway, the water broke over the hood. The car seemed to stop. I called to the chauffeur:
>
> "George, back it up quickly!"
>
> It was impossible to go. My mother begged to be allowed to walk out before the water should get to her neck. My father said, "Impossible; nearest house is half a mile away."
>
> Father told George to close the doors; with that one blew off; immediately followed by the lower half of the other. My car, higher powered, was standing in the garage and George wanted to take Mother in that, but she wouldn't leave Dad. I thought no; they must stay together. I began to think: Suppose this storm had been yesterday when Dad was coming back from New York! I don't know what I would have done with Mother.
>
> Water, water everywhere. No road to be seen, the whole forty acres. Nothing but rough waves blowing in every direction.

When the car stalled and the door was opened, ice-cold water dashed in; the car rocked and swayed. I thought it would blow over.

Eventually, with the aid of a truck and everyone pushing, the family Packard finally attained higher ground.

At Monument Square, Bridgehampton, the gilded eagle flew off the flagpole, leaving its perch there empty. Ernest Clowes, a newspaperman, who doubled as a stringer for the Weather Bureau, had earlier been concerned about the "soaking wet" air and the way "trees dipped" under mounting winds. Even as he attempted to phone meteorologists in the New York office, the line went dead. Now he listened to "the voice of the storm . . . a steady, almost organlike note of such intensity that it seemed as if the whole atmosphere were in harmonic vibration."

At the same time he watched "spray and all sorts of small items going by, almost horizontally, principally shreds of leaves torn in pieces from the trees. A barn, a chicken house would lift from its foundations and collapse or burst into fragments that flew away down the wind . . . unseen fingers seemed to pick shingles off roofs and scatter them."

It was perhaps worse yet at Westhampton, about half an hour's drive west of the Lafrentzes'. The George Burkhardts, for example, observed "the water hurtling over the dunes and swirling around the foundations of our house. . . . It would come in great surges, ebb away, and come again with greater intensity." Soon, it was obvious that they would have to make a run for the bridge over Moriches Bay into Westhampton. With their butler and his wife, Mr. and Mrs. Carl Dalin, a pekingese, and a spaniel, they "fought across the dunes, the tide belting us first around the ankles, then coming higher and higher."

To the two dogs, this was a real lark, "playing and enjoying the whole thing immensely," chasing sticks floating by, and yipping excitedly. Every time the Burkhardts and the Dalins thought they had gained a safe position, a wave would knock them down. Finally, the sea frothed over their heads, and the Burkhardts found themselves swimming. Neither Carl Dalin nor his wife knew how to swim, so they were forced to cling to poles or whatever objects floated past.

The servants drowned. The Burkhardts made it. One of the dogs, the spaniel, paddled through the ordeal, as his aquatic breed indicated he would. The pekingese was lost.

Police Chief Stanley Teller and Sergeant Timothy Robinson, of

Westhampton, herded twenty women, children, and older men into what appeared to be the strongest house within sight and on the highest land. They were ordered up to the third floor. Only one man, Wallace Halsey, appeared to have objections.

When the structure began to shake and rock under the blast of wind and sea, the group was moved to the roof. Soon that started to crumble, and the drenched assemblage was then brought back down to the third floor, now open to the storm. From the agonies and contortions of the building it was obvious that it had already left its foundations and was bobbing, like some misshapen, top-heavy vessel, with the flood. There was no visibility through the slanting rain and scud. "We're done for!" arose a recurrent cry. "She's breaking up!"

Miraculously, the house came to rest near Quogue, two miles from "embarkation" point, with all occupants safe. Halsey, who had been washed off, was picked up four miles distant, at Speonk.

A Westhampton butler, Livingston Gibson, rode the roof of an otherwise submerged house along the same rapids. He was relieved to jump onto a hillock, since his companions on the strange journey had included a chicken, a snake, and three rats, all of which had been seated, pensively, not far from him.

Staying with one's house, or with any house, was no guarantee of salvation. Some nineteen residents of Westhampton Beach perished in that very mistaken belief. Of the 150 homes there, 144 were crumpled into flotsam. Some had been sliced in half "with the precision of an ax." Others were swept out to sea to be torn into pieces by the currents and breakers. A number of women and children saved themselves by huddling behind dunes. They were found, half buried, in the evening. For others this desperate recourse only hastened death. The storm was capricious. Even the salties in their weather wisdom had been fooled by this one.

The fashionable Dunes Church, familiar setting of Southampton's blue-book weddings, was virtually reclaimed by the waters over which bells had so long pealed. Carved above the altar's wreckage was a passage from the 89th Psalm:

> Thou Rulest the Raging of the Sea
> Thou Stillest the Waves Thereof
> When They arise.

Fire Island, to the west, was marooned without electricity, communications, or drinking water. Entire new inlets were cut through the Moriches on Long Island. At Greenport the roof was whipped from a theater in which an audience of sixty was seated. The shipyard there was wrecked, to the last keel plate. At Saybrook, Connecticut, a house was blown a mile from its foundations, end over end. At Wesleyan University families had just left the chapel when the old stone tower collapsed. At Milford, Connecticut, all that testified to the presence of a schoolhouse were the desks, bolted to the cement floor. Everything else had blown away, like the gilt eagle on the pole at Bridgehampton.

The Bridgeport ferry was caught twelve miles out in the Sound. The *Park City* lost power when engine spaces were flooded. It was kept afloat, pending Coast Guard help, only by the two male passengers aboard helping with the pumps.

The *Bostonian* was only one of many trains that stalled or were knocked off the tracks during the afternoon. At Stonington, Connecticut, five cars of the train derailed on a viaduct near the beach. Engineer Eaton uncoupled part of the train, ordering all passengers into the two forward cars still on the rails, then inched his foreshortened "express" ahead, like a tugboat, pushing a fishing craft off the track as he attained higher ground. In this manner all but one of his passengers and a waiter were saved.

The fury "like the rising roar of a siren" hit New London about 3:30 P.M., knocking off the anemometer of a navy weather station when the velocity clocked ninety-eight miles per hour. The buoy tender *Tulip*, along with other craft and parts of piers, ended up in downtown areas of the city. Fire followed the flood, leveling one block of Bank Street and burning into the night. The beautiful Connecticut seaport hadn't been so roughed up since Benedict Arnold burned it in 1781, because it was a haven for privateering.

The Thunderbolt roller coaster, "New England's most thrilling ride," along with the entire Savin Rock amusement park outside of New Haven, simply "slipped into the sea." Wilcox's familiar pier was converted in minutes into a ragged line of piles, and white septic tanks marked where cottages had once reposed.

A woman on an exposed promontory at Watch Hill, Rhode Island, observed with deadly fascination a tidal wave boiling shoreward, "like a fogbank coming fast." To another, the awesome wave was like the approach, "covering everything, of a long roll of cotton." One woman, caught in this wave, encountered the cross arms of a telephone pole, the dangling wires of which wrapped themselves around her. Thus lashed, she floated into Little Narragansett Bay where she was unwound and freed, not badly hurt.

Less fortunate were the ten members of the church guild of Westerly, Rhode Island, a town that was hit with especial ferocity. Picnicking at the house of a member, all drowned when they sought refuge in a basement.

At Fisher's Island, Frances Woodward continued, "curious to see the houses you knew so well, the roofs under which you had lived tilt and courtsey gravely—and cease to exist." Next, she would recall, the tide showed signs of turning,

> if this surging gray waste could be called anything so familiar and commonplace as tide; turning back along outrageous ways where no tide had ever been; rippling six feet deep over fallen trees, through the Machine Company engines; sliding over what used to be the Foundry, receding from black-wet piles of fabric in the Velvet Mill, pulling branches and chairs and life buoys with it.
>
> On High, on Margin, on the highway across the tracks, small rowboats were floating free and men began to capture them, poling through the streets, feeling the tide ebb beneath them, feeling the wind slackening some. A crying gale now—something you could recognize for wind and put a name to. The rain began to fall like rain.

Richard Hawes, of Westport Harbor, finished lunch with his father in Fall River and was back at his office when his wife, "Gen," telephoned that the lights were out and parts of the chimney were beginning to blow away. He said he would come home and drive her and the two boys down "to see the surf." He hurried home, then left there with his family at four o'clock. Immediately he had reason to speculate on the soundness of his decision. It was "almost impossible to see anything through the windshield." Then the engine stopped.

"Keep her going, Dad, keep her going!" his oldest son, Dick, urged.

Mrs. Hawes, sensing the hopelessness of that effort, announced, "We're going to get out!" They found the water was well over their shoes when they did so.

"Gen said she would run into the Dennett house," Hawes would write, "and I shouted that they were not there and she had better go to Israel Brayton's house where she could get dry clothes." As she reached the Dennetts' porch, its roof "with a series of crackles like a machine gun rose in the air and folded over backward onto the bathing houses as if it were a hinged box cover." This so startled Mrs. Hawes that she kept running, holding her younger son, Sim, by the hand. She climbed a wall, then gained the Braytons' lawn. By now they were down on their hands and knees.

"At that moment," her husband added, "there was a terrific increase in the amount of wind, rain, and salt spray, and the Walsh house seemed to rise bodily in the air and turn completely over, collapsing on the road. A moment later John Brayton's house, with solemn dignity, moved from its foundation into the middle of the road, while my automobile was forced by the water backward into the pond. The water was then above the engine hood. It apparently crossed John Brayton's tennis court, the back nets of which had disappeared. From then on all sense of time was lost."

Cottages and homes were not the only casualties. Lighthouses in this bay region themselves suffered disproportionately. Well Rock Light at Point Judith was destroyed, along with the beacon at Charlestown, a few miles west. The light-tender's wife and son were lost from Prudence Island Light in Narragansett Bay as the tide rose twenty-five feet.

The same moving, "growling mass of water," with nothing to impede its progress, surged up the bay toward Providence, casually knocking over piers, houses, and utility poles and exploding a 300,000-cubic-foot gas tank.

Van Wyck Mason was now waiting at the Providence railroad station for his train to New York, his book galleys clutched tightly. "You can imagine my astonishment," the novelist would recall, "when the entire roof [of the station house] blew off. Lights went out. No trains were coming in. People screamed. I looked. The water was beginning to rise. It was ten feet high in the square in no time. People climbed to the tops of cars as it rose, then some were carried off. One woman tried to wade across the street while the torrent was at about the four-foot level. A man motioned to her. No sooner had she stepped off the curb than she was carried off down a sewer. Another woman who couldn't swim screamed pitifully for help from the top of her car. Nothing could be done. She was carried off.

"You could see the lights of cars under water. Quickly commenced the deafening roar of hundreds of short-circuited auto horns."

People leaned far out of the Biltmore Hotel on the station plaza and from the second floors of office buildings lowering ropes, tied clothing, umbrellas, anything, in an effort to lift up those floating below. Only the tops of streetcars protruded for a brief time above inundated downtown Providence. Then, it appeared to Mason, "the water started to subside almost as quickly as it commenced."

In other sections of Rhode Island's capital deer and elk wandered, lost and aimless. They had broken loose from Roger Williams Park.

With singular detachment Benedict Thielen, on Martha's Vineyard, watched trickles, "as if one had emptied a glass," grow to something much more alarming. The "slowness" of the buildup impressed him. He continued:

> Now the tops of the waves sent up spray from the dunes, and all over our land the water was flowing to the pond behind. It was no more than ankle deep, and there were many higher places that were still dry.
>
> But in the swishing sound of the flowing water there was now something different. There was a thin clicking sound of pebbles being carried along by the sea. This sound soon deepened until it became a dull rumbling as the stones that were beneath the sand were also uncovered and borne away. The heaviness and deepness of the sound increased, and now, from time to time, there were hard thuds against the foundation of the house as boulders struck it. The water still was deepening only slowly, but there was a sense of its increasing strength, and the sound of it was different from any we had ever heard before. It was then that we decided to leave.

With his wife he struck out across a pond for the opposite shore:

> The current carries us past . . . the filthy yellow water streams by, and a big clump of bushes in which my arms get entangled for a moment. It reminds us then of all the silly movies that I've ever seen, of all the broken dams, floods, storms, and charming young women . . . and stalwart young men battling for life.
>
> Up to a point you can describe things consecutively, but

beyond that there is no sequence of events. The things that happen have their reality only in the manner in which they exist in or momentarily impinge on the mind of the person caught up in their midst. The mind of that person does not see consecutively: it is impressed by a series of images which in themselves have no logical connection but exist only as isolated, unrelated phenomena. The mind, in art and in life, feels a basic need for some kind of arrangement of these unrelated phenomena. Suddenly deprived of this, it finds itself facing a horror and a loss that is far deeper than any mere physical distress of the moment. There is a kind of eerie surrealist dream quality about it.

Near him their cook, Josephine, was drowning: "I know about life-saving and try to swim backward holding her with one arm on my chest. I cannot move my legs with their water-filled boots. . . . I see the dark face sink in the water, then rise again. . . . The face is gone. A woman's hat with a green feather is floating, spinning slowly around in the water."

When Thielen, "utterly exhausted," finally collapsed onto some high ground, he saw "some cows . . . looking strangely firm and secure," contemplating him.

Harvard University's Blue Hill Observatory, at Milton, recorded a 186-mile-an-hour gust. Nonetheless, Boston was dealt no more than a glancing uppercut. At the Charlestown Navy Yard, "Old Ironsides," the *Constitution*, rocked at her permanent moorings, threatening to capsize, but the sturdy frigate from 1812 won once more.

In Blackstone, Massachusetts, across the border from Woonsocket, Rhode Island, eighteen-year-old Mary McCooey rode four hours atop a mattress after being washed out of her yard. It was sort of fun, confessed the daughter of Dr. James H. McCooey.

The storm smashed into populous Worcester, Massachusetts, about the same time it barreled into equally industrial Narragansett Bay. The clock tower of the First Unitarian Church, on Lincoln Square, swayed and righted itself and swayed again as the bells chimed discordantly. Finally, the tower went down in a clanging mass of wood, masonry, and inner workings. A realtor, Philip H. Duprey, looked out of his downtown office window to see his Cadillac being blown down the street. He wasn't even ready to trade it in, he reflected.

Twelve miles west, at Brookfield, passengers raced for the station after water rose above the car windows of a commuter train. East Brookfield was itself cut in two by the Quabaug River, forming yet another community. Two hundred inmates of the Hampden County jail in Springfield rioted, mortally afraid that the Connecticut River would drown them in their cells. The reassurance of heavily armed state troopers was needed before the prisoners quieted. At 5 P.M. the big blow was screaming through Hadley, north of Springfield. It ripped up Northfield Seminary, killing two girls as a chimney collapsed. Mt. Hermon School for Boys, a part of these twin secondary institutions founded by Dwight L. Moody, was also damaged.

The hurricane tore into Vermont, knocking down entire sugar-maple orchards and hacking swaths through the forests in the style of Paul Bunyan. In Rutland, as in other Vermont towns and cities, the storm awakened dormant, paved-over rivers and streams to burst through sidewalks and storefronts. In Windsor doctors delivered two girl babies by lantern light. The base station of the Mount Washington cog railway was torn up; higher elevations were untouched. Peterborough, New Hampshire, was set ablaze. Like New London, it would burn into the night, flames reflected in the swollen Contoocook River.

At 8 P.M. the hurricane was churning the placid waters of Lake Champlain into something evocative of Cape Horn at its wintriest. By midnight the "evil spirit," if not altogether exorcised, was surely out of breath and had become nothing worse than a squall over the wooded vastness of Canada.

All at once the scourge had passed. Children pattered out into the wet and littered streets again, with wonder and awe on their faces. Old people looked with disbelief at the clearing heavens as though they were witness to the resurrection. Dozens of communities in the five hardest-hit states—Connecticut, Rhode Island, Massachusetts, Vermont, and New Hampshire—were without food, water, light, or any sure means of moving from here to there. A candle couldn't be found, bought, or even stolen anywhere. Norwich, Vermont, would have to be supplied with food and medicine dropped by plane.

Rumors in the absence of better communications—100,000 phones were dead—had it that all lower portions of vulnerable Cape Cod had been washed into the sea and that Boston, inundated, was eroding into its own harbor. In many communities ham-radio operators tapped out the first bad or—not so often—good news. George P. Drowns, for one, advised Red Cross headquarters in Washington via a roundabout amateur relay of Westerly's rumored toll: ten persons dead, with fifty unaccounted for, and five hundred summer homes damaged or destroyed. Fortunately, he was in error. None died in Westerly, although damage was severe.

The National Guard moved in throughout New England's shattered and soggy centers of population. Looters had scarcely waited for the rain to stop. In Providence they were observed in chains passing back merchandise from inaccessible areas of broken stores.

The combination of wind and pounding of the sea had been sufficiently powerful to cause seismograph readings on the West Coast, but on Thursday morning New England was strangely silent, as with a gigantic hangover. Its landscape had been violently altered; sweeping sands occupied large areas where cottages had formerly rested; some wooded spots had been replaced by fields. Everywhere debris had collected, presupposing a multimillion-dollar cleanup.

Legends arose even before the advent of shovel and saw crews. Apocryphal perhaps was the experience of the town "character" of Westerly. A body closely resembling his own ragged features was found on the beach when the waters receded. When the man himself turned up, he was taken to view the corpse. He rubbed at the stubble on his chin as if in thought, then shook his head. "No," he allowed. "'T'ain't me."

They also told about the man in Westhampton who had received in the mail that morning a barometer he had previously ordered. When he saw that the needle was pointing to an area on the dial marked "hurricane," he decided it was faulty. After lunch he had started to rewrap the instrument when the dining-room windows blew in and the porch began to disintegrate.

There was also the wag who strolled about Boston Common wearing a sandwich board on which he had scribbled: "For 50 cents I will listen to *your* story of the hurricane." But there really wasn't much to chuckle at. It was time to take stock and to rebuild.

President Roosevelt opened the Treasury gates for relief, then ordered General Malin Craig, the Chief of Staff, to put the army at the disposal of any areas where heavy work was needed. The scope of damage, obscured by so many individual losses and tragedies, was no simple matter to measure, although it was apparent that more than six hundred had died, tens of thousands had been injured or sickened to some degree as a result, and 93,122 were left homeless. The Red Cross alone spent nearly $2,000,000 on some eighteen thousand relief applications. Structural damage included 2,500 barns leveled and 6,000 damaged, along with 7,500 "other" buildings including garages and sheds. Farmers, badly hit, reported 475 work animals lost, 1,000 cattle, more than 200 hogs, and 750,000 poultry. Salt plucked from Long Island Sound killed gardens and crops twenty miles inland. Windows in Montpelier, 120 miles from the sea, were caked with salt. Laborious fertilizing and plowing was the price for restoring blighted fields. Close to 27,000,000 trees, including much of the maple-sugar orchards of Vermont and historic elms and oaks of Connecticut, had been torn up by their roots and were virtually irreplaceable.

Plate-glass windows were shattered in astronomical quantities: 50,000, some estimated; 100,000 or even 200,000, according to others. Perhaps 100,000,000 feet of electric, telephone, and telegraph lines were down, together with the 31,000 poles on which the vast length had been strung. At least 26,000 automobiles and 2,605 boats were on casualty insurers' total-loss lists. The entire fishing fleet of Block Island had been sunk to the last trawler, plunging the economic health of the offshore community into bleak despair. Railroads were in bad shape. Milk from Vermont, the East's dairyland, had to be shipped via Maine and Montreal. It would take two weeks to fully restore New York–Boston service.

The winds had blown so hard that they dissolved vegetation, especially leaf mold, and splashed the pigmented mess against anything in the way. More than one incredulous resident found his house greenish in hue, irrespective of the color it had been the day before.

So thorough was the hurricane in its capacity for eradication that it scrubbed clean the last vestige of 190,000,000-year-old dinosaur tracks near Holyoke. This was a wrench to archaeologist and tourist alike.

All in all, the bill for this widespread and diversified damage would total close to $1,000,000,000. No one would ever know for sure. A close-packed, industrial civilization had been paralyzed in a few short hours as had never happened in the United States. The repercussions far transcended the immediate population of some ten million in the states involved.

Not even New England's "*Portland* blizzard" of 1898, which sank thousands of tons of coastal shipping including the side-wheeler that gave the storm a name, approximated the devastation of the hurricane. The destruction topped that of the San Francisco earthquake, the Chicago fire, and the Mississippi floods of 1927. Although the loss of life from the Galveston tidal wave was some ten times that of the 1938 hurricane, the disruption was confined to a relatively narrow area.

Churches had been handled roughly, as though nature herself had raged at the Deity. Of the 6,923 houses of worship in the five states affected, the majority had suffered some damage, aggregating at least $150,000,000. Seven churches in Connecticut were total losses, including the large Congregational Church in Glastonbury, which was insured for $65,000. For quite unfathomable reasons, however, clerical reporters found that the synagogues and Episcopal churches were largely undamaged.

Ministers would be left with much to ponder. What *were* the implications of this sudden and massive scourging? One, Dr. Phillips Endicott Osgood, of Emmanuel Church, Boston, readily saw parallels between "the hideous majestic waves coming crashing in" and the war crisis in Europe. The Reverend Henry W. Knickrehm, of Haven Methodist Episcopal Church, East Providence, was convinced that "God is probably heartbroken." The Reverend Ralph O. Harpole, of Park Place Church, Pawtucket, confessed that "it made us feel our littleness," and he dismissed the matter there.

Whatever the hurricane may have implied and however the Lord may have felt about it, the black shadow of the "evil spirit" had crossed the land as though in augury of worse fortunes yet to come. Even as these men of faith were weaving their Sunday rationales, President Beneš, in capitulating to Hitler and the statesmen of Britain and France, was pronouncing his own obituary for Europe: "Nothing else has remained, because we were *alone*." World War II was just a year distant.

Postscript: In 1969 hurricane Camille caused more than $1,000,-000,000 property damage to the Gulf Coast but claimed only one sixth of the lives of the 1938 storm. Better advance warning kept down the death toll.

8

Circus Fire at
Hartford, Connecticut, 1944

Military operations did not command all of the priorities of World War II. The less tangible factors of morale were also an important consideration. It was fact—and posters never allowed one to forget it —that without the home front there'd be no war front. Frills, from sweets and cigarettes to vacation areas and all forms of entertainment, persisted at least as second-level priorities. Since the circus rated highly, the giant among traveling, multi-attraction shows—Ringling Bros. and Barnum & Bailey—had kept close to peacetime schedules since the attack on Pearl Harbor. Extra allotments of gasoline, tires, rope, canvas, and other scarce commodities had been made available to the famous extravaganza created some three quarters of a century earlier by Phineas T. Barnum. However, the quality and quantity of merchandise wasn't the same as in prewar times. Canvas, as an example, had to be patched rather than replaced, and the old grades of tough, fire-resistant hemp ropes simply couldn't be found at any price on the civilian market.

The circus made do anyhow. By July, 1944, a light at the end of the long tunnel of war and scarcities began to appear. D-Day was a month past, and Allied armies were slashing well out of the Normandy beachheads into occupied France. Cherbourg had surrendered, and

"Caen," one of the gateways to Paris, was about to fall. The new V-1 flying bombs, however, had killed 2,752 Britons in three weeks. In the Pacific resistance on Saipan had almost ceased. The end was near for this major Japanese base of the Marianas.

The first week of this fateful month of the war the circus arrived in Hartford, Connecticut. It spread out its train of tents and wagons upon an empty expanse known as the Barbour Street Grounds. The animals themselves made up an impressive, mobile jungle—one thousand in all, including forty lions, thirty tigers, thirty leopards, twenty bears, and forty elephants, most of them in their wagon cages just south of the "big top." The undisputed tour de force was the huge gorilla, Gargantua, glowering at one and all through his tremendous den wagon. He seemed even larger and more menacing in the broad daylight.

The big top was just that: 520 feet long, weighing nineteen tons, with a seating capacity of more than thirteen thousand persons and said to be the largest hunk of canvas in the world. P. T. Barnum had always liked things big. Ringling Brothers was proud of that valuable tent. Recently it had been sprayed with paraffin diluted with gasoline, for both waterproofing and preservation. It could not make the canvas fireproof, however—in fact, quite the opposite.

Wartime transportation uncertainties and irregularities had canceled the opening matinee, Wednesday, July 5. The night performances, however, commenced on schedule. According to the Hartford *Courant*, the show was "bigger, better, and smarter than ever." The circus's own press agent could not have improved on the superlatives.

Thursday morning, preparations went forward for the first and last matinee of this two-day stand. Sawdust was smoothed over from the past night in the three main rings. The booths were readied again. The flag was run up at the peak of the big top, where it hung limp in the still summer air.

The bandsmen under their veteran leader, Merle Evans, were practicing. Rehearsing were such top-billed performers as the "Great Wallendas"; May Kovar, a Britisher with Alfred Court's famed big cats; and Emmett Kelly and Felix Adler, world-renowned clowns.

The elephants, staked out, consumed pail after pail of water until sweat trickled in unending rivulets down the foreheads of the handlers and boy helpers. There was ample reason. At noon the thermometer stood at 90°, Hartford's hottest and driest day of the year. One early arrival, Everett D. Dow, a reporter for the *Courant*, declared, "The intensity of the sunlight was excruciating." The fans kept coming anyhow. Between 1 and 2 P.M. they flocked onto the huge lot, from Hartford, its suburbs, and other cities as far away as New Haven and Danbury. The men were in shirt sleeves, the women in light cottons, children in sunsuits. A sprinkling of servicemen perspiring in uniforms and tight caps were guests of the circus. Some bought their popcorn, ice cream, or glazed apples and waited outside until the last minute, visiting the sideshows, although there was no menagerie top today. The canvas had baked all morning, and now it was stifling inside. Among those walking around, waiting for the first blare of the band music, was Mrs. Dorothea Felber with her eleven-year-old sister, Nancy Burnham. Dorothea, whose husband was with the army in New Guinea, had left her own two small children with her parents in nearby South Windsor.

When the grand march of elephants started, 6,789 admissions had been sold, a large but not a record crowd. Others still milled about outside.

At 1:45 P.M. Emmett Kelly, in a nearby dressing tent, heard the bugler sound first call on his cornet. This gave him forty-five more minutes to finish makeup and flap off for the "top" in his oversize clown shoes. As he shaped his bulbous nose, he found himself hoping that "it wouldn't melt in the blistering heat."

Miss Kovar was performing with her panthers, lions, and tigers. As soon as she shooed them back down the iron-barred runways to their cages, the Wallendas would climb and swing their way up to the high wires, "to shake hands with death," as their billing described it. There were five of them: Herman, Karl, Joe, Helen, and Henrietta. While at this dizzy height, they rode bicycles, clutched partners leaping and floating toward them through space, and performed seemingly impossible if not outlandish feats of balance on one foot, one hand, or on their heads, with nothing but a cable for a perch. Kelly was supposed to provide comic relief inside the center ring during this act—a counterpoint to split-second breathlessness. The clown, however, was having trouble with the putty for his nose. Just as he had feared, the stuff was too soft in the ninety-plus-degree heat, and he couldn't mold it quite right. He was late.

About 2:30 May Kovar, finished with the big cats, was snapping her whip over the heads of four panthers to hurry them down the enclosed runways while exiting with them on one side of the ring. Herman Wallenda, in his tight pants and wide waistband, was astride the tiny platform atop the center pole. He had bowed in the best theatrical tradition and was starting to fit his special bicycle onto the wire. Without the tire the rim clung snugly, like a railroad wheel on track. It was just a matter of perfect balance.

Merle Evans, atop the eight-foot-high bandstand, signaling for a dramatic pause, raised his baton. The eyes of the nearly seven thousand spectators were all focused upward. A hush swept over the big top. Then the leader dropped his stick, and the bandsmen blared into waltz music.

Herman Wallenda swung a leg over the seat of his flyweight bicycle. Then he hesitated. He had noticed something at the entrance, between the general-admission board stands and the grandstand chairs. The audience, too far below Wallenda to notice his stare or, certainly, the shadow that had etched his face, was aware of his stop-motion in the act of mounting the bicycle. However, they figured it to be part of the routine.

The band continued with "Waltzing Matilda." Emmett Kelly heard it as he padded out of his tent, mildly annoyed that he wasn't quite on time. His watch read 2:40, and he should have been below the high wires at least four minutes ago. Absolute punctuality was part of the circus performer's tradition.

Wallenda, from his lofty vantage point, had seen it first: a tiny tongue of flame at the general-admission entrance. But "it didn't seem to spread fast"—it was so slow, in fact, that apparently those seated beside the flare did not even notice. To Everett Dow, the reporter, in stands directly across the ring, it was "a horseshoe of flame." He looked to his right, then his left, and realized that "the full danger of the situation was grasped only by spectators seated most distant from the flames." They appeared "momentarily stupefied and incredulous."

Even as the flame started creeping up the sidewall of the tent, Wallenda thought there would be time to lash his bike onto the platform railing and make a more or less calm descent down the rope. As with Dow, he believed most of the crowd was "oblivious" to what was happening.

Intent on watching the exit of the last of the cats, Dorothea Felber was herself "oblivious" until she heard "Fire! Fire!" from a sudden "roar of voices." Outside, Emmett Kelly heard the same shout. He hastened his gait, wondering if the fire was not emanating from elsewhere than inside the big top.

Felix Adler, on a slightly later schedule, was still completing his own clown makeup when he listened to "a roar like the applause when one of the big acts comes off." He was at once puzzled, since he knew that May Kovar should be finished with her animals and that the Wallendas would not have finished their own act. To Adler "there shouldn't be applause." Instinctively the German-born clown suspected "something was wrong."

With meteoric acceleration the blaze that had been more or less smoldering leaped up the side and raced on to the peak—possibly being carried by the hemp ropes instead of the canvas. Wallenda realized that time had run out. He "hit" the rope and slid down toward the rings. The audience unfroze. Nearly seven thousand persons, leaving the chairs and the boards as one, raised their massed voices in a throaty wail of horror—the noise heard by Felix Adler. Now smelling smoke, the latter, half painted, half dressed, ran outside.

Emmett Kelly, trying to run but "making poor headway in my big, flapping clown shoes," looked down and realized he was toting a water bucket that he had, reflexively, picked up at the elephants' tethering area. Roustabouts raced into action—some toward the smoking big top, others toward the city fire boxes, still others dashing about aimlessly like swarms of bees without a queen. Kelly, already conscious of the hopelessness of fighting such an inferno with one bucket of water, heard "the grandstand chairs slamming inside the tent" and people commencing to stampede.

Merle Evans, his baton poised anew, had already passed the word to play "The Stars and Stripes Forever." This was a traditional circus signal of impending troubles. The bass-horn musician, W. J. O'Connor, looked up to be seized with the curious notion that some of the women and children appeared "kind of fascinated" by the moment.

May Kovar was shouting and cracking her whip through the smoke at the last of the wild animals. There remained the real danger that they might turn and rush back in. Their massed bulk and inertia conceivably could shatter the gates and thus augment the existing madness.

Herman Wallenda, followed by his "family" of four, had made good his escape, scrambling over the animal exit. Once clear, the five high-wire artists joined others of the troupe in trying to help the panic-stricken audience to safety.

The first of the six center poles, its top lashings eaten by the flames, swayed, then crashed across the tanbark. The people were jumping, some twelve feet or more from the top rows to the ground. Others slid down on impromptu chutes fashioned by the roustabouts as they slashed the sidewalls. They shouted at men and women starting to turn back, seeking members of their families: "Go on! You can't go back in there! Keep moving!"

Nancy had bolted at once, but her big sister, Dorothea, just "sat and sat," watching the flames across the tent, to her left. She was loath to start down the bleachers largely because of a lifelong fear of descending stairs or any steep area without a railing. "People," she would recall, "were trying to get out under the tent. Flames were spreading. Masses of people were running and pushing toward both exits."

Then, when she began to see "ropes of fire" falling from the roof, she decided it was time to get out. It wasn't easy, the way people were "stumbling and pushing." At the last bleacher she paused as a woman fell flat in front of her. Dorothea jumped down and helped her up.

A number of what Kelly recognized already to be "a frantic, milling mob" were halted as they had almost made good their escape by misdirected workmen or even other spectators who were trying to channel the exits into certain directions. One girl approached Kelly crying for her mother. "Listen, honey," he pleaded with her, "listen to the old man! You go way over there to the 'victory garden' and wait for your mommy. She'll come along soon."

Another pole crashed inside the roaring big top. Detective John A. Reardon, of the Hartford police, vainly· attempting to stop the tidal wave of panic, watched the tent beginning to collapse "in great flaming folds." Yet Bandmaster Evans kept leading his musicians, choking as they were from the billowing smoke. It looked already to Reardon that the band didn't stand a chance of ever "getting out of that place."

The flames had licked along the sawdust and were moving like rivulets of lava toward areas and other tents beyond the big top. One man was pushed abruptly away from a generator wagon, near the flames and itself burning. "Good God! Come with me!" he was told by the attendant. "This thing's liable to blow up!" As the dazed on-looker obeyed, childlike, a diesel caterpillar ground up, almost knocking over Emmett Kelly in its smoky progress, hooked up to the generator, and hauled it off. At a safer distance the performers beat out the flames with pieces of wood and with their bare hands.

Inside the big top Thomas E. Murphy, an editorial writer with the *Courant*, leading his five-year-old away from the flames, heard a nearby voice, "Take it easy! Walk out quietly!" Murphy thought that the crowd "seemed to subside." But only for an instant. Then they began pushing and screaming again.

"The din of shouting and shrieking," Murphy's colleague, Dow, continued, "mingled with the crash of falling grandstand chairs was deafening." Somewhere in the wild discord rasped the cries of frightened animals. In vain the reporter lifted his voice: "Keep steady. Keep your seats!"

But it was already too late for that. He joined the push. Two high-school boys who had accompanied him were by his side. It was difficult to make any progress at all, since the swarm of human beings was "coming like a cyclone." One of his young charges tripped over a chair, and people behind him at once started to pile up. Mothers were tossing children down from the upper stands, desperately hoping that wherever they landed, someone might catch them. The teen-ager with Dow then extricated himself, and the three scrambled up and over the grandstand. They slid down poles to the ground for a relatively un-obstructed final dash.

Shirley Snelgrove, whose parents, Mr. and Mrs. Ralph Snelgrove, of Plainville, had brought her to the circus as a thirteenth-birthday present, fell back when she couldn't keep up with her mother and father, sprinting across the steel animal trellis. Certain she was lost, she stumbled to the top of the bleachers and dropped down. Someone dragged her, already burned, from under the canvas. She beat out her smoldering garments and wandered away through the chaos to a grassy spot, just as the other girl, unhurt, had been directed by Kelly. Although Shirley could not know it now, her inability to surmount the lion and tiger runway had saved her life. But she was an orphan.

Many others had already perished as this strong barred barricade denied their bid for safety. In their panic almost none of the audience had noticed the two wide, unobstructed entrances at the far end of the tent, used by the performers. The spectators were vainly and instinctively struggling toward the congested route by which they had entered.

The members of the cast were performing heroically. At least one of the midgets was already burned from repeatedly darting, terrierlike, under the flaps either to lead those inside out or to plead with them to follow.

Rose Behee, a starlet with the circus, had seated her two small children on a bleachers bench before the show started. She kept going in looking for them. Each time, she brought others to safety, after despairing of finding her own little ones. Not until later did she locate them both, unharmed.

Other acts of heroism were being performed and encored from unexpected quarters. A thirteen-year-old crippled boy ripped a great hole with his jackknife in the canvas allowing as many as three hundred persons to pour through while he himself limped away. Ten-year-old Timothy Moynihan, son of a policeman, heard a soldier call, "Don't run, take it easy!" Timothy saw the serviceman holding up the edge of the tent, urging, "Come out this way." He helped the soldier hold up the flap while two dozen or more scrambled through to safety.

"My children, my children!" one woman was screaming. Then, one after another, she began clutching them to her side as all four of them, ranging in age from six to nine years, popped up like rabbits. Another mother, not nearly so thankful, was overheard complaining bitterly. Her young ones were safe, but she had lost her purse.

The flames had been roaring and crackling for at least five minutes now. Firemen, emergency police, Civil Defense workers, and Red Cross groups were arriving. The tent, however, was a 520-foot-long inferno, a "flaming forest of canvas," in the words of one witness. The holocaust could no more be extinguished than Vesuvius at the height of an eruption. Furthermore, the smoke was so thick that rescue teams couldn't even see who might still be inside.

"The canvas was nearly all burned away," Kelly continued, "and the center poles were crashing one by one. We ran to the horse troughs, filled four buckets, and threw the water on the fire."

Dorothea Felber reached the bandstand just after embers from a pole had set fire to the calliope. She walked out with Merle Evans and other bandsmen. Undaunted, the musicians played as they walked—

much as a jazz funeral procession in New Orleans—and then formed up to continue their brassy music outside.

To Dorothea it was "bedlam, terrible screaming and such pushing. Everyone was talking at once to everyone and running aimlessly. There had been panic inside the tent, but outside it was more shock and disbelief. I saw circus people everywhere trying to help."

Everyone in a "terrible" discord was yelling names of some loved one. They called, shouted, and screamed in crying, tearful tones. "No one," it seemed to Dorothea, "was able to find anyone. I saw the flames and felt the heat of the fire but kept on walking and roaming around for some time with no real direction."

A gust of wind from the southwest sounded a final requiem for the big top, which now lay crumpled on the July earth, a flaming, indistinguishable heap—reminiscent of the wreckage of the *Hindenburg*.

"I have lost my child!" "Have you seen my brother?" "I've lost my family!" These were the anguished phrases ringing in Dorothea's ears as she hurried through the streets and side streets bordering the circus grounds. She kept thinking, *"How* am I going to tell my family that Nancy is dead?"

She did not have much longer to speculate. She looked up to see Nancy, crying, running toward her. When she could manage words, Dorothea's little sister explained that she had simply run out the main entrance at the first alarm, apparently ahead of the first surge of people.

It was very difficult to find a telephone, since all who had escaped the fire were lined up in front of homes to use private phones. When finally Dorothea was able to call home, another sister, Barbara, didn't know what she meant by saying that she was "safe" or that they were trying to get home when they could. "I thought you were going to the circus," Barbara said. She hadn't heard the news, and in her own nervousness Dorothea hung up without further explanation.

Curiously, even those members of Ringling Brothers who had been combating the conflagration found the reality of the moment as hard to comprehend as did the circus-goers. The word continued to be spread from mouth to mouth, from the fat lady, the thin man, and the snake charmer to the clowns, magicians, roustabouts, and water boys, that everyone had "gotten out."

Knowledgeable as to the fluctuating conditions in the big top during performances, the circus people were thankful that the blaze had not started a few minutes later when the three rings, two stages, "the entire hippodrome oval would have been crowded with elephants, camels, horses, wagons, and close to the entire troupe."

Performers such as Kelly sat down, removed shoes, and put their feet in buckets of water. They dabbed their scorched faces with the cream used for removing makeup. Not until they had been listening to the wail of ambulance and fire sirens for several minutes was the tragedy brought home. Then they began to watch doctors, first-aid people, and firemen carrying bodies from where the bleachers and grandstands had been.

Kelly, walking past the ruins of the big top, noticed a clown doll lying in the charred sawdust, and, as he would write, "that moment was when the tension . . . broke over me in a wave, and I couldn't keep from crying any longer." There had been train wrecks, storms, wild animals running loose, and "all the other misfortunes that are part of outdoor trouping," but before, "the people who died or got hurt were mostly our own. The terrible thing about the fire was that the victims had been our customers and that so many of them were kids."

At that moment, the ending of "the longest afternoon of my life," Emmett Kelly, minus his putty nose, his big, painted grin, and his oversize shoes, was one of the world's saddest clowns.

For others the day's denouement was dramatized by relief and thankfulness. Dorothea and Nancy found their friends who had driven them to the circus waiting in the parking lot. They "cried and talked, and I guess we were all in a state of shock."

Once free of the seemingly inextricable traffic jam and driving across the East Hartford bridge, Dorothea noticed her mother driving the other way. They yelled and blew the horn and finally attracted the older woman's attention. She had not been home when Dorothea called, had heard the word on the radio, and was hurrying to the Connecticut Armory on Broad Street, already set up as a morgue. "I was trying to remember what you and Nancy were wearing," Dorothea's mother admitted later. The girls then drove home with their mother, in silence.

The fire was not the first to level a circus. Hitherto, however, spectators seemed to have led a charmed life in spite of far flimsier and much more inflammable equipment of past decades. The worst previous blaze had hit Barnum and Bailey while at winter quarters in Bridgeport in

1887. It had incinerated virtually the entire circus except thirty elephants and one lion named Nimrod. The flames, which almost put the show permanently out of business, could be seen for miles. A flash fire in Huntsville, Alabama, in 1916 destroyed eighty-four horses, tents, and wagons. In 1942 more than forty animals perished in a blaze at Cleveland.

If the Hartford catastrophe had not happened in wartime, the death count might have been greater still. Blood plasma, flown in from cities as far west as Chicago and as far south as Atlanta, was stockpiled in abnormally great supply. Operating teams and relays of nurses with plasma bottles and burn jellies worked around the clock at hospitals in and near Hartford.

Lessons in preventing fatalities when a great portion of the body was scorched—even upward of 75 percent—had been learned not only on the battlefields but in the wake of the *Hindenburg* explosion and, before that, in 1934, following the *Morro Castle*'s burning off the New Jersey coast. Even so, of the nearly 700 who had been hurt, 168 would die of their burns, of suffocation, or from complications such as pneumonia. Of the dead, about one-fourth had perished beside the cast-iron bars of the big cats' runways. Those who failed to surmount the formidable barrier on the first try were trampled in the surging accumulation of human beings. Wallenda was familiar with the very few stiles or crossover points, but how many of the audience were acrobats?

For several days identification continued. Child and adult alike were victims. The well-known—for example, Dean Edwin G. Woodward, thirty-three, of the College of Agriculture, University of Connecticut—along with the scarcely known were claimed and brought to some familiar plot for burial.

Finally, the blanket rows in the Connecticut Armory dwindled to one: a girl about nine, blond, blue-eyed, untouched by the flames, a victim of suffocation. She became only "Little Miss 1565," from her number. The police placed hundreds of phone calls, newspapers ran gratis ads, and spot announcements were heard over radio—all seeking for any clue that might provide a hint as to her identity. But no one has ever come forward to claim her.

The child was buried by the Hartford Fire Department in a nonsectarian cemetery in Wilson, a Hartford suburb, with a simple tombstone inscribed: "Little Miss 1565." Each July 6, a minister, a retired policeman or fireman, or some other concerned individual drives out to the plot and places a wreath on the grave of a little girl who somehow had made her way to a circus one Wednesday afternoon in a long-ago July.

Meanwhile, with the big top in ashes and the identified dead buried, two major considerations remained: Who was to blame, and what was the immediate cause?

Police, merely the instruments of higher law-enforcement bodies, are expected to move in with manifest haste after such catastrophes as this and arrest at least somebody. And they did—on instructions of the district attorney. Six officials of the circus corporation, of varying echelons of importance, were charged with criminal negligence. They included George Smith, the general manager, James A. Haley, the executive vice-president, and Leonard Aylesworth, the chief canvasman. Robert Ringling, the president, was in Chicago at the time.

What physical assets of the circus remained were seized by the Connecticut courts as security against the many damage suits to be filed. It looked even to the most myopic as though "the greatest show on earth" was now about as dead as the Romans' Circus Maximus. But just when the clowns and the roustabouts and the billed stars such as the Wallendas and May Kovar were about to pack up and look for bookings outside of the circus, Jim Haley pulled what seemed tor everyone in the troupe a rabbit out of his hat. He produced a $500,000 insurance policy drawn—he did not say just why—a few months earlier and another $500,000 in cash reserves. The show was kept out of bankruptcy with this $1,000,000 bond deposited with a court-appointed arbitrator.

The wagons—some still scorched—with their animals and their performers, fat ladies, midgets, skinny men, and sword swallowers, rolled out of the darkest chapter in circus history. Ringling would never pitch tent again in Hartford, yet on August 4, less than a month after the fire, the "Greatest Show on Earth" did strike up the band in Akron's Rubber Bowl. It continued under the open sky in fair grounds and ball parks around the country until it closed in October in New Orleans and limped back finally to winter quarters in Sarasota.

On October 20 another disaster occurred in Cleveland when a liquid-gas storage plant exploded, claiming 135 lives, comparable to the Hartford catastrophe.

Meanwhile, Hartford police joined with insurance investigators and the F.B.I. in attempting to pinpoint the source of the fire. True it was that the canvas was aging and had been treated with a most combustible mixture of paraffin and gasoline. The hemp ropes, not of prewar quality, tended to be carriers of flame rather than buffers. They conceivably hastened the movement of the blaze to the tent peaks. Then, too, what about the factor of dry grass or an electrical short circuit? Or the blazing generator wagon? Had that really been set afire secondarily?

Thus, while there was scant mystery about how the fire had spread, the major question of how it started remained unanswered. Years later, a mental patient in Ohio who had been employed briefly by the circus in 1944 claimed he had started the conflagration "for a thrill." There was no substantiating his erratic boast.

To Everett Dow, the reporter, now town clerk in West Hartford, sabotage "doesn't seem to me to be the answer." He continues (in a letter to the author):

> You must remember that there was no menagerie top that two-day setup in Hartford and people were circulating around the lot even while the show was on. It seems that it would have been very difficult for an arsonist to go unobserved in lighting the fire which apparently started in the tent wall diagonally across the arena from where I sat.
>
> In a nonconclusive sort of way it has always seemed to me that a lighted cigarette butt discarded in litter, probably by a "townie," started the fire. Canvas is very difficult to ignite.
>
> In fact, I have seen circus workmen putting out their cigarettes by rubbing them against the canvas tent wall rather than throwing them in litter, which is invariably at the bottom of the big-top wall.
>
> The day was terrifically hot . . . a lighted cigarette butt tossed into litter could easily have started a blaze at the bottom of the tent wall which could have been unobserved in the intense sunlight until it had become, with the help of the paraffin-treated canvas, impossible to extinguish.

To this day, no one has suggested any better explanation.

The circus went back on the road and stayed in business, although the legal complexities continued. Five of the six charged were convicted and sentenced to short jail terms. Irrespective of the considerations of justice or otherwise, a greater legal tilt persisted within the circus corporation itself—a struggle for control. It finally concluded with John Ringling North in command.

Ten years later, on July 6, 1954, the books were at long last closed. The circus mailed a check for $100,000 to the receivership in final settlement for the $4,000,000 death claims. "I deeply appreciate the splendid spirit of cooperation from the people of Connecticut . . . in its effort to mitigate the pain and suffering attendant upon the disaster," wrote John North.

An understanding state judicial system had kept the circus out of bankruptcy, allowing it both to remain in business and to make good on reasonable debts to the utmost of its ability. Probably no enterprise in the United States had ever been staggered to its foundations so mortally and come back swinging at the bell.

9

Explosion in
Texas City, 1947

> Hardly without exception all persons concerned with the handling, stowage, and transportation of the cargo displayed a lack of knowledge of the provisions and regulations governing the safety of the operations. . . .
>
> Control of smoking on deck and in the holds was lax. . . . The fire could have been extinguished in its early stages. . . .
>
> —Coast Guard Board of Inquiry

The origins of that particular investigation were routine and disarming, even as the sunny summer days preceding the fire in Hartford. On the morning of Friday, April 11, 1947, the S.S. *Grand Camp*, which was the former American Liberty ship *Benjamin R. Curtis*, now owned by the French Line, shoved her squat bulk through the flat blue waters of Galveston Channel to tie up at Pier O, North Slip, in Texas City, Texas. Under the command of Captain Charles de Guillebon, the 7,176-ton freighter was a die-stamp duplicate of hundreds of other Liberty ships—seagoing cargo bins of World War II, produced and launched far faster than the U-boats or the Luftwaffe could sink them. What they lacked in graceful lines or speed was amply compensated in dependability.

Tramplike, this freight car of the sea-lanes had paused here and there at Gulf ports and by the time she reached Texas City was already halfway down to her Plimsoll. The rather remarkable assortment in her five cavernous holds included 380 bales of compressed cotton, picked up in Houston, 59,000 bales of pure sisal binder twine, 2,500 bales of tobacco leaf, 9,334 bags of shelled peanuts, two hundred boxes of oil-well or agricultural machinery, and sixteen cases of small-arms ammunition consigned to La Guaira, Venezuela.

The *Grand Camp* was warped to Pier O to top off her considerable cargo with approximately 2,500 tons of nitrates, packed in one-hundred-pound six-ply paper bags, each of which was stamped in black letters "Fertilizer—Ammonium Nitrate, Nitrogen 32.5%." It represented a Marshall Plan gift to Belgium and the Netherlands as well as France.

At I P.M. that same day stevedores commenced the tedious process of loading the bagged fertilizer. This was a French ship, and the signs were all in that language: "Defense de Fumer" for example, on deck and in the holds. *If* any one of the longshoremen understood what "Defense de Fumer" meant, he did not so indicate by his response. Most of the men chain-smoked, aboard the vessels and on the wharves where the signs *were* in English. The stevedores knew better, but they didn't care, and no one wanted to admonish them to obey the rules. Their union was strong and tough, and it didn't take much provocation to call a strike. Then the shipper faced mounting costs from idle dock time.

For that matter, the tobacco habit was not the only example of disobedience of regulations. Stowage itself proceeded in the same sloppy pattern. For example, if a bag of the fertilizer was ripped or broken open, Coast Guard ordinances demanded that it be repaired or refilled and the spilled contents cleared away. When they broke—and this was from time to time inevitable with such a cargo—the bags were simply left where they were, their contents slopping onto and around adjacent sacks.

The fact that this material was directly associated with agriculture and that more than 75,000 tons of ammonium nitrate had been loaded out of Texas City in the past year conceivably lulled the stevedores into a false security. Perhaps if they had known that the so-called fertilizer had originated as by-products or "compounds" from three

U.S. Army ordnance plants, two in Nebraska and one in Iowa, they might have evinced increased respect for what was passing through their hands.

There was also the psyche itself of Texas City: busy, vital, bearing no resemblance to the match-stick town that fielded the backwash of the Galveston tidal wave. Its population had soared from five thousand to eighteen thousand during the war, and that growth was continuing. The world's largest tin smelter was in operation, along with Monsanto's multimillion-dollar plant for styrene. It was a trailblazer, constructed in the war out of the ravenous demand for synthetic rubber. The Martian-like towers involved in catalytic cracking of high-octane gasoline raised themselves all along the waterfront, a part of the picture of postwar industry. Just like the Lone Star State, everything about Texas City was big and becoming bigger each week. The Chamber of Commerce, advertising for new businesses to move to what they tagged as the "Port of Opportunity," didn't have to exaggerate too much in describing the city's lusty potential.

The *Grand Camp* loaded during five working days. At 5 P.M. Tuesday, April 15, No. 4 hatch, aft, was closed for the night. One "draft," or cargo hoist, of bags was left in the middle of a working "square" of the hatch waiting to be stowed around the hold the following morning.

At 8 A.M. Wednesday, the sixteenth, the gangs were back to finish up. The day was sunny and clear under the cleansing influence of a familiar "norther" blowing in strong. The stevedores went to work. At 8:15, or no more than two or three minutes afterward, one of the longshoremen noticed a wisp of smoke emerging from the starboard side of the hold between the side plates of the Liberty and the wood cargo battens, or "sweatbands." It appeared that the source was farther down between the fertilizer bags.

Word was passed topside, bringing crewmen and four portable soda-acid fire extinguishers. The smoke disappeared. Then, in moments, it started up again, from between the one-hundred-pound bags of what was basically one of the most explosive substances in existence, known chemically as NH_4NO_3. This implication, however, even with a known fire smoldering somewhere deep in the bowels of the ship, still wasn't driven home to the men in Hold No. 4.

Attempts to quench the smoke continued desultorily, much in the same spirit of apathy and ignorance as was evinced by the ticket taker at the gangway of the *Eastland*, who persisted in allowing picnickers to pour on board even after he had noticed the steamer was overcrowded and that there was a list.

A summons went out for pails. A few—used for drinking water—were lowered into the hold. At least one was empty. A longshoreman shouted up the obvious: He wanted *full* buckets. The quip echoed back down: "Y'wanted *buckets*, didn't ya? Y'didn't say water, too, did ya?" He laughed at his own wit. Others joined in.

Spurts of flame became visible along the sides of Hold No. 4. An alarm was sounded by blowing the ship's whistle, while a hose was unrolled partway down toward the smoldering fire. Although the engine room reported the main water pumps were working, the *Grand Camp*'s first officer ordered that no water be turned on. He did not want to risk damaging the cargo, he explained.

The conflagration by this time—it was nearly 8:30 A.M.—was gaining headway. There was so much smoke that neither crewmen nor stevedores could remain in Hold No. 4. Coughing, shouting back and forth, eyes watering, they came up on deck.

Captain Guillebon appeared. He ordered the hatch closed and tarpaulin battened over the wooden cover and then wet down to make the material fit more snugly. Next, he ordered live steam into the ship's smothering system, through vents in the holds. Although steam was long used to blanket ship fires, it was not indicated for explosives. It would only heat up such materials and measurably lower the flash or ignition point. Ammonium nitrate would decompose at 392° F. and boil at 410°.

At the same time Guillebon ordered the cases of small-arms ammunition in adjacent No. 5 hold to be moved to the far side, away from No. 4. Three cases were lugged up and placed aft of the deckhouse.

Obviously, the fire was worsening, since the tarpaulin on No. 4 hold billowed upward, then ripped, allowing thick orange-colored smoke to escape. The volume of these clouds was so impressive that the attention of surrounding areas was called to the dock. Across the slip, the location of the Monsanto plant, H. K. Eckert, the manager, rubbed his eyes and observed to an assistant standing beside him, "Gosh, that orange smoke is pretty!" Deciding he wanted a picture of it, he sent for his camera.

The spectacle at the same time was suggesting photography to others at the marine terminal. One was a mate aboard the *High Flyer*, a C-2 type vessel slightly larger than a Liberty, moored seven hundred feet from the *Grand Camp*, loaded with partially assembled railroad cars, sulfur, and ammonium nitrate. She was at the moment a "dead ship," owing to inspection of her turbine.

As the mate, camera in hand, wandered over to Pier O, loading of the *High Flyer*, owned by Lykes Brothers, was suspended. The order was also passed to close hatches, lead out hoses, and man fire stations.

Slightly after 8:30 Pete Suderman, union boss of the stevedores, ordered his men off the *Grand Camp*. At 8:33 they were followed by the entire crew of the burning Liberty on instructions of the master. As a matter of fact, he himself had to go ashore anyhow to find a telephone, since there were no fire-alarm boxes on the pier. There was also only one fire main.

No one was ever quite certain how the first alarm was sounded— whether Guillebon himself reached a phone or Mrs. Maude Bieg, switchboard operator at the Texas City Terminal Railway Company, had seen the smoke and on her own initiative called the city's Volunteer Fire Department. The Terminal Railway operated one-half mile of the waterfront property, including freight yards and warehouses.

Certainly, some twenty-five minutes after the first discovery of the fire, a number of individuals in the area were roused to action. Harley Bowen, for one, a foreman at the terminal, looked up from his desk to see an employee, Harvey Menge, racing toward him: "Mr. Bowen," he cried out of breath from running, "there is a big fire in Warehouse O!"

The two jumped into a car, collected Henry Baumgartner, volunteer fire chief also employed at the terminal, and drove to the *Grand Camp*. It required just one glance to evoke a concerned comment from Baumgartner: "This is a dangerous fire. We need all the help we can get!"

Baumgartner was a big, husky man in his forties, a favorite of the waterfront. Already he was perspiring from exertion, and his ample brow was creased with worry. "All the help" wasn't much, however; principally the new fourteen-thousand-dollar pumper and maybe two dozen volunteers who could respond on an instant's notice.

Another executive of the railway, Grant Wheaton, seated in the office of "Swede" Sandberg, a vice-president, himself became aware of the blaze. When he reached for the phone, Mrs. Bieg was already ringing him. "They want the Galveston fireboat," she said.

Wheaton, grabbing his hat, replied: "Call the Texas City Fire Department! Tell the powerhouse to sound the siren! Get me the chief of the Galveston Fire Department on the phone!" He was connected with Galveston and requested a fireboat. Next, Wheaton called the two principal towboat companies in the area and ordered "all tugs available, especially those equipped with fire-fighting apparatus."

The *Albatross* and *Propeller*, already manned with standby crews, tossed off their lines from a Galveston dock. In minutes the greenish bay waters were frothing at their sterns. Another tug, the *Pan I*, of the Pan American Refining Company, had just docked two barges, each carrying eighty thousand barrels of oil. Her master, Leonard Fuller, was ordered to get clear, since the *Pan I* carried no fire-fighting apparatus. He decided to tarry, however, to see what was going on.

He was joined by many others that early morning. Although there had been numerous more or less minor ship and warehouse fires, they still drew a crowd. All, too, were possessed by a common illusion, expressed by W. A. Johnson, owner of a materials company in the dock area—they didn't "seem to dream" that the Liberty could explode.

Texas City's leading citizen, sixty-year-old Henry J. "Mike" Mikesha, also president of the terminal organization, was on the scene. He was, with Baumgartner, among the relatively few who were genuinely worried. "Send some of the dock fire squads to move inflammables to the opposite side of Warehouse O," he ordered. "Watch for burning paper, open up all gates, and generally clear lanes for the trucks when they arrive."

When Harley Bowen sent for keys to unlock a large door of the warehouse facing the burning vessel, he found it was solidly blocked anyhow with stacked flour sacks. The same side was also two or three deep with the curious summoned by the fire whistle—already too many and too insistent for John Fuerst, the chief policeman, to control. John pushed his cap back onto his head and shrugged in a gesture of despair. The orange clouds mounted.

"Flames and smoke were pouring up out of one of her hatches," Grant Wheaton, at the scene, would recall, "making the hatchways look like a huge chimney." Then he hurried back to his office to find J. C.

Tompkins, a vice-president of Lykes, on the phone from Galveston and worrying about their ship, the *High Flyer*. Although both men agreed the *High Flyer* was "in no particular danger as yet," Tompkins said he was going to dispatch two tugs anyhow, to move her "if necessary."

By approximately 8:45 two pieces of apparatus from the Texas City Volunteer Fire Department had arrived. The men lost no time in coupling up their hoses, and soon the sun glinted from long streams of water arcing from the pier onto the blazing ship.

Some children, out of school that morning, piped their appreciation of the spectacle as they clutched their mothers' hands. There were about four hundred spectators on the wharf. None would ever know the exact count.

A few minutes before 9 A.M. two more engines arrived—and this was all Texas City's Volunteer Fire Department possessed. Counting Chief Baumgartner, twenty-seven volunteer firemen were hard at work, and it seemed as though progress were being made. The deck plates were so hot they sizzled and steamed under the streams of water, but the smoke was thinning. Even so, the adjacent Republic Oil Refining Company sent a couple of truckloads of foamite and men to direct it toward that burning hatch. Monsanto quickly followed suit.

Captain Fuller, of the *Pan I*, moved aboard the tug *Record*, which carried a ship-to-shore radio. He heard that the two Galveston tugs were en route. Also, on the AM band he listened to Station KGBC warning all residents to stay away from dockside—a warning that produced an opposite effect. Townspeople—in some cases whole families —kept arriving through the several terminal gates, carrying soda and sandwiches. Above their heads curled not only that strange orange smoke but smoldering scraps of paper bags—like fireflies or burning leaves wafted under a sudden autumn wind.

That longshoremen were leaving the entire dock area might have been a portent to others. Some went home; others progressed no farther than Frank's Café, a favorite waterfront rendezvous. Those stevedores who gave vent to their fears in the hearing of spectators indicated that their worries centered on the cases of ammunition, revealing an ignorance of the nearly 100-percent safety of small-arms shells. They required rifle or pistol hammers or pins for detonation.

Now, droning in and out of smoke clouds were two small airplanes, a pilot and a passenger in each, themselves bent on sight-seeing. It was a unique vantage point.

Satisfied that he had all the photographs he wanted for the moment, the mate from the *High Flyer* started back to his ship, nodding to Swede Sandberg as he strolled. The latter had just observed to Suderman, the longshoremen's boss: "Gosh, it's 9:07, and we don't have any sign of tugboats!"

"Why don't you go out to the T-head," Pete Suderman suggested. "You'll probably see them coming around the bend of the channel."

Actually, the tugs were in view to anyone on the end of the pier, the "T-head." Sandberg decided to continue on to his office. There he phoned Tompkins, over at Lykes, to bring him up to date on the fire and the situation on the *High Flyer*. He joked about the "alarmists" and their worries over the cases of small-arms ammunition.

Swede's diminishing concern seemed warranted. Workers at Monsanto began returning to their jobs. Eckert, figuring he had obtained the best pictures that would be made, now that the smoke was abating, put his camera away. Ralph A. Ford, foreman carpenter at the same styrene plant, shooed his men back with the casual aside: "The fire's about out."

The clock stood at just 9:12 A.M., and time had run out.

Without warning, the *Grand Camp* vanished in a massive eruption of orange smoke and flame—towering so high that it knocked the two sightseeing planes out of the sky, atomizing them and their four occupants. There was a vibrating rumble, as if an immense summer thunderstorm had struck.

Of the several hundred spectators and every member of the fire department on the scene, including Mike Mikesha and Baumgartner who just disappeared in the atomlike blast, only Harley Bowen was spared, probably because he was blown into the water, then up again and onto the wharf, where "everything" seemed to be "in total darkness."

Just a few hundred feet away the tug *Record* was hit broadside by the shock wave. Captain Fuller, from the *Pan I*, first struck on the head by a window frame, came under a shower of mixed debris that lent the impression "it was raining iron." He dived under a mattress knocked off a bunk in the pilothouse.

Mrs. Madelaine Rockefeller, working in the storeroom of Monsanto as it was hit by bricklike objects that "fell thick and fast," crawled under a large table. Then, "like waves on the beach, oil and water rushed in, reviving me. The next thing I noticed was a one-hundred-foot area near me afire. All I wanted was to get away before the benzol tanks caught fire."

She stumbled out of the half-collapsed, burning building with a bloody-faced man, arm in arm, and into an "utter silence" that "was awful." Another employee, Mrs. Adeline Flanikin, crawled out to find "the whole place down around me."

"A pluperfect hell," a police sergeant logged, and a witness in the streets called it "a vision of hell," watching an immense black cloud that covered everything and blotted out the sun. It was observed many miles away. The concussion itself was felt 160 miles distant, in Palestine, Texas.

In Texas City every window was shattered, and every home or business property was in some way scarred. Structures such as Frank's Café, in close proximity to the waterfront, collapsed at once, burying all who happened to be inside.

A tidal wave at least fifteen feet high surged up from the harbor, lifting a 150-foot barge laden with hydrochloric acid and depositing it more than one hundred feet farther away, on land. Spectators had been observed moments before on the spot where it smashed down, like a meteor. The ships *High Flyer* and *Wilson B. Keene*, another Liberty, torn from their moorings, banged into each other, drifted about, and finally stopped like runaway horses that had come to the realization that there was no place to go.

Parts of the *Grand Camp* ranging in size from rivets to a sixty-ton chunk of the superstructure rocketed down as far as two miles from Pier O. Some of these red-hot missiles pierced gasoline storage tanks on the rim of the warehouses, exploding or setting fire to eight of them. Tanks of benzene, propane, and ethyl at Monsanto, also holed, sent the highly inflammable liquid gushing in all directions, over wharves, ground, and water. In moments they had become blistering rivers of fire, consuming all in their path.

The entire cargo of 59,000 bales of pure sisal binder twine had been blasted into the heavens like Fourth of July rocket displays. Fragmented and ablaze, spider-web particles of twine wafted down on homes, lawns, and stores in Galveston, five miles distant. There, too, the building housing the office of Tompkins, the Lykes vice-president, shook so violently that he and his secretary were both thrown onto the floor. He had just been dictating a message on the fire for New Orleans headquarters.

As they stood up and straightened out their clothing, Tompkins commented wryly: "Don't send that one. There are some changes. . . ."

Meanwhile, water and vaporized oil as well joined the fall from out of the sky. Far heavier objects, not directly related to the disintegrated ship, were equally lethal. A safe, for example, loosened on the top floor of a swaying building, crashed through to the office below, instantly killing the occupant.

Edgar M. Queeny, Monsanto board chairman, who at once enplaned for the scene, would write:

> Our warehouse—a steel and brick structure—was flattened; not a splinter remained upright. The main power plant was similarly crushed. As the blast fanned out, walls of manufacturing buildings fell, windows of the plant office and laboratories shattered, roofs were ripped off, and pipe lines carrying inflammable liquids were torn apart. A huge wave, rushing in from the basin where the ship had rested, inundated the area.
>
> Savage and cruel fires, feeding on these inflammable liquids, scalded those who had survived the blast and were fleeing to safety; they cremated those who had fallen, and melted and twisted steel supports and girders.

People, just as they had in earlier disasters, reacted in individual ways, even though some, in a daze, didn't react at all for a measurable time. Many retrogressed to childhood, screaming for little objects like their screwdrivers or other tools, or their hats, as though such items possessed inherent saving or curative properties.

Everywhere were screaming, half-naked, dying people; a few, even while bleeding, protested they were "all right." Many, like Captain Guillebon and all but seven of his crew, vanished without trace.

When at least some of "the sounds died away," Grant Wheaton, knocked down and bloodied, staggered to his feet. "My head felt numb," he would recall. "I could see nothing from my right eye; a red film of blood seemed to cover my left. . . . I looked up and saw the sky through holes in the roof. Stumbling over debris, I went to the front door."

He heard someone call his name. Then Sandberg and Mrs. Bieg appeared. The latter had remained long enough at her switchboard to make one last plea: "For God's sake, send the Red Cross."

"I'm going to have to lie down," he told them, and the two, without meaning to, eased him into two inches of oil and water.

All tended to lose a relationship to reality and to their normal patterns of conduct and inhibitions. One woman, in Texas City, trying on a corset in a lingerie shop, wandered out onto the sidewalk in the corset and her shoes—and nothing else. Another walked out of what was left of the terminal offices carrying ten million dollars of insurance policies in a bedsheet.

Others, blocks away from the blast, found that most of their clothes had been swept off their bodies as though suddenly snipped away by giant shears. Other men and women were momentarily blinded. A few shocked, but not physically hurt, began crawling under the delusion that their legs had been broken or possibly blown off. "A kind of shell-shocked madness seized the town," a psychologist would observe.

Storekeepers left their doors and, in some instances, cash registers wide open as they rushed into the streets to find out what was happening. Schools that were in session quickly emptied as children raced outside through raining glass and fiery debris to their homes.

In the Mexican and Negro section, where most of the homes were flimsily constructed, the carnage was barely short of complete. One black ghetto, less than a mile from this nonatomic "ground zero," was almost totally wiped out. Those who could move at all joined the exodus north and west, away from the fury.

Since fire mains were ruptured, there was no water pressure even for reserves of firemen now en route from neighboring communities. The shock had burst pipes even inside of homes, which were now being drenched.

The whole waterfront was ablaze—including the five principal warehouses—and more than half of the buildings and piers had already been reduced to rubble. The dead were everywhere. The dense black smoke pouring out of the twisted remains of the Monsanto plant furnished a cerement to the area, making it difficult for the survivors to move about at all. Warehouses O and A contained shipments of sulfur. Now afire, its noxious fumes added to the horror and perils of the moment.

Miraculously Pete Suderman was among the survivors, although he was severely injured. He had been standing so close to the ship when it exploded that two stevedores beside him were instantly killed. Sandberg, meanwhile, had bandaged his own head and led Grant Wheaton to a truck he had commandeered, one of the few operable vehicles of any description. He gathered up other casualties he encountered and headed for town.

There were not nearly enough beds in the diminutive Texas City hospital nor in the clinics, themselves badly battered and without electricity. However, Houston, Galveston, Corpus Christi, and even Dallas, 250 miles distant, were rushing ambulances and medical and Red Cross teams. Army relief workers from Fort Sam Houston were already boarding planes in San Antonio. Soldiers from Fort Crockett, Galveston, were speeding across the causeway. A quick-thinking yardman at Houston uncoupled railroad tank cars, had them filled with water and dispatched to Texas City.

The Gulf Coast hurricane emergency plans were put into effect, especially in Galveston County. What was left of the wartime Civilian Defense was being frantically mobilized by Mayor J. C. Trahan, of Texas City, himself an army veteran. The explosion had reminded him of nothing so much as "an artillery barrage."

As in other disasters of great scope, the quick and the dead posed a mounting problem. Stretchers bearing the living were placed in the city auditorium after the hospital overflowed, then in the park behind City Hall. The critically injured, predominantly severe burn and fracture cases, were rushed to hospitals in Galveston, and the less severely injured were taken to the city auditorium in Texas City. The army hospital at Fort Crockett in Galveston was reactivated for the emergency. A constant stream of ambulances, station wagons, and buses rushed victims to Galveston hospitals throughout the day. Citizens converged on the two locations with blankets, towels, and rudimentary first-aid supplies. Buses, trucks, station wagons, and many private automobiles rolled into the stricken dock area on the prowl for the wounded. A loud-speaker mounted on a truck moved among the growing throngs rasping out instructions. The Coast Guard buoy tender *Iris* began shuttling the injured to Galveston. It was joined by smaller harbor craft, searching the waters around the burning piers.

When the dead were recovered, their bodies were taken to a garage; their names, if identified, were then scribbled on a blackboard outside. Ropes were stretched to keep the crowds from pushing inside.

A young woman sang out a man's name. "Dead," came the response from inside.

She was heard to murmur, "I danced with him last night," before she turned away.

The garage was too small. Soon, the high-school gymnasium and the bowling alleys were put into service.

Telephone workers, who had been on a nationwide strike, returned to work to handle an astronomical number of calls crackling to and from Texas City.

In Galveston Tompkins was trying to obtain tugs to haul the *High Flyer*, now emptied of her crew, out to sea. No one was interested, for fear of new explosions.

Well-known names appeared by afternoon: General Jonathan Wainwright, the nation's former highest-ranking Japanese P.O.W., now commanding the Fourth Army; Hal Boyle, the war correspondent; even the comedian, Jack Benny.

"I have never seen a greater tragedy in all my experience," Wainwright declared. To Hal Boyle, the scene of devastation resembled nothing so much as Nagasaki after the drop of the first A-bomb. Benny, for once, was speechless.

The afternoon moved on. At least one of the flaming oil tanks fizzled out. Bulldozers were pushing rubble in medium-sized mounds. It looked like the situation was returning to a semblance of normalcy.

Then, when it was nearly six o'clock, Sandberg, back at the docks, was accosted by a man, shouting, "Mr. Sandberg, the *High Flyer*'s on fire!"

The word spread. Coast guardsmen who had been on and off the *High Flyer* confirmed that the ship, which had sustained widespread damage from the *Grand Camp* explosion, was indeed hot. Chief Arthur Meyers, from the Galveston Lifeboat Station, reported that "the woodwork [of the *High Flyer*] was burning pretty well." It was among the more tragic understatements of a most tragic day.

Darkness settled down on the city. Fires smoldered in the dockside and within the tank farms. There were no floodlights to aid the fire fighters and rescue teams, since the entire emergency supply of army searchlights had been destroyed in one of the warehouses. Even so, they dug away through the debris hunting for anyone who could manifest even a feeble hint of life. Plasma was being flown, railroaded, and driven into a wide area surrounding the disaster apex, along with penicillin. Something like 500,000 units were consumed each hour in an effort to ward off gas gangrene.

As the uncertain evening wore on, the understandable confusion within the shattered purlieus of Texas City was augmented by conflicting orders. The police dispatched a sound truck, warning of a second explosion. It was followed by substitute firemen from other communities saying there was really nothing more to fear. Some householders and storekeepers commenced to replace broken panes of glass. The result was inevitable. Individuals together with groups, families, and random clusters surged back and forth, in and out of the city, like a tidal cross-rip.

About 7:45 P.M. army authorities ordered the evacuation of the waterfront. However, diametrically opposite instructions from sources that proved impossible to trace sent four tugs out of Galveston toward the disaster area, and by 11 P.M. two tugs were at the scene. Swede Sandberg himself met them and supplied the crew with oxygen masks. A hawser was secured to the *High Flyer*; it tightened, then snapped. Someone had forgotten that the anchor was down.

Since there was no steam up on the C-2, Nos. 2, 3, and 4 holds of which were still smoking, acetylene torches were used to burn through the tough cast-iron anchor chain. This was not an operation that could be accomplished in a few minutes—or even half an hour.

At 12:05 Pat Flaherty, announcer for KPRC, Texas City, long since groggy from bulletins, had yet one more to flash onto the air: "There is an impending danger of another explosion in the dock area!"

A dogged little band of some two hundred persons, including Red Cross and other volunteers still digging for survivors, began to move back from the rubble of the waterfront in response to increasingly insistent orders, "Clear the area!"

About 1 A.M. a Roman-candle effect began shooting skyward from the burning *High Flyer*. Her side plates were glowing amber. The tugs threw off the towlines and churned away, as someone shouted, "Get the hell out of here. This damn ship's gonna blow up!"

A policeman on the dock was heard to observe, "We've been run out of here two or three times today. Everybody says there is going to be another explosion, and it hasn't happened yet." Luckily the remaining volunteers heeded the warning and dashed to City Hall.

At 1:05 it happened. The *High Flyer* went up in a mushroom of flame and smoke. Locke Mouton, Galveston school principal and Red Cross volunteer, avowed he could never forget it.

A four-ton turbine landed on the pump house of Republic Oil Refinery. Another fragment went through a Salvation Army canteen truck. The surviving Liberty ship, the *Wilson B. Keene*, was torn in two. A three-hundred-foot section was projected upward. It turned end over end, then came hurtling down onto a row of freight cars on a siding. The destruction of Warehouses A and B was completed. From behind the barge that earlier had been blown ashore, Sandberg "could hear the hot steel hitting the sides."

At City Hall, several miles away, where the auditorium floor was covered with stretcher cases on army cots, a powerful draft sucked boxes of supplies along the corridors moments before the shock wave shook the building and caused serious structural damage to the auditorium ceiling and roof. The stretcher cases were moved to the park outside under the eerie lights of hesitating generators and the accompaniment of wailing sirens on missions of mercy.

Then, at long last, the carnage was over, with only one additional known death from the second detonation. As Sandberg ventured out from his shelter and shuffled once more past the litter and fires, realizing he had lost many friends in the past hours, he "felt like the man walking the last mile to the electric chair." When he arrived at a dispensary, people blanched. The word had preceded Sandberg that Swede was dead. He asked for a drink of bourbon. A nurse on duty poured him an entire glass, and "it didn't bother me at all."

Not until the following Tuesday were the last fires fully extinguished. On May 11 the final body was exhumed from the dock area, some ten days after the first ship since the explosion had tied up in Texas City.

The toll was at least 560 dead, with 120 missing, 3,000 injured, and 2,500 homeless. The property damage was far in excess of fifty million dollars.

"Stunned and grief-stricken," editorialized the Houston *Post*, "one asks *why* such a thing should happen. But it is not given to us to know. . . ." The Coast Guard, however, was not permitted through its prerogatives to shrug off its own conclusions quite so rhetorically. Its inquiry observed, in part:

The methods of combating the fire on the *Grand Camp* in its early stages were futile. The procedure of closing the hatch and sealing the ventilators increased the danger potentiality of the fires and caused a serious delay in the later introduction of water into this hold. The introduction of steam resulted in raising the temperature of the mass of the cargo in the hold. The action of the Second Captain of the *Grand Camp* in ordering that no water from the ship's fire hose be applied to the fire in its early stages resulted in eliminating all opportunity of the city fire department to combat the fire upon their arrival.

The investigation's best guess was that the explosion was caused by "unauthorized smoking in the hold" (probably igniting first the sulfur cargo). One cigarette, in other words, had all but leveled a port city, even as another cigarette may have consumed the big top in Hartford, or, though less probable, have exploded the dirigible *Hindenburg*. The tobacco habit hardly seemed justified.

The task of cleaning up the wreckage and of rebuilding remained. Monsanto, which had lost 154 of its employees, at once appropriated half a million dollars to care for their survivors and for the 200 injured. Proportionately, the chemical company, a mere bystander, had suffered the worst, and yet Monsanto had construction crews on the scene in three days.

Ahead lay a wrangle in the courts: 8,484 plaintiffs filing 2,735 suits, totaling nearly a quarter of a billion dollars. Even so, the claims were probably no greater than the scope and fury of the explosions themselves.

The defendant was the United States Government, since the ammonium nitrate had originated in army ordnance plants. In addition, the United States and France each filed suits against the other, mutually charging the "negligence" of the other party. Then the Terminal Company sued the ten insurance companies that refused to honor some $3,250,000 in damage claims, based on the technicality of whether the loss was occasioned more from an explosion than fire. The Terminal Company finally won, on its contention that explosions were the prime cause.

The major claims seesawed all the way to the Supreme Court, which found that the Federal Government was *not* liable. The army, ruled the jurists of the land's highest court, had made no secret of the dangerous nature of this cargo, and all who handled it had every reason to be aware of the same thing. However, influential Texans carried the fight for compensation to Congress. A special act was passed and signed by President Dwight D. Eisenhower through which the army, acting merely as an agent of the government, was to settle claims not to exceed in toto $16,500,000.

Nearly ten years after the explosion, in February, 1957, the last settlement was made: $25,000 to Mrs. Ann Thirion, of France, the widow of Jean Thirion, of the *Grand Camp*. It had required a whole decade, just as had been the case after the Hartford circus fire, to close the books on the Texas City disaster.

Today, Texas City, with more than double the population of 1947, plus new schools, new churches, and new stores, no longer handles "dry" cargo—just petroleum, which is far less sensitive in its crude state than ammonium nitrate. Whether this is happenstance or expediency is not readily reconciled. The reminders, nonetheless, linger at Slip O, Berth B, in the shape of twisted, barnacle-covered pilings and cables—mute warnings perhaps of what happened one day in April when Texas City once moved dry cargo.

10

Thanksgiving Eve
Train Wreck, 1950

It was a cold, bright Thanksgiving Eve, Wednesday, November 22, 1950, two days before a full moon. For many of Long Island's commuter battalions this was the beginning of a long holiday weekend, and everyone was anxious to get home.

Two Long Island Rail Road trains carrying this workaday genre, plus a sprinkling of late shoppers, were pounding through the tenement jungle along Lefferts Avenue in the Richmond Hill section of the borough of Queens. Each train was made up of twelve cars, most of them self-propelled, with their own powerful electric motors, similar to trolleys. The first, No. 780, the familiar if hardly beloved "6:09," now about thirteen minutes out of Penn Station bound for Hempstead in Nassau County, was packed with more than one thousand riders. Originally running one minute late, Motorman William W. Murphy, sixty-one-year-old veteran of forty-five years of railroading, had poured on the "juice" along the straightaways of this four-track main line with the result that the 6:09 was now on schedule. The second train was No. 174, the "6:13" out of the same Victorian terminal on the West Side of midtown Manhattan, and bound for a slightly farther destination, Babylon, in sprawling Suffolk County, which stretched all the way eastward to lonely Montauk Point. This train carried twelve hundred commuters, many of them standing in the aisles. At the throttle was Benjamin J. Pokorny, a few years the junior of Bill Murphy. The 6:13 was on time.

Although not one of the more than two thousand souls aboard the two expresses probably accorded the fact a thought, they rode with history. One of the first railroads in the nation, the Long Island went into service in 1834, aimed at establishing a "through line, Brooklyn to Boston." It was the greatest single factor in the colonization of hitherto remote Long Island.

Lately, boredom, discomfiture, and danger had been dominant among the Long Island's passengers. A succession of breakdowns, interminable delays, and relatively minor accidents had culminated the past February 17 in a sideswiping of two trains at Rockville Centre when 32 persons were killed and 101 injured. Death had taken an unexpected time-out in August when two Long Island trains collided head-on at Huntington, injuring 121 persons.

Nationwide, including the Rockville Centre disaster, 83 persons had lost their lives in four train wrecks thus far in 1950, and 300 had been injured. Yet the average commuter persisted as a fatalist. Stop and start, jerk and jar, was beat and discord, if not quite lullaby, of his or her existence.

Less adaptable was the occasional rider—the late shopper, for example—who visited the city only rarely. Tonight, as usual, there were a few such exceptions, among them George L. Brown, forty-five-year-old laundry operator from Baldwin, and his son, Stephen, eighteen. The senior Brown had met Stephen in New York. The latter was just home from Bluefield Junior College, in West Virginia, for the holidays. The two had celebrated homecoming with lunch and sight-seeing.

There was, as well, Max Woliner, forty, of New Hyde Park, Long Island, avowedly taking his last train ride. He had been saving all year for an automobile. With the accumulation plus a raise at the office, he had arranged to purchase the vehicle and would take delivery on Friday. "How I hate to ride on that darned old railroad," he had observed to his wife that morning. "What a delight it'll be when all I have to do is jump into the car and drive to the subway."

Within two miles of Jamaica, the first stop for both trains, the Hempstead express received a slowdown signal at C tower, almost immediately altered to "approach," which meant that Murphy could accelerate to thirty miles per hour. He drove his train some 3,500 feet farther to a slightly elevated section of the quadruple track, along an embankment beside 126th Street, near Hillside Avenue. Here, at "Jay" (for Jamaica) tower, No. 114R, a "restricting" light ordered him to cut back to fifteen miles per hour.

Aboard the train, Helen Nugent, of Rockville Centre, riding backward, reacted as most passengers—if indeed they reacted at all—as the 6:09's forward motion began to be retarded once more. It seemed to her "the normal slowdown at this point," approaching the Jamaica station. The "slowdown," however, was considerably more than normal. The brakes grabbed, stopping the 6:09 dead. The standees were jolted against one another as they reached out for the nearest seat backs—an unpleasantly familiar rough-and-tumble of their life of transportation. Harry Rothstein, of Merrick, adjusted his glasses and kept right on reading his newspaper.

Fred C. Meigl, of the New York City Fire Department, standing in the forward part of the rear car next to the conductor, braced himself and then relaxed and watched a flagman open a door. The flagman was holding a lantern or possibly a flashlight.

During the same past two to three minutes, Pokorny had halted his No. 174 at C tower, then "proceeded" in accordance with the same signals at fifteen miles per hour.

Up ahead beside the tracks, on 126th Street, the William Stakers were sitting down to dinner in their home. The lights of the stalled Hempstead express shone outside of their front windows, but there was no more reason to pay any attention to this train than to the thousands, possibly tens of thousands, that had passed their house since they had lived there. In the back of Will Staker's mind was a vague concern for the furnace that had been acting up, and he was wondering if he'd have to call a repairman.

In the cab of the 6:09 Motorman Murphy fiddled with the air-pressure valves, hoping that he could release the brakes. He wasn't having much success. Neither was the flagman in getting out warning flares and torpedoes to put back, as required, on the tracks behind the train. The failure to do so, or slowness in accomplishment, was now like the signing of a formal death warrant.

Motorman Pokorny had already rolled past C tower when the signal flashed on, warning that a train or some obstruction was in the block.

He had no way of knowing that the signals a few hundred feet behind him had changed, for there were no automatic repeaters in these trains, as, for example, in the engines of long-distance passenger expresses. (Automatic repeaters, known to engineers as cab signal control, are as basic as they are effective. Each signal tower sends electric impulses onto the tracks, the phases of which vary with the actual message of position of the signal disks. A "pickup bar" on the engine receives these impulses continually from the track, and small duplicate disk lights in the cab faithfully repeat the signal ahead which, if for example there is fog, might be invisible to the engineer. In addition, the engineer is given only four seconds to "hit the brakes" if the signal so orders. If, for some reason, he fails to do so, the same repeater mechanism shuts off his power and hits the brakes for him. The system is supposed to be 100-percent foolproof.)

Without the benefit of automatic repeaters to guide him, Pokorny read the signal about half a mile up the tracks of "Jay" tower which at the moment was advising the stopped No. 780 to "approach" Jamaica—that is, at speeds up to thirty miles per hour. He obviously did not see the rear lights of the train ahead of him and on the same track. He accelerated, as it would seem in the memory of some of his riders, to ten or fifteen miles per hour over the limit.

Pokorny had something like forty seconds to close the distance between the two trains. It was 6:26 this crisp, clear Thanksgiving Eve, and time's sands, just as at Texas City three years earlier, had almost run through.

The passengers in the rear car of the Hempstead train first noticed a bright light coming up behind them and swelling until it flooded the car, "like a hundred flashbulbs popping at once," by one estimation. It reflected off their newspapers and the heads and backs of passengers with the fiercely bright quality of a magnesium flare. The flagman of the forward train—far too late—blinked his puny flashlight at the onrushing headlight of the 6:13. From then on, no one would be precise as to what happened or the exact sequence of following events.

It was all over as fast as the detonation of a bomb, as the first car of the Babylon express completely telescoped the last coach of the 6:09 to Hempstead, then came to a smoking, crumbling halt. Several hundred feet back—it was later established—Pokorny had applied his brakes but to no avail. This act of the motorman would be his last.

The two cars, in effect fused together, represented the core of fury and destruction. The other coaches, if they left the rails at all, for the most part tilted and stayed where they were as the lights went out.

The way the collision impressed or affected the passengers in the two trains was as varied as the individual or his or her positioning from the impact point. Fred Meigl, the New York fireman who had been standing in the rear car next to the conductor, found the two of them on the aisle and sliding forward at great speed. "I was lucky," he said later. "The lights went out, and glass crashed in. Everybody was yelling and screaming."

Rothstein, who had been reading, said, "I lost my glasses, lost my paper as the train tumbled and everybody fell forward. It was awful."

Dave Nugent, a publicity representative of the Long Island Rail Road, who also happened to be forward in the last car, was conscious of "a dead silence" before he fell down and blacked out. Helen Nugent, who had been aware only of a "normal slowdown," heard "a sickening thud," then: "I was thrown against the seat in front of me and blacked out for a minute. When I got up, everybody was screaming and running to the exits. Blood was streaming down my face. I thought I was badly hurt." Actually, she was suffering only from a nosebleed.

Sherwood Faubel, of Hempstead, was asleep in the last car when he was awakened by "a loud noise." He was thrown forward and showered by glass: "I tried to call out from the wreckage. Everything was dark . . . people yelled and screamed."

John Walters, a correspondent for the London *Mirror*, living in Garden City, was in the middle of the halted train. Other than the startling effect of "a roar and an explosion," Walters was not especially shaken. He walked out of the car and started back along the embankment, onto which other passengers were jumping and running. Under the flat shadows cast by the nearly full moon, Walters observed "the most dreadful sight I've seen since the air raids of London. At one window I saw the face, quite still, of a woman. She seemed to be peering out, but she was obviously dead."

Arms and legs protruded through broken windows, with voices in the darkened coaches screaming for help. Others were noticed by Walters "just sitting" while fellow commuters climbed with singular detachment over their still forms. The correspondent wondered if the latter were dead.

Another newspaperman, William H. Good, from Merrick, who

worked on *The New York Times* advertising staff, had been standing in the eighth car of the Babylon express. He believed that "all of a sudden the brakes were jammed on," and he tumbled into the aisle. He groped outside to find much the same scenes as had Walters: no sounds from inside the two cars that had become virtually one, "bloody hands hanging out of windows . . . at first glance, I saw ten bodies."

Residents of the neighborhood, meanwhile, themselves shaken out of the relaxation of a pre-Thanksgiving meal, were converging on the embankment. The Stakers called the police emergency number, then commenced leading those who appeared to be more badly hurt into their small home. Will Staker warmed up his car, figuring he'd better carry some of the injured to nearby Queens General Hospital. Soon, their living and dining rooms resembled first-aid centers. Their small gray rugs, sofas, chairs, and table covers became splattered with blood.

Harold Coyle, a nearby tavern-owner, helping passengers out of the cars, found many to be bewildered, irrespective of whether they showed physical evidences of injury.

"Where am I?" one middle-aged gentleman asked him.

"What happened?" several inquired.

Quite a few worried disproportionately about inconsequentials, such as the packages they had lately carried, their hats, or even their newspapers. One woman, Alice Sheals, of Baldwin, in the third car of the Babylon express, was bearing home a perishable and, in part, a fragile cargo: two bottles of champagne and a dozen eggs. Unhurt, she feared to leave her coach because of the electrified third rail. When she was finally assured that she could safely alight, she handed her packages to someone—then never saw either again. Many survivors would remember her pacing up and down the embankment that evening, inquiring for her bundles.

Those hurt, shivering, or merely distraught believed it to be a very long time indeed before the wail of sirens heralded the arrival of fire engines, bearing floodlights, ambulances, police vans, gas and electric utility crews, Red Cross and hospital teams, Civil Defense volunteers, all manner of rescue and emergency parties. Actually, they were on the scene in minutes and ministering to the badly hurt—even the ambulances from more distant Kings County Hospital, Bellevue on Manhattan's East Side, and Fordham in the Bronx.

All were in time to free the slightly injured from the wreckage, such as Sherwood Faubel, of Hempstead. They, in turn, were assisted by the lucky passengers—Martin Kramer, of Freeport, for example, who, except for this evening, usually sat in the lead car of the 6:13.

Transfusions of plasma were effected at the wreck and in nearby living rooms such as the Stakers'. There was plenty to go around in spite of totally unfounded rumors that plasma was being exhausted and commercial blood banks or pay donors would have to be tapped. Two interns from Queens General, Dr. Paul E. Soffer, twenty-six, and Dr. Arnold R. Sanders, thirty, operated into the night, attempting to reach those trapped in the wreckage but alive. Soffer himself performed two amputations within the twisted coaches as Sanders passed him hypodermics, scalpels, and other instruments. As Dr. Sanders and Dr. Soffer fought to save lives otherwise forfeited, "burners" pressed in with acetylene torches, cutting through the jungle of broken, bent metal searching for both the dead and the living.

Another physician expressed his own semidespairing diagnosis: The whole affair was a "bloody, bloody mess . . . it couldn't have been worse!" There seemed scant basis for disputing him.

By 9 P.M. the throngs of curious had swelled to five thousand, then melted off as the night grew colder, leaving mostly friends and relatives, waiting and hoping. Under the impassive moonlight and the floodlights mounted along the tracks, the scene presented an aspect of almost total unreality.

Priests were still administering last rites to blanketed forms as the remaining injured were freed from the wreckage and carried on stretchers over the boards that had been placed across the slippery embankment and into waiting ambulances. Finally, the last siren had echoed into silence through Queens's vast dwelling land.

Remaining behind were the mute, waiting lines of black vans from the county morgue or the somewhat more ornate but equally somber private hearses. Before the final one of these funereal vehicles rolled off, seventy-seven victims would have been removed from the wreck. Among them were George Brown, who had been celebrating the return of his son, Stephen, who perished by his father's side, as well as Max Woliner. Now the money Woliner had saved to purchase an automobile would have to be used for his funeral expenses. The Long Island Rail Road that Max had tried so hard to circumvent had, after all, prevailed—and in its own way.

In addition to the dead, 318 had been injured, 14 critically. This

Richmond Hill, or "Jamaica," wreck—as the Interstate Commerce Commission would label it—was bad enough, yet it was not the worst in the first half of the twentieth century. In fact, the record of American railroading the past fifty years had been considerably less than reassuring—thousands of accidents, of varying degrees of seriousness annually, according to the I.C.C.

The worst had occurred during World War I—in July, 1918, near Nashville, Tennessee, when 101 persons, mostly workers at a powder plant, had perished. A local of the Nashville, Chattanooga and St. Louis Railway had collided head-on with an express train.

In November, a few days before the Armistice had stilled if not altogether resolved "the war to end all wars," ninety-seven had died when the Brighton Beach subway express jumped the track in Brooklyn near the Malbone Street tunnel.

Not quite a decade earlier, March 1, 1910, ninety-six were killed in a freak accident near Wellington, Washington. An avalanche hurled the Great Northern's Spokane express along with a second train into a canyon beside Cascade Tunnel. On top of this tragedy fifty-five more died in a Rock Island Railroad derailment near Marshalltown, Iowa, on March 21. The train had been backing at the time to bypass a freight wreck on the main line.

Among the many more calamities of the rails, forty-seven lost their lives in June, 1938, when the Chicago, Milwaukee and St. Paul *Olympian Flyer* plunged through a bridge washout over Custer Creek, Montana. Another famous train, the Southern Pacific's *City of San Francisco*, was derailed in August, 1939, near Elko, Nevada. It hurtled into the Humboldt River Canyon, taking twenty-four lives. Sabotage was suspected.

Outside of Cuyahoga Falls, Ohio, in 1940, forty-three died when a suburban passenger self-propelled car smashed into a freight train. The years during World War II were especially catastrophic. If extenuations of defense expediency and wear were in many respects logical, they were scant consolation to the many bereaved. Three wartime wrecks by themselves in 1943 claimed 179 lives; four in 1944 claimed 161 lives. The worst involved the Pennsylvania Railroad in September, 1943, when the *Congressional Limited* jumped the tracks at Frankford Junction, outside of Philadelphia, killing eighty. A broken coupling was blamed.

In April, 1946, a total of forty-six persons perished when a second train section of the Burlington's *Exposition Flyer* hit the first near Napierville, Illinois—much as the Richmond Hill disaster, four years later.

In addition to the I.C.C., Congress, the State of New York, the borough of Queens, and innumerable private investigative bodies not excepting insurance companies and railroad unions sifted, probed, debated, and argued the Richmond Hill disaster. The conclusion of the I.C.C.—and not disputed—was frustratingly basic: human error. Motorman Pokorny, who had perished at the controls, asserted the commission, was obeying the wrong signal, that ahead of him. He then sealed his doom and that of the others by failing to apply the brakes in time once he had presumably spotted the rear lanterns of the 6:09. "Disobedience of signals!" was the verdict, in short.

11

Midair Collision, 1960

It was snowing over New York that third Friday in December, 1960. For practical purposes visibility was zero. For airline procedure, oriented to instruments, visual clarity was largely inconsequential, or so the operations books said. What it all meant was that the many travelers flying home or away for the holidays might be somewhat delayed in holding patterns. But Christmas was a week off with all the festivities implicit, and a few minutes added to a journey also seemed to be inconsequential.

Inbound toward Manhattan that morning of December 16 were hundreds if not thousands of human beings whose backgrounds and reasons for being where they were at a given instant of time could be duplicated or approximated only on another airline passenger list. For example: Dayton, Ohio, originating Trans World Airlines Flight 266, due out of Port Columbus Airport at 9 A.M. Its equipment, in manifest contradiction to the company's current slogan—"the Superjet Airline"—was that grande dame of the airways, a four-engine propeller craft dating to World War II, the creaking but dependable "*Connie.*" Already aboard or boarding the venerable *Constellation* at Ohio's capital city were seven guided-missile experts from Wright-Patterson Air Force Base, Dayton; a young couple carrying their fourteen-day-old infant; an attorney; a chemist; half a dozen salesmen and advertising people; and four Ohio State University students returning for Christmas, including one co-ed who seemingly was seized with a premonition at the very last minute. Pretty Nancy Briggs, nineteen-year-old daughter of the Kenneth Briggses, of Springfield, Massachusetts, told her "steady" seeing her off that she was afraid she would never see him again. He laughed at her fears.

There was another, Walter D. Hunnicutt, of Columbus, who had never missed a Christmas party at his old firm, National Dairy Products, in New York. He had called ahead, then canceled out—no premonitions, just the weather. Hunnicutt was a retired type and loathed wet, snowy days.

There was yet another passenger, also retired—from the police force—Everett L. McSavaney, who turned about-face at the ramp. Doing part-time law-enforcement work, McSavaney was en route to return a prisoner to Columbus. A phone call had just informed him to take another flight, scheduled for Newark. TWA-266 had a LaGuardia destination.

There were also some who, if their original plans had been followed, would not or should not have been aboard at all. And this random circumstance itself was no exception along the commercial airways.

Richard Bitters, the lean, thirty-three-year-old former reporter for the Columbus *Dispatch* turned director of the Ohio University Fund, had set his business trip to New York for the previous day, Thursday, the fifteenth, but had delayed one more day to attend a faculty party. Dick, father of three, had saved enough to buy a new home in the North Hill suburb long planned by himself and his wife, Martha. Bitters hurried to Port Columbus Airport early Friday morning, without a reservation. When he was promised a seat on TWA-266, he considered himself fortunate.

Much the same set of circumstances caused Raymond Walsh, forty-three, president of Wesleyan University Press, Middletown, Connecticut, to cancel a 4 P.M. flight on Thursday. He had not wound up a tight round of appointments and held no prospects for doing so that late afternoon or evening.

A change of heart relative to his future had spurred Vincent Flood, of East Orange, New Jersey, onto the same flight. Young Vincent had just decided after four months as a novice in St. Joseph Priory, a

Dominican order, that he did not wish to become a priest. He was going home to see his parents, the Patrick Floods, who did not know of his change of mind or his trip home.

In addition, there were those long-booked individuals who had not changed their plans whatsoever—for example, the Garry Myers, who published the Columbus monthly *Highlights for Children*. They had left their own five children at home.

In all, there were thirty-nine passengers, twelve from the Columbus area, aboard when TWA-266 was "buttoned up." The *Connie*, as customary, carried a crew of five: a captain, a first officer, a flight engineer, and two stewardesses. Captain David A. Wollam was a thirty-nine-year-old veteran of more than 14,500 flying hours, commencing on the airlines with the old DC-3.

The LaGuardia flight announced "wheels up" at nine o'clock, into cold, bright skies. Dave Wollam advised his passengers, as part of standard welcoming procedure, that the estimated time to LaGuardia would be one hour and thirty-two minutes, at an altitude of seven thousand feet. Flying under Air Traffic Control on I.F.R. (Instrument Flight Rules), the *Constellation* would follow the VOR navigational, so-called omniranges, to Appleton, Ohio, then check over Johnstown, Pennsylvania, east of Pittsburgh. Somewhere over the Ohio-Pennsylvania line the four propellers would commence to bite into mist, then thicker clouds, until the *Connie* would become lost to the earth below.

In Chicago, just eleven minutes after TWA-266's takeoff, a United Air Lines (the "Best West") lumbering DC-8 jet, Flight No. 826, lifted its immense bulk of 107 tons off O'Hare International's lengthy runway—destination, Idlewild Airport, Queens (later to be renamed Kennedy International). Among the seventy-six passengers were a scattering of those who, like their counterparts on the TWA flight, had not been long booked on UAL-826. Frank Dileo was one.

Frank's father, Charles Dileo, an accountant living in Floral Park, Long Island, had wired his twenty-one-year-old son, a senior at the University of Utah, money for the trip. It was confusing to the elder Dileo, since he was certain he had mailed Frank his Christmas air ticket a month ago. Then United had advised him that *if* his son booked on the jet flight, Frank needed further passage. Whether the confusion concerned the type of plane, or nonstandby status, or a misplaced original ticket, the exact reasons were not forthcoming.

Milton La Riviere, of Greenwich, Connecticut, put his daughter, Peggy, eighteen, a student at Barat College of the Sacred Heart, Lake Forest, Illinois, on the jet instead of himself. He had completed business with the Electro-Motive Division of General Motors in La Grange, and he could use the extra time to make a few more calls before arranging a later flight for himself. Besides, he wanted Peggy to have the best, such as this fast, comfortable jet.

There was also John N. Tuttle, forty-seven-year-old fruit-products corporation executive of Montvale, New Jersey, who had not planned to return home until a day or two later. He had telegraphed his wife, Grace, at home with their ten-year-old Timothy, that he had just benefited by a cancellation and was on his way. He had booked out of Los Angeles where the plane, as Flight 856, originated.

A bad cold and sore throat had kept Stevie Baltz, eleven, of Wilmette, Illinois, home on Wednesday when the sixth-grader had been scheduled to fly to New York with his mother, Phyllis Baltz. The son of William S. Baltz, Admiral Corporation executive, Stevie was going to visit his grandparents in Yonkers, New York. Now, two days late, Stevie started off alone, jauntily dressed in a gray suit and matching gray hat, with a bright feather stuck in the band.

On the opposite perimeter of chance and planning, however, were travelers such as Mrs. Edwige Dumalski, of Oak Park, Illinois, and her two young children en route to France for a visit with her mother. Her husband, William H., was a training and education instructor with United.

There was Alvin Sokolski, thirty-four-year-old television producer and bridegroom, of Baltimore, who had endeavored to wind up his business in Colorado Springs and make *this* flight for certain.

There was a grandmother booked well in advance, journeying to see her grandson for the first time, plus at least one lawyer and several salesmen.

Flight 826 carried a crew of seven, commanded by forty-six-year-old Captain Robert H. Sawyer, who had amassed nearly twenty thousand flying hours in two decades of flying. An Air Transport Command pilot in World War II, Bob Sawyer lived on a horse ranch near Los Angeles with his wife and three daughters.

Accompanied by his first and second officers, Captain Sawyer had piloted the flight since the West Coast. Among the four stewardesses were Patricia Keller, twenty-six, who had joined United the previous summer, and twenty-two-year-old Augustine Ferrar who had switched flights several times with other girls to be home on Christmas with her parents, the Frank Ferrars, of Columbus.

Sawyer's announcement had become routine enough for those accustomed to the jet airliners. The flight level would be 27,000 feet and the time to Idlewild, one hour and twenty-nine minutes, at a speed of approximately six hundred miles per hour. In other words, the DC-8, covering approximately one-third again the distance of TWA-266, would make the flight in three minutes less estimated time than the *Connie*, throbbing eastward from Columbus.

Meanwhile, far removed in time, space, and life habits from those aboard either of the two flights were five persons in particular, each a resident of Brooklyn. They had already gone to work this snowy, bleak Friday, each to his own station on Sterling Place, a drab street that lay within a run-down residential area of Brooklyn—Park Slope—an anachronism of shabby, four-story tenements and dimly lit stores, which not even the falling snowflakes could gloss with any ephemeral softness, much less majesty.

One of these Brooklynites was the ward of the three-story, gabled Pillar of Fire Church, the dingy edifice of the holiness or fundamentalist denomination—ninety-year-old Wallace Edward Lewis. Caretaker those days when his rheumatism wasn't acting up, the old man stumped about the chilly, bare, unprepossessing place, sweeping floors and dusting pews in anticipation of the trickle of worshipers who might be expected to attend services during the forthcoming weekend.

Two—whose combined age was still only a fraction of Wallace Lewis's—were outside, shuffling their feet across the frosty sidewalk, swinging their arms, and brushing accumulating snow from the Christmas trees they hoped to sell within the next seven days. Standing in front of a vacant store were John Oppericano, thirty-four, and Joseph Colacano. The latter, in spite of a mere five years' age difference, was Oppericano's nephew.

The fourth was a sanitation-department worker, Charles J. Cooper, who happened to be the same age as Oppericano. His task this morning: shoveling snow from the sidewalks. The fifth, Albert Layer, had just opened his butcher shop at 138 Sterling Place.

Within sound of Flatbush Avenue's traffic roar and also intersecting that major artery, as well as Seventh Avenue to the south, Sterling Place harbored considerable primary education, as if, by some curious chemistry, to compensate for what it failed to offer in all outward grace. There was—at 49 Sterling Place—St. Augustine's Parochial School, where one thousand children not many minutes previously had answered the final morning bell of this week. Another school, Berkeley Institute, two blocks south of Sterling Place on Lincoln Place, was attended by four hundred.

So another wet, wintry morning had commenced over Park Slope. . . .

When TWA-266 left the flat fields of Ohio for Pennsylvania's rough and ore-rich hills, it also swept its passengers toward an opaque world. Ahead, New York Air Route Traffic Control Center (A.R.T.C.C.) counted some fifty planes crisscrossing the cloudy wastes within a radius of thirty miles from Manhattan, like the hub of a many-spoked wheel, and extending in altitude from 300 feet to 18,000 feet. One pilot reported "on top" at 31,000 feet—six miles high. Others called in to say they were "between layers" at 4,000 to 5,000 feet and, again, from 13,000 to 15,000 feet. Otherwise, the considerable assemblage of aircraft stacked at many altitudes within A.R.T.C.C.'s lofty home cote was invisible one to another.

Partly because of the congestion ahead and partly because of the worsening weather en route, the *Connie*'s altitude was altered to 17,000 feet by Airways Traffic Control—10,000 above the filed plan, a slow climb for the old propeller craft. Then another 2,000 feet was added until—over Selinsgrove, Pennsylvania, sixty miles north of Harrisburg and about one hour out of Columbus—266 was struggling eastward at 19,000 feet.

Captain Dave Wollam now checked in with A.R.T.C.C., New York. He was cleared to descent in stages, crossing Allentown, Pennsylvania, at 11,000 feet. Wollam throttled back. About fifteen minutes later, at 10:19, he advised New York that 266 was passing Allentown—or so his instruments advised—at 11,000 feet, just as instructed. There had been no visual reference with anything since the plane passed the Ohio-Pennsylvania border. In response the New York center informed Captain Wollam that radar contact was now established. He was cleared to Linden Intersection, a congested electronic crossroads high above

U.S. Highway 1 just south of Newark and requested to "stand by for descent."

At 10:12 A.M. and exactly 110 miles west of Allentown, still at 27,000 feet, United 826 made a routine approach report to A.R.T.C.C. "United 826, roger," the center replied. "Have your progress. Radar service not available, descend to and maintain flight level 250 [25,000 feet]. Over."

Captain Bob Sawyer acknowledged, "Leaving flight level 270 [27,000 feet]," at approximately 10:14. One minute later New York advised, "United 826 clearance limit is Preston [also in northern New Jersey, west of Sandy Hook] Intersection . . . direct to Robbins-ville . . . maintain flight level 250."

Seven minutes later, at 10:21, Sawyer called Aeronautical Radio, Inc. (ARINC), which operated United's radio systems, advising that "No. 2 navigation receiver accessory unit inoperative."

This information, that 826 was operating on only one omnirange receiver, was acknowledged by ARINC and relayed to United. Since these big jets had duplicate navigational facilities, and in various types, and since the pilot had not called at once for radar monitoring, it was assumed that the flight was in no trouble. Air Route Traffic Control was not informed by ARINC of this seeming slight malfunction of the DC-8's great flying laboratory of electronic gear.

At the same time New York control center issued the flight clearance to descend to 13,000 feet—that is, 12,000 feet or slightly more than two miles lower than the plane's latest level. Sawyer wasn't pleased. "We'd rather hold upstairs," he replied. In this choice he was simply reflecting the old pilot's dictum that every thousand feet of altitude is equal to that much more life insurance.

Two minutes later, at approximately 10:23, Bob Sawyer added, "If we're going to have a delay, we would rather hold upstairs than down. We're going to need three quarters of a mile. Do you have the weather handy?"

The center's reply was almost immediate. "No, but I'll get it. There have been no delays until now."

In a few seconds Sawyer or his first officer, Robert W. Fiebing, forty, also a California horse rancher, reported that 826 was over Allentown at 25,000 feet—just four minutes behind TWA-266.

At 10:23 Dave Wollam, flying the latter, was receiving the

LaGuardia weather: "Measured five hundred overcast, one mile visibility in light snow, surface wind northwest fifteen knots, altimeter setting 29.66." Wollam acknowledged and requested the runway in use. The center replied that I.L.S. (Instrument Landing System, or "cross-pointer" from the configuration of the cockpit dial) approaches were being made to Runway 4 and that the localizer beam was "inoperative." At 10:24 the *Connie* was cleared to leave 10,000 and report at 9,000 feet.

Two minutes later Wollam confirmed that he was passing the Solberg, New Jersey, VOR at 9,000 feet, in the Linden holding pattern, a long oval, racetracklike course, over the New Jersey meadows immediately south of Newark. At approximately 10:27 the center advised termination of radar control, instructing Flight 266 to contact LaGuardia Approach Control. This was done on the frequency indicated.

"Maintain 9,000," LaGuardia ordered, "I.L.S. Runway 4, landing Runway 4, no delay is expected. The wind is northeast fifteen, altimeter 29.65 . . . visibility one mile, light snow. Stand by."

Two minutes previously, aboard United, Sawyer was receiving Idlewild weather which was slightly better than LaGuardia, with fifteen hundred feet overcast, light rain, and fog but still not the three-quarter-mile visibility on the runway that the U.A.L. pilot wanted. The DC-8 captain then advised, "We're starting down."

At 10:25 the center offered Sawyer a slightly amended route to Preston holding pattern, observing, "It'll be a little bit quicker." The alteration, comparable to cutting across the corner of a field, shortened the distance from the jet's present position, just east of Allentown, to the Preston Intersection by eleven miles.

A minute later UAL-826, now under radar guidance, was cleared to descend to 11,000 feet. In two more minutes the radar screen revealed that the jet was only fifteen miles from "Victor 123," the airway Sawyer must intercept for his shortcut to Preston. At the same time, 10:28, Dave Wollam, on TWA-266, was cleared to 8,000 feet. A minute and a half later he confirmed that the *Connie* was now at that altitude. LaGuardia approach control instructed 266 to maintain present heading and reduce speed for a radar vector to the final approach course.

By 10:32 Wollam, reporting 6,000 feet, was ordered down to 5,000. Half a minute later he was told to turn right to 150 degrees, as the approach control at the same time advised that its radar showed "traffic . . . 2:30 [o'clock relative position], six miles northeastbound."

At 10:30 New York Center had asked Sawyer, "Look like you'll be able to make Preston at 5,000?"

The United 826 captain replied he would try.

At 10:32, while Wollam in the *Connie* was himself starting down for 5,000 feet, the center again called United: "If holding is necessary at Preston, southwest one minute pattern right turns . . . the only delay will be in descent."

"Roger, no delay," Sawyer responded and a minute later reported passing 6,000 feet on his altimeter.

The center came in, "826, I'm sorry I broke you up. Was that you reporting leaving 6,000 or 5,000?"

"Affirmative" was Sawyer's reply.

Then, from the center, "Roger, and you received the holding instructions at Preston; radar service is terminated. Contact Idlewild Approach Control."

Sawyer acknowledged with a "Good day." The time was approximately 10:33:27.

On board the big jet those passengers with faces pressed close to the windows were rewarded with quick glimpses of the ground through rifts in the mountainous cloud banks. Stevie Baltz, for one, looking at the snowscape below, saw at once the similarity: "a picture out of a fairy book . . . a beautiful sight."

Dave Wollam acknowledged the report of traffic "six miles northeastbound"—a "target" that was approaching from the south, toward the *Constellation*'s right side.

A few seconds later, LaGuardia Approach Control requested the flight's altitude and received the reply "500." Since this sounded like a garble, LaGuardia asked if 5,500 was correct. The TWA captain replied in the affirmative.

At 10:33:14 LaGuardia called a clearance to continue down to 1,500 feet. This was acknowledged. At 10:33:21 LaGuardia instructed TWA to "turn left now heading 130"—that is, on a southeast course. Wollam acknowledged by repeating the direction. At 10:33:26 LaGuardia came in again during this almost uninterrupted ground-to-plane conversation: "Roger, that appears to be jet traffic off your right now three o'clock at one mile northeastbound."

Thus, the "jet traffic" previously reported was closing the distance, having covered five miles in about a minute since the last report. The surveillance radar in use could inform of these factors but not altitude. Two seconds later, at 10:33:28, Bob Sawyer was calling: "Idlewild Approach Control, United 826, approaching Preston at 5,000." Idlewild replied, "United 826, this is Idlewild Approach Control. Maintain 5,000. Little or no delay at Preston. Idlewild landing Runway 4 right. I.L.S. in use. Idlewild weather, six hundred scattered; estimated fifteen hundred overcast; visibility one-half mile, light rain and fog. Altimeter 29.63. Over." The transmission was not acknowledged. Idlewild asked United 826 to reply.

LaGuardia approach, working the TWA flight, at the same time heard a sound that seemed to be that of an open microphone, but no words. At 10:33:43 the controller continued: "Trans World 266, turn left, one zero zero"—that is, from a southeast course back toward an easterly heading.

It was too late. Stevie Baltz, like the other passengers on both planes, did not know quite what had happened, though the little boy was aware that "all of a sudden there was an explosion, the plane started to fall . . . and people started to scream. I held onto my seat. . . ."

On New Dorp, Staten Island, near the army's Miller (helicopter) Field, a resident, Mrs. Edward Brody, glanced out of the window and saw a plane, or at least parts of plane, emerging out of the snow and murk: "I saw it coming right at us. I ran upstairs to get my daughters. Then it stopped."

It sounded to another housewife like "a thousand dishes coming from the sky." A florist, Paul Kleinau, watched it "tail down, four propellers up and whirling helplessly," then screamed, "My God!" and found he was continuing to scream, uncontrollably. Yet another witness agreed: "It went down in a terrible way . . . one wing gone, and it turned over and over very slowly."

Colonel E. M. Howan, commanding the small military base, kept looking until the crippled *Constellation*—actually falling in three pieces—smashed into the landing field, 150 feet from two schools and numerous houses, as though the pilot were somehow in control. "God brought that plane in," Colonel Howan thought as he raced toward the crash site, now a pyre of flames. Soldiers commandeered a flatbed truck and followed a snowplow toward the wreck.

LaGuardia radar had observed two "targets" merging and had then seen one quickly disappear from the scope while another continued somewhat erratically northeast for a distance of eight to ten miles.

In the Park Slope section of Brooklyn Mrs. Henrietta Enright, at 122 Sterling Place, was awakened by "a whistling sound." Mrs. Henry McCaddin, in an upstairs room of her husband's funeral parlor on Seventh Avenue, was one of several persons who were startled by what they thought was "a large bolt of lightning."

Brother Conrad Barnes, in St. Augustine's School, looked out of a classroom window to see a plane "six hundred feet in the air, a wisp of black smoke coming from the right wing." Although it appeared to be attempting to make Prospect Park, Brother Conrad told his class of forty-three boys to "put their heads on their desk and pray."

The boys, if they had had time to begin even a short prayer, had not done so in vain. The falling United jet banked to the right, plummeting down like a meteor, slashed and careened across several four-story brownstone tenements, then sheared off the steeply gabled roof of the Pillar of Fire Church, before, finally, as though the great aircraft possessed an inherent will for immolation, hurtling into the intersection of Sterling Place and Seventh Avenue.

The aft section of the passenger cabin, breaking free, slid some one hundred yards before coming to rest. Like a fragmentation bomb, the 107-ton airliner had disintegrated—engines, parts of engines, housings, the flight deck, tail section, seats, wings, parts of wings, windows, people scattering the length and breadth of Sterling Place. Sixty-three thousand pounds of mail aboard, including 120,000 letters, augmented the conflagration. The flaming fuel at once ignited the Pillar of Fire Church—as if in affirmation of its own torrid prophecy—ten tenements, several shops, McCaddin's funeral establishment, and innumerable parked or moving automobiles and trucks.

A huge crater was blasted at the Seventh Avenue intersection where United 826 had first hit and exploded.

As fire bells in St. Augustine's School and Berkeley Institute rang to evacuate the premises, four priests raced from church to what seemed to be the largest remaining section of the fuselage, to do what they could.

"The heat was terrific," the Reverend Raymond Morgan, assistant pastor of St. Augustine's, would recall. "The flames were shooting three stories high. We couldn't get near the plane, so we helped people out of the threatened houses."

Fire alarm after fire alarm was pulled. In minutes companies from all over Brooklyn were noisily responding. It looked and sounded as though the entire Park Slope area were a wilderness of flame and smoke.

Not at once was a seeming miracle of salvation perceived—a little boy, bleeding from the nose but to all appearances not badly hurt, lying in a snowdrift. As soon as he was discovered, he was surrounded by dwellers of the area, who put blankets over him and held umbrellas against the falling snow as they gazed in mingled awe and disbelief. Stevie Baltz spoke, dreamily but clearly, telling about the "fairy book" from the air preceding the "explosion." He asked one woman if he was going to die. She assured him he would not as she told him she had a son his age. On his wrist he still wore his watch. It had stopped at 10:37—four minutes after the last transmission from either airliner. He worried about that watch and inquired several times if it was all right.

At Miller Field, on Staten Island, five passengers were pulled from the wreckage alive. They died en route to a hospital. No others aboard the TWA plane had survived even that brief period.

The word had quickly spread to Manhattan's air terminals, where people awaited friends and relatives on both flights. Dazed, Milton La Riviere, who had seen Peggy off on UAL-826 short hours earlier and had himself arrived in New York, repeated to reservations personnel at Idlewild, "I'm just waiting for my daughter. . . ." Most shared his numbed disbelief. Mrs. Ruth Sokolski, the bride of Alvin, the television producer, just shook her head when she received the first telephoned message. And the Patrick Floods, of East Orange—Vincent hadn't even told him he was returning from St. Joseph Priory. . . . There had to be *some* mistake, hadn't there? And Dick Bitters just *might not* have been on *that* plane, as *might not* many others. Unfortunately, they were. . . .

That so many from the Columbus area had perished at once staggered the capacity even of newspapermen to convey their own assessments adequately. For want of possibly more adequate expression, a writer on the Columbus *Dispatch* began: "The Community bows today in sorrow. . . ."

That afternoon Stevie's parents were at his bedside in Brooklyn's Methodist Hospital. "The next time I fly," he whispered, "I want to be my own pilot flying my own plane." Soon he dropped off to sleep.

The next morning the eleven-year-old died. No one appeared more distressed than the hospital chaplain himself, who wept to reporters as he reiterated: "When you do everything—everything—and you lose out . . . God!"

It was Saturday—and the fifty-seventh anniversary of man-made flight. A number of commemorative observances at Kitty Hawk and elsewhere were canceled. Among the worst domestic air disasters in United States history, the collision had claimed 128 lives, plus 6 more on the ground, including the aged caretaker of the Pillar of Fire Church, the Christmas tree sellers, the snow shoveler, and the butcher.

Singularly, the same number of crew and passengers had perished in 1956 over the Painted Desert, near Tuba City, California, when a United and a TWA plane had come together in clear air, with no attendant traffic congestion.

Before this black Saturday, December 17, 1960, was out, an airforce plane would crash in Munich, killing twenty aboard and thirty on the ground.

The collision, together with eight other accidents involving scheduled airlines in the United States, would make 1960 the worst year in history—307 dead—and a sobering record that, fortunately, has not been equaled to this date. Although, for example, 305 died in ten accidents in 1968, air-transport officials point out that by then scheduled airlines were flying three times as many passenger miles as in 1960. In 1970 there were only two deaths, with a sharp peak to 174 in 1971.

The Civil Aeronautics Board would come up with a logical-sounding opinion that the United 826, after being given its eleven-mile shortcut to the Preston holding pattern, was actually *past* that intersection when the crew believed they were coming up on it, at 10:33:28. "Idlewild Approach Control, United 826, approaching Preston at 5,000. . . ." Further, the C.A.B. noted, "this revised routing was not relayed by the New York Center to Idlewild Approach Control."

Both planes were flying at approximately 5,000 feet at the moment of impact, the United plane presumably the "jet traffic . . . three o'clock at one mile northeastbound," colliding with the TWA *Connie*, at the latter's "right rear quarter," flying southeast. Normally, the two holding patterns, Linden and Preston, offered at least ten miles separation even on their closest legs. However, Flight 826 was not actually flying the pattern at the time of the last transmission. The board concluded:

> . . . The probable cause of this accident was that United 826 proceeded beyond its clearance limit and the confines of the airspace allocated to the flight by Air Traffic Control. A contributing factor was in the high rate of speed of the United DC-8 [computed at 301 knots, compared with the *Constellation*'s 160 knots] as it approached the Preston Intersection, coupled with the change of clearance which reduced the en route distance along Victor 123 [the omnirange course] by approximately eleven miles. . . . The crew . . . did not take note of the change of time and distance. . . .

The one faulty receiver reported by Captain Sawyer on the United plane was not considered a contributing factor.

Other than the inevitable legal actions to come, the midair collision over Brooklyn, December 16, 1960, was "locked up" so far as federal investigators were concerned. Recommendations for operational changes would evolve later.

But all of the rationalizations or extenuations—that, for example, the fatality rate was but 0.76 that year measured against more than forty billion passenger miles—did not bring back one dead passenger or crew member, much less those caught on Sterling Place, or dry one tear of any of the many left behind. In fact, statistics tended to accentuate and then magnify the feeling of frustration if not as well bitterness—*why*, with billions of passenger miles, did they have to be on those *two* particular doomed flights? It was inescapably human nature to speculate.

If Dick Bitters had not delayed in order to attend a faculty party. . . . *If* Vincent Flood had perhaps elected to remain a novitiate and not return home. . . . *If* Raymond Walsh had been less conscientious about finishing up his appointments. . . . *If* Milton La Riviere had himself taken that plane and allowed his daughter to board the other. . . . *If* Stevie Baltz hadn't come down with a sore throat. . . . *If* Augustine Ferrar had been less serious of spending Christmas with her family. . . . If, if, if. . . .

But it had happened. It was all over. No one could turn back the clock. When TWA-266 and UAL-826 were "wheels up" that wintry December morning, 1960, certain, irreversible destiny flew with them.

12

Earthquake in
Alaska, 1964

March 27, 1964, was Good Friday. In the majority of states this holy day just prior to Easter Sunday was traditionally a precursor of spring, when homeowners began to open windows, initiate cleaning projects, and shop for garden supplies. The weekend of the Crucifixion and Resurrection held a number of connotations.

In Alaska, the forty-ninth and largest state, Christians among the quarter million inhabitants were conducting Good Friday observances. Most schools were out, as elsewhere, and the general mood was that of a semiholiday. In the evening the play *Our Town* was to be presented by the Little Theater Group of the Anchorage Community College.

Otherwise, the approach of Easter in Alaska was markedly dissimilar to the same time period in the other states. Winter locked the Arctic and sub-Arctic land. Large and small centers of habitation remained blanketed in white. In many areas snow was falling. The thermometer registered 24° in Anchorage; in Barrow, 250 miles north of the Arctic Circle, temperatures remained congealingly below zero. Only along the southern rim bordering the Gulf of Alaska, from Cordova and Valdez west to Anchorage, Seward, and Kodiak Island, warmed somewhat by the Japanese current, were clusters of population beginning to anticipate spring, much less summer, ephemeral as either would be.

In Valdez, an old gold-rush town—"the Switzerland of America," so dubbed because of its scenery—merchants were preparing for the tourists. In Cordova, "clam capital of the world," with a population of about eleven hundred people, the same approximate size as Valdez, fishermen were readying nets and clam tongs, even as they were on Kodiak Island 450 miles to the southwest.

With all of its mineral and saltwater wealth, however, Alaska has historically rebuffed habitation. The bitter weather has remained one reason, but only one. Another—geology—has condemned it to sit astride volcanoes.

This vast land embracing nearly 600,000 square miles—twice that of Texas—lies within the great volcanic mountain arc rimming the northern Pacific west to the Kuriles and Japan. "Circle of fire" in Eskimo lore, this arc from North America to Asia has been assaulted by earthquakes, tremors, and tidal waves, dating back to early Russian records.

In 1788 the czarist colony at Three Saints Bay on Kodiak Island was inundated by a tsunami, or tidal wave, following a quake. The same island was shaken violently in 1866, just two years before Alaska was purchased by the United States.

As inhabitants of less volcanic sections of the United States might remark in passing on the strength of an exceptionally violent windstorm, "sourdoughs"—when they listened to the dishes rattle and felt the floor tremble—would ask, "Did you feel *that*?"

The shakes, even so, generally came as a surprise. There might be a mild, preliminary tremor, permitting householders to move outside in the event the main shock knocked plaster off the ceiling or heavier fittings from the walls. More often, the primary jolt came unheralded.

Alaska's largest city, Anchorage, seven times the size of Juneau, the state capital (550 miles to the east), was itself constructed upon unfelicitous ground. In 1960 a U.S. Geological Survey publication had warned that much of the city on Cook Inlet, to the west of Prince William Sound, was "built over a hazardous layer of unstable clay." The admonition, little read, went wholly unheeded.

Good Friday had been just that to the sixty thousand residents of bustling, modern Anchorage. Whether or not he or she had worshiped at the familiar three-hour service, commencing at noon, much of the day had been spent in shopping or selling. By dusk most of the inhabitants, including shopkeepers, were home or going home, leaving down-town and its bars to the "Oly Joes"—the Indians or Eskimos, speaking almost no English, but able to order their Olympia beer by telling the bartender, "Oly, Joe."

Paula Slaymaker, fourteen-year-old eighth-grader at Ora Dee Clark Junior High, was one of many schoolchildren who had the day, or most of the day, off and had consumed it in shopping, especially at Penney's new and popular department store. A few minutes before 5:30 P.M., laden with packages, she was being driven by her mother, Mrs. Ronald Slaymaker, up the driveway of their home on the east side of Anchorage. A light snow was falling, the streets were slick, and another cold, dark Alaskan evening was moving in. Mrs. Slaymaker had stopped the car, seemingly, when a strange thing happened: The auto began backing up by itself on the perfectly level drive. . . .

At College, a town of fewer than two thousand inhabitants near Fairbanks, some two hundred miles north of Anchorage, Jack Town-send had the watch at the Coast and Geodetic Survey office. Without warning the seismograph needle, or pen—measurer of earth tremors —took a tremendous jump across the continuous graph roll. Then the entire instrument shook so that no recording was possible. Beneath Townsend the very earth "seemed to ripple."

In fact, it was "rippling" along the whole five-hundred-mile arc from Cordova to Kodiak. At Kodiak Ed Naughton, working in the family bakery—which marketed "Russian Rye" bread nationally—braced himself against the vibrations, then "beat it" when he saw the walls starting to "go in and out, the floor undulating." A woman cus-tomer who had been in the shop ran for her automobile, then paused when she saw that it was "bouncing up and down." She stumbled and fell to the ground.

Naughton, the son of an Illinois native who had arrived during the turn-of-the-century gold rush, was reminded of nothing so much as being adrift in "a ten-man rubber life raft in rough seas."

To the northeast, in Valdez on Prince William Sound, a crewman on the 10,815-ton motor vessel *Chena*, which was unloading, watched in horror as three dock workers, a man with his young son and daugh-ter who had been standing on the dock, suddenly vanished. One minute "the dock was there. . . . The next minute it wasn't."

As tall buildings in Anchorage swayed back and forth ten to twelve feet at the top, a doctor who had been dictating into his tape recorder paused, still pressing down the button, and, unintentionally, created a priceless sound track of an earthquake's rumbling voice.

Those in areas or in houses that must have been built with the possibilities of violent earth tremors in mind paused in their evening meal or preparations for it and observed, "I think we're having a shake." When generally accustomed to firm floors, one found it hard to orient to their acting like roller coasters.

In St. Mary's Nursing Home, an old sourdough, all but falling out of his rocking chair, confided to Sister Superior Barbara Ellen, "I've been through a lot of earthquakes here, but it looks like this is going to be a humdinger!" It was.

"Get out! Get out!" Paula Slaymaker's mother shouted, and the occupants fled the car.

In the Turnagain-by-the-Sea district of expensive homes in southwest Anchorage, a large section of bluff overlooking Cook Inlet collapsed, slid down fifty feet, much of it frothing on into the sea—houses crumbling in thunderlike roars and plunging in brick and wooden splinters into the water.

Mrs. Craig Taylor watched giant chunks of earth flake away just across the street from her own home and vanish. She ran inside to telephone "someone" about this catastrophic sight, then discovered the instrument was dead. The woman jumped into her car, slammed the door, backed down the driveway, then noticed to her horror that the street was cut by yawning chasms at both ends. She saw yet another incongruous sight: a neighbor and his family crawling hand over hand up and over the precipice that had been the middle of his front yard.

Others of "easy living" Turnagain had fled their residences as the structures started "rolling just like a ship"—or so it felt to Mrs. Robert McCready.

Downtown at Fourth Avenue, land dropped eleven feet or more and slid horizontally fourteen feet. In the L Street area thirty city blocks experienced similar sliding. Fissures in the ground six feet wide and one hundred feet long opened and closed, while the earth visibly heaved like ocean waves. The Four Seasons luxury apartment house crashed in on itself as though it had been made of match sticks. Workmen had been inside rather late, "knocking off" only because it was

Good Friday. J. C. Penney's modern department store crumpled, several people inside losing their lives as concrete slabs fell upon them. The reactions of Chancey Croft and his wife, driving along Fourth Avenue, were less than singular. He thought at first that "a flat tire or broken wheel" was causing his automobile to act so erratically. Of an exact turn of mind, Croft became aware that the car was "rocking quite a bit in a north-south direction."

When next he watched a crack a foot wide open up in the street at "the left edge of our automobile," the couple had no doubt of what was going on. They abandoned their machine to watch "the north side of Fourth Avenue sinking very slowly," as were adjacent buildings. The Crofts pitched in to aid occupants to escape from the structures that were acting in so odd a manner.

Ninety-foot treetops dipped back and forth against the snowy ground like pendulums.

Leaving her office in Anchorage, Delphine Haley, twenty-eight, was caught in an elevator that jammed as the building swayed and "groaned." She had to fight her way out of the escape hatch on the car's roof and then crawl through a floor door she forced open before she could reach a stairway. And all the while the building kept in violent motion.

The Government Hill Elementary School on a bluff in the northeast section broke in two, with half of it and part of the playground sinking several feet.

In all parts of Anchorage the story was the same: If one did not have something to hang onto—like straps in a subway train—he or she was hurled to the floor or to the snowy ground.

At Valdez the water rushed out of the harbor without warning and seemingly with the speed of light. The big freighter *Chena* struck bottom with a thud, momentarily stranded, as crewmen still aboard her clung to anything with a life-or-death grip. Before these same salts were able to drop anchor—in an amazing display of nerve and seamanship—the vessel hit bottom twice more under the impact of sucessive tidal waves. She ended up in the middle of the harbor. Thirty had died in the port area, the highest loss of life in any one place.

In Chenega, Seward, Kodiak, Whittier, Portage, Cordova, Seldovia, and Homer, the inhabitants watched similar tortured surface reactions to a shifting of the earth's crust some twelve and a half miles below the surface. The epicenter was located eighty miles east of Anchorage in Prince William Sound—measured in strength on the Richter scale at least to 8.6 or .3 heavier than the San Francisco quake. The main jolt lasted about four and a half minutes, then its waves were off, toward all points of the compass. Indeed, the shocks were of sufficient strength to be recorded anywhere in the world, provided the proper instruments existed.

The diminishing effects rolled across the North American continent in a few minutes, knocking out many sensitive seismographs as it swept forward. Just eight minutes after the first shock in Anchorage, the surface of the earth in Washington, D.C., more than 8,500 miles east of "ground zero" in Prince William Sound, rose and fell two inches. Although this subsequent phenomenon could be recorded, it could be neither observed nor felt. The ground had risen four inches at Houston, Texas. The water level of a four-foot-deep well in Milwaukee surged momentarily up to twelve and a half feet.

The pummeling in Alaska, however, was not finished; nor were the secondary effects. In Seward, south of Anchorage, and at Whittier, between Seward and Anchorage, ruptured petroleum storage tanks spewed gasoline onto the waterfront and soon were blazing fiercely. Nearby homes were quickly consumed, others menaced.

Thirty minutes after the first jolt, the initial tsunami hit Kodiak, like a weird, fast-rising tide, twenty-two feet above mean low water. Ed Naughton had hurried to his residence just below the city reservoir to check on his wife and son. When he ascertained both were fine and his home still sound, he started back toward the bakery. The main shop was standing, but an annex close to the harbor was already gone, possibly struck by a heavy crab boat, among the many vessels, some as large as two hundred tons, hurled inland by the huge combers.

From safer heights Ed could discern in the darkness the silhouettes of mast tips and boat keels being tossed about in the harbor by what presumably was a giant whirlpool. More than half of the fishing fleet was lost—swept out to sea or, shattered, ending up in all parts of the town and island.

At Cordova the great waves stole houses and boats. Ten cabins at nearby Point Whitshed floated off, as one observer would note, "in a precise line like coaches of a train." One resident, returning to see if his cabin was still astride its foundations, was himself carried away by the second tsunami.

At Chenega, across Prince William Sound from Cordova, a wall of water ninety feet high destroyed all but one school and one house, drowning one third of the seventy-six inhabitants. At Whittier Mr. McDonald likened the rising water to a "black cloud boiling out of the Passage Canal." Thirteen persons had already perished in Whittier.

The tsunamis moved south and west at four hundred miles per hour. Warnings were flashed ahead, but not soon enough to save four children sleeping with their parents on an Oregon beach. The wave crashed ashore at Crescent City, California, on the Oregon border, at midnight. Sheriff Oswald Hovgaard watched "the whole harbor come up in the air!" Before it came down again, fifty-six business and residential blocks had been wrecked and twelve persons killed.

Civil Defense sirens wailed across the Pacific in Hawaii to warn people to seek higher ground. Many were evacuated from coastal areas. Before dawn, however, even in the distant, sixteen-hundred-mile-long Hawaiian "ridge," the fury that had arisen from the depths of Prince William Sound had spent itself—like some huge and infuriated drunkard finally grown weary from his own excesses. The earth and the surrounding seas were as calm as though nothing or very little had actually transpired.

It was time for the fortunate, such as the Slaymakers and the Naughtons, to offer shelter to those whose luck had run out and had no shelter against the cold sub-Arctic night. It was time to take stock, to lick wounds, and, even, to think about rebuilding. The city manager of Anchorage, W. Harrison, drily observed, "We're in a hell of a mess!"

As that first night wore on, almost every type of group—civilian, military, or quasi-military from the Alaska Scouts (or National Guard) and Civilian Defense to the Red Cross and pink-cheeked Explorer Scouts—was projected into action. Their numbers were vast.

Douglas Clure, Anchorage's Civil Defense Director, struggled through the blacked-out streets, uncertain of fissures in his path, to find his offices in a shambles and no means of communication (or so he thought at first) other than the state-police radio net, a tribute to its own operators. With no idea of how many persons were dead or injured, Clure set out to bring medical supplies to the Presbyterian Community Hospital.

"We could not communicate with anything except by radio," he would recall, "and by this time there were two commercial radio stations that were operable and working. . . . Our first effort was to get public utility groups. We needed people for communications—particularly telephones—and those who could perform certain rescue functions. We needed ambulances. . . ."

Military aid from Elmendorf, Fort Richardson, and other bases in Alaska was at once sought and obtained. Soldiers, guardsmen, sailors, and airmen were arriving in Anchorage, as well as in the other stricken towns and cities, well before dawn. Ski patrols and mountain troops were alerted to probe into remote areas, including the tracks of the disrupted Alaska Railroad. Also before dawn military transport planes were taking off from bases as far distant as Ellington, Texas, laden with doctors, nurses, food, clothing, and medical supplies. On the return leg they were prepared to bring the injured back to hospitals in Seattle, Portland, or elsewhere.

The Military Affiliate Radio System (MARS) was in full-speed operation within sixty minutes of the first tremor. Military communications personnel and signal battalions worked with civilian companies to restore communications and to assure continuous service. Military tank trailers were supplying water to greater Anchorage before 9 P.M., and purification units were being loaded onto aircraft in Fort Lewis, Washington. Both Elmendorf and Fort Richardson, situated as they were in greater Anchorage, unlocked barracks space for displaced persons. Beds were made and chow lines opened by midevening to shelter and feed as many as five thousand.

By the request of Governor William Egan and city officials, troops from both of the large bases were patrolling downtown Anchorage by 8 P.M. The whole business area had been closed off. Gas leaks, unknown crevices, and buildings that threatened to cave in made the streets and sidewalks hazardous. Military trucks, bulldozers, and cranes crunched over snow through the glare of searchlights not only to clear access routes but to free people trapped in the rubble. A number of lives were saved by this operation. Gasoline flowing from ruptured storage tanks in several cities was hosed down by firemen and emergency crews—as one more effort to stabilize what threatened during those early hours to degenerate into chaos.

Foremost, perhaps, of the all-abiding if irrational fears of those within the five-hundred-mile shock arc was that the earth would open once again and swallow them up—this time for sure! Secondly, if another seismic sea wave did not snatch them off into the deep, a subsequent mud slide would. So, in weariness, trepidation, and sorrow, Alaskans poked through the rubble of their ice-locked towns and cities. Could they reweave the shattered dreams of pioneering in the far north?

Monday arrived. It was Seward Day, the ninety-seventh anniversary of the Alaskan Purchase. None, this year, would find heart or time to celebrate. "We have been subject to no heavier blow" was the assessment of the governor of Alaska.

He was right in some respects—in the magnitude, for example, of the "shake"—wrong in others. Because of a quirk in timing—the tremor occurring at the close of the business day and on a partial holiday at that—and a geographically sparse population, the loss in life was extremely low: 115 dead. And virtually all of those injured would make complete recoveries. Even the property damage—over $300,000,000 in toto—was insignificant compared to what would have happened had the epicenter been beneath downtown Los Angeles, Seattle, or even Denver, Colorado.

The major loss was sustained in Anchorage, where 215 homes were demolished, together with 157 commercial establishments. Yet only nine persons had succumbed in Anchorage, less than one-third the death rate in Valdez.

Attracting more national attention was the hurt done to industry— to the canneries and their vessels, especially the king-crab fisheries, and to communications such as highways, telephone lines, and the Alaskan Railroad, which was severed, crushed, and covered by earth in many places, its bridges torn away. Nearly 30 percent of the highway bridges were gone. The Kodiak Naval Base suffered the greatest destruction among military or federal installations, the loss amounting to more than ten million dollars.

But money was fast on its way. The Federal Treasury opened its gates. President Lyndon B. Johnson appointed a special committee to investigate, to recommend, and to keep the money pouring northward. He was not alone. The Red Cross—as was to be expected—the Salvation Army, the Veterans of Foreign Wars, the American Legion, Rotary Clubs, all manner of church groups, and even the Ford Motor Company became obsessed, seemingly, with one purpose: to speed rescue funds into the forty-ninth state. Allentown, Pennsylvania, dispatched a truckload of housewares over the Alcan Highway.

Thus, the meaning of the Good Friday earthquake was as far-reaching as it was diffuse. Certainly, it would far transcend its sum total to Paula Slaymaker and others of her general age group—no school for two weeks.

Plans to move the geographically unstable downtown area southward would be too disruptive to the economy, businessmen said, so federal officials made money available to rebuild existing structures in the slide area but not to construct new ones. A four-million-dollar earth buttress was constructed to stabilize part of the Fourth Avenue slide.

Then, in February, 1967, the Federal Housing Administration removed its restrictions on mortgage insurance in two high-risk residential areas. The L Street slide area remained ineligible for federal funds, but new buildings have been constructed atop the slide itself. An apartment house has been built in the high-risk area adjacent to the slide, all with private financing.

Six years after Alaska had rebuilt, a somewhat negative note was struck—unexpectedly—from an equally unanticipated quarter: the National Research Council of the National Academy of Sciences, a "private organization" chartered in 1863 by Congress with the stated responsibility for advising the Federal Government in scientific matters. A team of social scientists sent to Alaska after the earthquake published in 1970 the second in a projected eight-volume series, this one dealing with human reactions.*

> The picture that emerges [the introduction states] is markedly at variance with the public notion of man's behavior in catastrophic events and with the singular quality of the earthquake as a great geophysical event. . . . Stripped of myth, the record of behavior during and immediately after the earthquake is of positive, but not unique actions.

Alaska had its normal share, the report says, of "heroes, wise men, and fools."

In a disaster, the report asserts, people do first those things they are trained to do rather than "the things that are most urgent." Thus, firemen look for fires to extinguish, policemen direct traffic and guard

---

* National Academy of Sciences, *The Great Alaska Earthquake: Human Ecology*, Washington, D.C., 1970.

against law violations, utility workers restore utilities, and administrators hold meetings. For the fire department, first priority in Alaska was to look for fires and maintain a state of fire readiness. It engaged in some rescue work, but this was said to have stopped at 8 P.M., and "no effort was made to take on novel tasks" such as search and rescue.

Protecting property seems to take priority over rescuing people, asserts the study, and the danger of looting is exaggerated in the public mind. Under normal conditions, the report states, if a child is lost or a person is trapped in a shattered building, massive efforts are started immediately to find or to rescue the victim. But in Anchorage, the writers charged, search and rescue was delayed until the next morning, more than twelve hours after the 5:36 P.M. quake. "Manpower that could have been used for systematic search and rescue efforts was devoted instead to the prevention of looting. The mobilization for the guarding of damaged areas . . . was reasonably rapid and coordinated, but the search-and-rescue activity was not." The report conceded, however, that these control activities, which were the first concern of many public officials, included efforts to protect lives by keeping people out of dangerous areas.

The behavior of Alaskans during the disaster was typical of behavior in such situations elsewhere, the committee asserts. Large numbers of people worked "heroically" for long periods without much food or rest and shared their homes, clothing, and food with others less fortunate without regard to class or status. Local "heroes" emerged who exercised leadership at crucial points. But as soon as the first emergency problems were under control, attitudes were found to have shifted toward expecting or even demanding outside help. Firms that offered supplies "free for the duration" asked for reimbursement. Workmen demanded pay for overtime.

Within an hour Alaskans requested aid from the military and depended on it very heavily. State and federal money was avidly sought, and delegations went to Washington to "lobby" for an omnibus bill to deal with local economic woes. Many individuals expressed hope that F.H.A. mortgages would be "forgiven" (as they eventually were, except for the first one thousand dollars due).

In the aggregate, the report finds, "Alaskans bore little in the way of losses," and the inflow of federal funds exceeded some of the loss estimates. Private property damage of $77,000,000, for example, was relieved by federal expenditures of $114,000,000 through September, 1966.

Where economic interests are involved, "lessons learned from a disaster are not learned for long," the research committee found. Although reconstruction provided "a needed stimulus to a lagging economy" and population climbed, the opportunity to reconstruct in a substantially better way was not well utilized. Despite the wide use of urban renewal funds, no substantial relocation or changes in land use developed at any of the communities except at Valdez and in some of the villages.

The designations of risk areas that were promulgated after the earthquake have not yet been found to be codified into the local land-use practice of any one of the four communities for which they were provided. "Natural-disaster plans have not been developed to any degree, nor is it clear what steps have been taken to ensure better construction practices," the report states.

The Alaska earthquake, "one of the greatest geophysical events," had little long-term effect, either good or bad, on the land or the people, the researchers concluded. A national policy aimed at reducing earthquake losses is needed now, because "before the end of this century it is virtually certain that *one or more major earthquakes will occur on the North American continent.*"

Thus, the major lesson of the Alaska earthquake should be the need for a comprehensive policy to reduce losses in future earthquakes, which might not be so "fortunately timed or located." Discouraging unsafe building locations and types of construction "ought to be a normal function of those agencies that govern where and how people build."

The report recommends that a national policy be modeled on the Unified National Program for Managing Flood Losses that was developed by a task force of the Bureau of the Budget. This policy, which must be known and thoroughly understood in advance, should include guarantees to local governments against loss of revenues, earthquake insurance and mortgage indemnification, interest rates on special long-term loans for business, restrictions on federal financing in the relocation of privately owned real property, and restrictions to be applied in locating new federally aided construction. "The dispersal of population and human works into areas of high seismic potential is accelerating," the report says. "We will have to labor mightily merely to keep future losses at present levels."

In sum, the report concludes:

> An influenza epidemic might have killed more people, the closing of a military base has had greater economic and social impact, accumulated destruction by fire has already equaled that of the earthquake in some communities. The earthquake had on balance little long-term human impact—evidence of the resiliency of the social fabric.

But it had. Per capita income surged from a prequake average of $2,850 to $3,154 by 1965. Everywhere was urban renewal—and so much so, in fact, that a street was built right through the site of Ed Naughton's bakery. Modern steel, chrome, and glass office buildings reared their many stories over Anchorage's shaky soil. Penney's rebuilt a four-million-dollar store, anticipating the Paula Slaymakers of generations to come, after the school bells rang their afternoon "amens," plus some other customers, too. Walter Hickel, the new governor, erected a $2,500,000 luxury hotel.

Alaska generally, along the fated five-hundred-mile arc, and specifically in Anchorage and its purlieus, lived again, more lavishly and robustly even than San Francisco after its own ordeal by upheaval and fire. In comfort and ever-bourgeoning modernity the forty-ninth state awaited the next time a wife or a husband or a child might look up and query, "Did you feel that?"

13

Buffalo Creek, Rapid City,
Agnes, 1972

In 1972 the rains came.

Late in February, after an incessant downpour and the melting of
heavy winter snows, a one-hundred-foot-high, mile-long "slag" or
mine-waste dam—known only as No. 3—in the southwest tip of West
Virginia gave way. It was a catastrophe that really should have surprised no one, since it had never been suggested that No. 3 was especially secure, much less durable.

It happened so quickly that it was close to impossible to flee. The
time was eight o'clock Saturday morning, February 26; the place, a
town named Man.

Many who lived along Buffalo Creek were in their yards or starting
on their day's errands when they saw the cascade of water and mud
rolling their way. The crest appeared to be an unreal thirty feel tall.
Wallace Adkins's experience was more or less typical. His first reaction was to load up his car. The engine would not start. Nonetheless,
Wallace kept herding his children into the vehicle. He was, in fact,
assisting his wife into the front seat when the water "just carried her
away." Struggling against the savage pull of the flood, he managed to
save the rest of his family by wading and swimming.

Alvid Davis rescued two of his boys, though his wife and youngest
son were lost, and friends two miles downstream saved his seventeen-

year-old daughter. James Burleson, his wife, and their fifteen-year-old son fought their way to high ground. There, amid the debris of homes and trees, they waited for eighteen hours until rescue arrived. A pregnant woman screaming, "Please save my baby!" was flown by helicopter to the Man Appalachian Regional Hospital.

And so it went. By the time Buffalo Creek had spent its fury, 118 were dead, more than 800 were injured and upward of 4,000—children and adults—were without homes in fourteen small mining communities strung along a fourteen-mile stretch of the bleak, obscure waterway.

Appalled and enraged by the extent of the disaster, Representative Ken Hechler, of West Virginia, stated in Congress, while asking the Corps of Engineers to press an inquiry:

"It is outrageous that the Bureau of Mines and other federal and state agencies have failed to demonstrate sufficient concern for the protection of the safety of the people who work in the mines and live in mining communities. I have been fighting with strip miners for several years in the Buffalo Creek Valley, attempting to stop them from allowing mud and sludge to slide down onto peoples' lawns and into their driveways.

"In one case, the Island Creek Coal Company, after officials visited the site of a slag heap at Proctor Hollow near Amherstdale, agreed to purchase some of the houses in the immediate path of some mud slides. The houses were subsequently condemned.

"As I looked through Buffalo Creek Valley, it struck me again that the entire valley is honeycombed with strip mines and wastes from deep mines so that the soil can no longer hold water. The people are the prisoners of the coal industry.

"It is significant that the only building left intact in one Buffalo Creek community was the company store.

"For too long the coal industry has polluted the air, water, and politics of West Virginia. Federal and state officials have handled the coal industry with kid gloves and allowed the industry to get away with murder, whether it concerns mine safety or strip mining or slag piles. Whenever anybody points out the evils of strip mining or the threats to human safety caused by ancient coal company practices, those federal and state officials responsible for protecting the public will scream, 'Energy crisis!' or, 'We need the jobs!' "

The congressman was quickly challenged by Elburt F. Osborn,

director of the Bureau of Mines, who testified before a senatorial sub-committee that the bureau had never possessed the authority attributed to it. Noting that the bureau was "not aware of the rapid rise of water behind Dam No. 3 on February 24, 25, and 26, Osborn continued, "Even if we had been aware, I must emphasize . . . that persons expert in the construction of dams would not have known that the dam would fail until almost immediately prior to its collapse.

"Even if a bureau coal mine inspector had been at the dam site as the water rose, his authority would have been limited to the issuance of an imminent danger order, withdrawing the miners working on the mine property. The finding . . . would not have prevented the retaining dam from failing, nor would it have been applicable to persons off the mine property in the path of the flood."

Osborn suggested that the most effective means of insuring against future Buffalo Creeks was the passage of pending legislation known as the administration's Mined Area Protection Bill.

Such disasters, however, would occur again—to dams "safe" or "unsafe," to "good" and "bad" dams.

The spring was as wet in South Dakota as had been the winter in West Virginia and, for that matter, much of the East Coast. In early June the Black Hills were characteristically lush, but the earth was sodden.

By Saturday morning, the tenth of that month, ten inches of rain had fallen in the previous twenty-four hours upon Rapid City, on the eastern borders of the Black Hills, and its 44,000 residents. Tourists en route during the summer to the hills or to Mount Rushmore National Memorial knew Rapid City on Interstate 90 as the only significant population center after Sioux Falls, 330 barren and sometimes blistering miles to the east.

Then the dam on Canyon Lake in the western section of Rapid City cracked, turning gentle Rapid Creek into the same sort of murderous, towering torrent as Buffalo Creek. Once again, on another fateful Saturday, there was no warning—just the surging wall of water. First the creek was shoulder-high, but scant moments later the swollen, turbulent stream was carrying away houses, especially the many mobile homes in the area. A witness watched "a blue thirty-to-forty-foot house trailer riding the large wave like a surfboard." The agonizing scenes of West Virginia were repeated as members of families were snatched away within reach of others. One could not easily surmount the force of the water.

The Whidbey Island Amateur Radio Club, in Washington, comprising many "ham" operators, carried much of the load of emergency messages relayed from a similar station in Rapid City to Red Cross and Civil Defense workers elsewhere. Via this roundabout network, many Rapid City families received the first word about the safety of their members. (The Whidbey group, with its several stations, had also maintained contact with Alaska operators during the 1964 earthquake.)

When the final tallies were completed, it appeared that 226 persons had lost their lives in Rapid City, with damage set at approximately $120,000,000. Among the dead were three sergeants from adjacent Ellsworth Air Force Base, engaged in rescue efforts. A fellow serviceman, working with the trio, Sergeant George O'Dell, saw "a wall of water coming down the creek toward us. Some people managed to climb a tall tree near the house," but the other three sergeants were swept to their deaths.

Several hundred mobile homes rushed in by governmental emergency purchase did much to provide temporary shelter to the some one thousand homeless, including families attached to the air-force base. The new owners were promised a rent-free year.

Rapid City, South Dakota however, was soon pushed out of the news space in America's dailies by the first hurricane of the season— "Agnes"—which was cavorting around the Caribbean even as Rapid City was starting to mop up.

Florida's east, then west, coast went on alert, a familiar procedure to the residents of this semitropical state. Capricious as any of her breed of "circular disturbances," this storm wandered into the Gulf of Mexico, headed north, and then howled ashore between Panama City and Apalachicola in western Florida, doing some, but not spectacular, damage.

Agnes drifted inland, up over the Alabama-Georgia border, and as June passed the midpoint, there seemed every reason to conclude that Agnes would blow herself out and become nothing more than a late spring rain.

Just like the hurricane of 1938, however, this one of 1972 would not die—and for good reason. The earth of the eastern section of the country remained saturated from the wet spring. Agnes could gulp all the water she wanted to refuel her demonic power.

Lost sight of for several days and all but ignored, Agnes, like a spurned harlot, smashed furiously into southwest Virginia on Wednesday, June 21. She had soaked up tens of thousands of tons of water in the interim which, without much accompanying wind, she dumped on the Old Dominion, Maryland, the District of Columbia, Pennsylvania, and New York State in the ensuing four days. According to the Oceanic and Atmospheric Administration, this quantity of water was estimated at 25.5 cubic miles, 28.1 trillion gallons, sufficient to fill a lake of sixty-seven square miles, two thousand feet deep.

As had been the case with the Alaskan quake and other disaster situations, it became obvious that the military, especially the National Guard and Reserve units, would have to hasten to the aid of the populace. The first hint of the extent of the required assistance came when the polluted waters of the James started pouring over Richmond's filtration plant.

By incredible happenstance, visiting state guard engineers had been demonstrating heavy-capacity water purification units at Camp A. P. Hill for Governor A. Linwood Holton. Within a few days the same machinery was trucked into Byrd Park, Richmond, to supply pure drinking water for nearly 250,000 residents of Virginia's capital city and surrounding Henrico County. Otherwise, they would have gone thirsty.

The Defense Civil Preparedness Agency, organized only the previous month and reporting to Secretary of Defense Melvin Laird, was suddenly faced with a challenge of wartime magnitude.

North of Richmond, astride Route I-95 to Washington, Quantico-based marines had themselves "moved out" to combat an immeasurably powerful enemy, which was assaulting in multisectors and was seemingly vulnerable to no counterattacks. The nation's capital itself was drenched with water. A number of secondary bridges were severed. One or two suburbs to the south suffered momentarily from water shortages. A small shopping center in historic nearby Alexandria, Virginia, was burned out because fire trucks could not get in to fight the flames. Otherwise, Washington, D.C., was scarcely in the category of a "disaster area."

That Pennsylvania was going to bear far more than its measure of the fury of Agnes was first obvious to those living or working in Harrisburg as they watched the Susquehanna River "slobber" over its low banks toward the state capital's downtown district. The temples of state government were on somewhat higher ground and appeared in no imminent peril, although Governor Milton Shapp's executive mansion was soon under water to the first-floor ceiling.

Pottstown, thirty-five miles west of Philadelphia, on the Schuylkill, was experiencing trouble. A navy helicopter squadron, HC-2, based at Lakehurst, New Jersey, was instructed by disaster control at Pottstown to stand by. Moments later, HC-2, along with sister marine and army squadrons also home-coted at the navy's onetime lighter-than-air station, was airborne.

Commander Mike Marriott, squadron "exec," piloting the lead chopper, was the first over flooded Pottstown. He would comment that in his fifteen years of flying he had never encountered "tougher" conditions—and that was probably an understatement. "There were hightension power lines," he would report, "and tall trees, all of which had to be spotted in the dark. . . . I think everyone in Pottstown has a forty-foot television antenna."

People cringed in the dark, some waving only candles, on roofs, in second- or third-story windows, even on the high branches of tall trees. Marriott lowered a net to one man stranded on the roof of his home. Apparently, the latter remembered something he wanted to take along, but before he went back down the skylight, he wrapped the rescue cable around the chimney, figuring no doubt he wouldn't lose the chopper that way. "A gust of wind came along," the officer continued, "buffeting the helo, causing it to give a hard yank on the line. Fortunately, the chimney came down, not the helo."

He had, perhaps, every right to leave the man on his rooftop. But Commander Marriott did not operate that way. He hovered above the house until he completed his rescue.

However, neither Pottstown, Harrisburg, nor Scranton, on the Lackawanna, but a city of sixty thousand a scant fifteen miles below Scranton was to become the tragic core of destruction among all the cities, towns, and crossroads of the East upon which Agnes spewed her watery venom. Wilkes-Barre, a drab industrial and Saturday-marketing center astride the northerly reaches of the Susquehanna, rested secure behind dikes constructed after the flood of 1936, with an engineered margin of four feet above the thirty-four-foot crest then. "We could not bring ourselves to believe that the river might break through," Jim Lee, editor of the Wilkes-Barre *Times-Leader and Evening News,* admitted to the author.

Yet warnings were spread on June 22 throughout the beautiful Wyoming Valley, extending some fifteen miles from Pittston, just below Scranton, to Nanticoke, south of Wilkes-Barre. Many were evacuated from this so-called Valley with a Heart. Those who elected to remain worked unremittingly to sandbag the banks of the river.

The Susquehanna first crested during the night of June 22, and the people started back to their homes. Then the civil-defense sirens sounded again the next day. Workers dropped their sandbags and fled. The Susquehanna surged through the dikes into Wilkes-Barre and on down the Wyoming Valley, inundating homes—some thirteen thousand beyond repair—farms, innumerable bridges, commercial buildings, and entire communities, cutting a swath forty-five times the river's normal width.

It was apparent even in the confused crisis moments that close to half of the valley's 200,000 residents would have to be rescued. The call went out to many quarters in many sections of the East. The Coast Guard, for one, unlimbered skiffs and whaleboats from many stations, north to New London, Connecticut, and south to Cape May, New Jersey, and sent them rushing toward Wilkes-Barre in trucks and trailers.

Rank was forgotten in the armed services. Brigadier General Ethel A. Hoefle, chief nurse of the air force and one of its two women generals, hopped an evacuation flight and went to work.

The rushing waters came up so fast toward a forty-foot crest that hundreds took to rooftops and other high places, with no sure idea of what to do next. They waited patiently in long lines, reminding at least one helicopter pilot of "a row of wheat" beneath him.

The performers of Strates Shows clambered to the car tops of their train, which, by monstrous bad fortune, had rolled into Wilkes-Barre a few hours earlier. They could not move until helicopters arrived to pluck them off.

In another part of the city, Airman Herbert Brinkert looked down from his helicopter at a cluster of people on the second-story back porch of a house surrounded by ample old trees and power lines. Almost brushing poles and trees, the chopper moved in. A line was dropped, and a woman was hauled aboard. "The lady started screaming that her baby was still down below," recalled Petty Officer Ken Elliott. "I wasn't sure if she was hysterical or if she just wanted to be heard above the noise of the helicopter. Anyway, I didn't think that anyone else could bring up the baby and hold onto the sling at the same time." So Elliott swung himself down on the crewman's sling and brought up ". . . well, the babies, four of 'em, and seven more adults."

Public Square, the business heart of Wilkes-Barre, was a deep, foul lake. Display windows of stores were covered to the name boards. The orchestra of a theater had applauded its last matinee, now resembling an ornate but filthy swimming poll. First floors of office buildings were awash with desks, chairs, file cabinets, typewriters, notebooks, pencils, erasers, paper, in mockery of man's penchant for neatness and order. Just around the corner, rolls of newsprint stored in the basement of the *Times-Leader* had swollen with meteoric speed to rupture pipes and threaten the very foundations of an otherwise substantial edifice. On another level the presses were soaked, gummed with mud and silt. Reporters, however, true to their tradition of pertinacity and innovation, merely moved to a higher story in the building. Drier presses elsewhere would roll out the next edition.

The waters were coldly impartial. Dr. Francis J. Michelini, president of Wilkes College, was congratulating himself that the campus had missed the worst of the catastrophe when the river inched in, flooding all fifty-eight buildings. The library lost 53,000 volumes. The Music Hall lost two new Steinway grand pianos and a new organ, with a total value of $35,000. The college had "scrimped and saved" to purchase those musical instruments, Dr. Michelini declared, as close to tears as an emotionally disciplined man can be.

Warehouses in the wholesale district along with scattered homes in residential areas caught fire, possibly from ruptured gas lines and short-circuited electric wires, and were destroyed. Fire trucks could not plow through the flooded, debris-filled streets to their aid.

The waters manifested no respect even for the dead. At Forty Fort, a small suburb on the northern edge of the city, two thousand graves from a small cemetery dating back to Revolutionary times were scoured out, taking away even bronze caskets and tearing apart mausoleums weighing tons. "I saw a wave," asserted the elderly caretaker, John Novak, "eight to ten feet high come across the flats, and on it coffins bobbed like surfboards."

Corpses and coffins alike from this once pleasant-appearing place of rest were strewn all over the countryside, and one came to rest on the back porch of a resident of Wilkes-Barre. The sights and the stench at Forty Fort boggled the mind's capacity for description. The cemetery, which had contained the remains of Elinor Wylie, the poet, and her grandfather, Henry Morton Hoyt, a governor of Pennsylvania, was still awash when the Graves Registration Section of an army reserve unit was given the unenviable task of retrieving the dead and cleaning up the place.

Streets, stretching in every direction from Public Square, Wilkes-Barre, were deep canals, a turgid Venice where only boats could navigate. Automobiles, trucks, and buses not only were wrecked but became free-floating objects of menace, bowling over or punching holes in walls with casual devastation or otherwise mutilating whatever stood in their path. Automobile dealers reported entire car inventories erased from their books.

Looting began even while the dark waters coursed through the streets, but it soon halted as increasing numbers of the armed military, especially the Pennsylvania National Guard, arrived on the scene. Bayoneted rifles, spiked boots, or menacing looks did not, however, deter the second wave—rodents, those historic camp followers of plague and disaster.

In the first few days, five hundred individuals were bitten by rats. The more seriously infected were airlifted to hospitals in Harrisburg. Others were "air-evac'd" because of injuries and illnesses. Humans necessarily commanded first priority, but animals were not altogether forgotten. Arriving at Lakehurst, New Jersey, for example, were eleven dogs, thirteen cats, a raccoon, and two ducks, although some might have speculated that the latter pair could have held their own in a wet environment.

Lights were out, clean drinking water was scarce, and instant communication, such as by telephone, was largely in the realm of memory. People needed food, clothing, and shelter.

According to Colonel J. M. Van Name, task-force commander for the 79th Army Reserve Command charged with "supporting" the entire Wyoming Valley, "This is complicated in the sense that the supplies and logistics furnished were not directly related to military personnel alone, but had to cover males, females, and babies. In other words, diapers and sanitary napkins became crucial items in the course of the operation, and these are not normally handled through military channels."

The bulk of these supplies funneled in by air from Willow Grove, Pennsylvania. There, by an especially unhappy chance of timing, two air reserve lumbering transports—"Hercules"—had been sabotaged prior to the flood by young people who scribbled on the noses of the old planes, "Bread and Not Bombs." Seemingly, any fool could have concluded at a glance that these slow-moving freighters of the airways could no more be employed in combat than the Wright brothers' first model. These vandals, however, were manifestly very special kinds of fools.

Crews of the 913th Tactical Airlift Group by means of devotion, skill, and around-the-clock labor repaired a third "Hercules," or C-130, and sped it toward Wilkes-Barre, laden with several tons of food, medical supplies, cots, mattresses, and blankets, and prepared to carry people and their immediate possessions to safety.

All in all, Wilkes-Barre was ruined, and few residents had possessed the foresight, or money, to carry flood insurance. For that matter, many who had suffered great damage complained that their insurers had never bothered to tell them that "flood" was specifically excluded—in small print, to be sure—from their so-called comprehensive policies. Others who might have considered having such protection could not afford the expensive premiums.

When the author visited Wilkes-Barre a month or more following the disaster, it remained under martial law, swarming with national guardsmen, reservists, regulars, state troopers, and police and sheriffs from surrounding municipalities. The city was prostrate, reeking with death and decay, reminiscent of Naples in 1944, which the author entered not long after the Germans had been driven out.

Mounds of sodden merchandise were still piled in the streets in front of silt-stained stores. The owners mopped and hosed with an attitude of mingled shock and apathy, giving an observer the impression that they did not expect ever to complete the chore. It seemed quite unnecessary when roaming M.P.'s looked with latent menace at a passerby who chanced to pause beside one of these shapeless goods heaps. Nothing survived that was worth the trouble or risk of looting.

Headquarters for emergency housing, for food, and for the registry of skilled workers such as electricians had been established in Public Square. A rock band performed with muted enthusiasm in an obvious effort to relieve the ennui and despair of long days and nights. At certain high schools and other designated spots typhoid shots were available.

On Interstate 81 and beside the highways leading into Wilkes-Barre, at the motels, restaurants, and shopping complexes located on higher ground, there appeared a mundane sense of normalcy, but the center of the city remained in shock and numbed with unreality. An old man walking a little girl beside the gaunt walls of a burned-out warehouse commented dreamily, "I used to sit there in the sun and eat my lunch. . . ."

One homeowner had scribbled the semi-despairing sign in front of his shattered abode, "This way to the Dump!" Others, trying to brighten their hopes, flew the American flag from dawn to dark amid the clutter of their yards and porches. Yet others bravely printed on the windows of their stores or offices: "Rebuild we will."

The National Guard in the first two weeks alone carried away 68,000 tons of debris to "sanitary landfills." This figure kept being augmented. Some 1,500,000 pounds of food and supplies were air-dropped into central points of the Wyoming Valley.

Psychiatrists were in demand, from the tensions resulting when families and neighbors were compelled to double up. It was hoped that Uncle Sam's one-year-rent-free mobile homes would go far toward alleviating this personal anxiety, if not claustrophobia as well.

Westward from Wilkes-Barre, communities experienced their own peculiar problems, all resulting from nature's rampage. At Milton, Pennsylvania, national guardsmen reported to their armory to find that much of their equipment, including uniforms, had been inundated. Undaunted, they made use of those items of their "gear" that had been kept at home and went on duty. One of their first challenges was considerable.

A six-thousand-ton-capacity propane gas tank was leaking. What did one do in such a precarious situation? "We had to work fast to avoid an explosion," recalled Colonel Boyd S. Farver, commanding the

164th Service Battalion of the Pennsylvania National Guard. They called similar propane installations around the East before they found out how to stop the leak.

Not quite one hundred miles to the northwest, the Chemung River, a tributary of the Susquehanna, had flooded the Elmira-Corning-Horseheads triangle of New York State, across the Pennsylvania border. Houses, washed from foundations, were swept across the Chemung Valley to come to rest against a ridge of hills—like the litter from a public beach in the evening breeze.

Especially hurt was the well-known Corning Glass Works and Corning Museum, home of Steuben glass and other quality glass and ceramics. Damaged were 65 miles of movie film, 7,000 slides, and 120,000 negatives, dating back to the making of the Mount Palomar Observatory lens in the 1930's. There was also a photorecord of certain heat-resistant ceramics for the early Project Mercury space flights. However, the Eastman Kodak Company, in nearby Rochester, hoped to salvage much of the irreplaceable film through delicate washing.

From large, unaffected cities such as Rochester and Buffalo came volunteers to aid in the seemingly infinite task of cleanup—the Richard Vinals, for just two, from a church group in the eastern environs of Rochester. It was calculated that 130 hours of continuous labor were necessary to clean just one floor of one house. "There was plenty of work still to be done one month after the flood," wrote Mrs. Barbara Vinal, "but we were impressed with the progress already made. We cleaned mud and water out of a basement, scrubbed floors and stairs, cleaned a kitchen.

"All of us agreed that the most important contribution we made to the two families we helped was to provide incentive, a breath of fresh air. They are constantly fighting that feeling of despair, a feeling the house can never be made livable again.

"Some of our group were working in homes more severely damaged. They ripped out walls, pulled up floors, helped with carpentry and rewiring. I still try to visualize entire basements and first floors under water and cannot do it."

By September more than ten thousand volunteers, both amateur and professional, had aided in this kind of work in Wilkes-Barre alone. But it was not nearly enough.

With the winds of autumn waiting somewhere across the western slopes of the Alleghenies, the city still had not come back. It looked as though massive federal assistance was the only prescription that might effect a full cure. Governor Shapp accused George Romney, Secretary of Housing and Urban Development, of a lack of support. Romney, in turn, retorted that the Pennsylvania executive was "totally unrealistic." Romney was summoned to the White House, and it began to appear that his tenure in the Cabinet was in the balance.

However, very few people in Wilkes-Barre were concerned about the political future of Romney, Shapp, or Richard Nixon himself. All they thought or cared about was the urgent need for assistance, and it could not arrive too soon. The real tragedy was that politics had further muddied the wreckage of Wilkes-Barre and the fortunes of its people.

After she had died over Canada, Agnes left some three billion dollars in property destruction in 142 counties and 25 cities along 4,500 miles of major rivers and 9,000 streams. The losses incurred by Pennsylvania alone were close to one-half the total of the economic damage and dislocation. The damage to crops amounted to $132,000,000. In addition, 2,400 farm buildings were damaged or destroyed, and other equipment, including fences, were ruined beyond count. Approximately 5,800 individual businesses were "seriously devastated."

In the storm's wake close to half a million persons were without electricity for varying lengths of time, and a somewhat lesser number were plagued by a lack of water or a means of communication or transport. About 330,000 people were driven from their homes, and approximately 500,000 suffered some damage—luckless residents of the five thousand square miles of inundated real estate encompassing 233 counties and cities in seven states. The fact that only 118 persons perished—according to the best available count—compared to the hundreds who died in the 1938 hurricane and the thousands at Galveston, was a tribute to advance warning and well-coordinated, prompt emergency efforts.

The dollar tag on the damage was astronomic. In fact, the three-billion-dollar figure, as mentioned above, projected by the Office of Emergency Preparedness, made Agnes the costliest single disaster in American history. Late in August, President Nixon signed a Disaster Relief Supplemental Appropriation of nearly $1.6 billion. This sum added to another one billion dollars from state, local, and private relief was further described by O.E.P. as representing almost double the combined total expenditures for five of the largest previous disasters, commencing with hurricane Camille in 1969. G. A. Lincoln, O.E.P. director, noted with reference to the moneys to be provided through various federal, state, and county agencies, "This is by far the largest federal outlay ever to assist states to spring back into first-class shape."

Interim assessments attested to the latitude of the damage: $186,-000,000 to federal-aid highways, including interstates, plus another $382,000,000 to state road systems. Bridges were the hardest hit, with 150 destroyed in Pennsylvania alone. At least one, however, the Pinetown Covered Bridge, near Lancaster, was retrieved and towed back to its proper location by a house-moving firm.

The upsetting of nature's complex balance wrought havoc in the crabbing and oyster industry of Chesapeake Bay. The onrush of fresh water and silt diluted the necessary percentage of salinization on the bay bottom. If this did not destroy the shellfish and even the otherwise tough clams, pollutants did. Fishermen went on relief, along with some 100,000 other men and women thrown out of work because of damage to their places of employment. Even the National Park Service was hurt to the tune of twelve million dollars.

So it went, and no one in or out of the Federal Government could say when the books might be closed on the toll taken by Agnes. As Director Lincoln observed, 1972 had been "unique in the history of large-scale disasters." President Nixon had declared thirty-two major disasters since January 1—twice the figure for any comparable early calendar year on record. It was enough to cause one to look at the heavens and wonder. Many sought an answer in the Bible. Others discovered a new meaning in the Forty-sixth Psalm in the Book of Common Prayer, of the Protestant Episcopal Church:

> God is our hope and our strength; a very present help in trouble. Therefore will we not fear, though the earth be moved, and though the hills be carried into the midst of the sea; though the waters thereof rage and swell; and though the mountains shake at the tempest of the same. The rivers of the flood thereof shall make glad the city of God.

Bibliographical Notes

CHAPTER I. THE DRAFT RIOTS, 1863

Considerable documentation exists on the New York draft riots, although much written shortly after the fact is impassioned, scanty, and contradictory. Original material can be found in these among other newspapers: the *Evening Star*, Washington, D.C.; the *National Intelligencer*, Washington, D.C.; the New York *Herald*; *The New York Times*; and the New York *Tribune*. *Harper's Weekly*, *Leslie's Illustrated Weekly*, and *Harper's Monthly*, January, 1867, are included among the periodicals reporting the riots.

Books for the period on the subject include:

Barnes, David M. *The Draft Riots in New York*. New York: Baker and Godwin, 1863.

Dickinson, Anna. *What Answer?* Boston: Ticknor and Fields, 1868.

Eye-Witness Reports. *The Bloody Week*. New York: Coutant and Baker, 1863.

Headley, Joel T. *The Great Riots in New York*. New York: E. B. Treat Co., 1873.

Mitchell, Edward B. *Memoirs of an Editor*. New York: Scribner's, 1924.

Stoddard, William O. *The Volcano under the City*. New York: Fords, Howard and Hulbert, 1887.

Some dispatches pertaining to the riots also can be found in *Official Records, War of the Rebellion*, U.S. Government Printing Office, Washington, D.C., 1890–1891. James McCague has written the most recent book-length study of the riots, *The Second Rebellion* (New York: The Dial Press, Inc., 1968). The principal repository of original research was and remains the New-York Historical Society.

CHAPTER 2. GALVESTON TIDAL WAVE, 1900

So far as can be ascertained, the last of those adults who survived the tidal wave are since deceased. Some, such as Isaac Cline, moved on subsequently to other careers. He took up oil painting and was a familiar goateed figure in the artist colony of New Orleans until his death, at ninety-three years of age, in 1955. His brother, Joseph, died within eight days in a Texas hospital.

John Edward Weems, of Waco, Texas, has written the definitive book on the disaster, *A Weekend in September* (New York: Henry Holt, 1957). He also wrote an article on the same subject in *American Heritage Magazine*, October, 1968. The author is indebted to Mr. Weems for his kindness in making certain of his photographs available. He also appreciated the good services of Bob Delehite, Archives Division, Rosenberg Library, Galveston.

Other books and periodicals:

Cline, Isaac Monroe. *Storms, Floods and Sunshine*. New Orleans: Pelican Publishing Co., 1945.
Cline, Dr. Joseph L. *When the Heavens Frowned*. Dallas: Mathis, Van Nort Co., 1946.
Helm, Thomas. *Hurricanes: Weather at Its Worst*. New York: Dodd, Mead, 1967.
Lester, Paul. *The Great Galveston Disaster*. Privately printed, 1900.
Ousley, Clarence. *Galveston in 1900*. Atlanta: William P. Chase, 1900.

Among magazines with articles bearing on the tidal wave are *Cosmopolitan*, November, 1900, and the *North American Review*, Winter, 1938. The Houston *Post* and the Galveston *Post*, as might be expected, carry the best coverage of the daily press.

CHAPTER 3. DISASTER AT MONONGAH, 1907

Many persons and organizations assisted in the research for this chapter, a subject that has somehow escaped public recall these many years. The author first wishes to thank three who were there, still living in Monongah: Robert J. Brooks, Clay Fullen, and Andrew Urban. Although he was an infant at the time, Urban heard his father, Pete, recount his escape so many times that he almost came to believe that he himself was present.

The senior Urban's luck ran out in 1926 when a part of the same mine caved in on him. Pat McDonnell, on the other hand, who was at the mine entrance by the coal cars, survived further labor and later was chief of police in Monongah.

Representatives of the contemporary scene of Monongah who also helped include Joe James Bavely, a historian; Dominic Mike, the town barber; Joe Scalley, shoemaker and collector of relics; and the Sisters of the Catholic Convent.

Monongah, with a population today of about twelve hundred, has no working mines, Nos. 6 and 8 having been closed in 1956—now depleted, or "gob" areas. The workers have left or found jobs in factories, shops, or businesses in the Fairmont area. About half of Monongah burned down the year after the disaster. In 1928 the community was rocked by labor unrest and instances of suspected sabotage.

Others who made possible this documentary account include John Duncan, on the staff of Representative Robert H. Mollohan, of Fairmont; Rex Locke, editor of the *United Mine Workers Journal*, who made available a fiftieth-anniversary article on the disaster; and Donald Poland, safety coordinator for the U.M.W. in Fairmont, West Virginia. The latter procured a copy of the comprehensive report of the explosion by Frank Hass, the Fairmont Coal Company's chief engineer. Poland had a narrow escape a few days before the author interviewed him in a runaway mine-shaft elevator. This was at Farmington, West Virginia.

Poland, a sturdy, pragmatic veteran of the mines, has come to believe that although total safety is theoretically attainable, it is impossible by practical yardsticks. He cited his near accident, which could have been fatal, as an example of continuing human error.

Robert O. Swenarton, handling public affairs for the Bureau of Mines, kindly read this chapter for factual accuracy, especially with respect to mining terminology.

M. A. Marchetti, chief of the Division of Production and Distribution, Bureau of Mines, Pittsburgh, made available photographs of the times.

John Veasey, managing editor of the Fairmont *Times*, produced old files of that paper. Also consulted were the Pittsburgh *Dispatch*, the Wheeling *Register*, and *The New York Times*. The *Literary Digest* (December, 1907), *Review of Reviews* (February, 1908), and *World's Work* (February, 1909) contained articles pertaining to the explosion. The only two books pertaining to the subject are a report, *History of the Monongah Mines Relief Fund*, published privately by the committee, 1910, and Humphrey, H. B., *Historical Summary of Coal-Mine Explosions in the United States, 1810–1958* (Washington, D.C.: Bureau of Mines, U.S. Government Printing Office, 1960).

For those interested in one man's perspective of violence in the minefields during the first half of this century, *Bloodletting in Appalachia*, by Howard B. Lee, former attorney general of West Virginia, is recommended. The book was published in 1969 by the University of West Virginia, Morgantown.

In May, 1972, ninety-one died in the Sunshine silver mine in Idaho, eliciting an outcry from Congress, especially from Ken Hechler, Democratic Representative from West Virginia—somewhat in the tradition of Matt Neely, the guardsman at Monongah who went on to become a United States Senator and crusader for mine safety. Among Representative Hechler's charges was one with an old if familiar ring— that mine companies still have no adequate means of ascertaining how many human beings are below the surface of the earth at any given time or their precise location.

CHAPTER 4. *Eastland* ROLLS OVER, 1915

Primary source material for this chapter was obtained in the Chicago dailies, especially the *News* and the *Tribune*, and the periodicals *Literary Digest, Outlook*, and *Survey*.

No book has ever been written on this especially needless tragedy, possibly because of the unrelieved horror of it all. By the same token, no author has put the Iroquois Theater tragedy between book covers. Chapters or reference matter can be found in these general books:

Boyer, Dwight. *True Tales of the Great Lakes.* New York: Dodd, Mead, 1971.
Buchanan, Lamont. *Ships of Steam.* New York: The McGraw-Hill Book Company, Inc., 1956.
Hoehling, A. A. *They Sailed into Oblivion.* New York: Yoseloff, 1959.
Kartman, Ben, ed. *Disaster.* New York: Pellegrini and Cudahy, 1948.

The author is also indebted to Alexander Crosby Brown, author and editor, of Newport News, Virginia, and John Lochhead, of the Mariners Museum, Newport News. His quest for survivors went unrewarded, although one cannot necessarily deduce from this alone that none from the *Eastland* still live.

As brought out in the chapter, the legal echoes continued for a score of years, long after a new generation had appeared on Chicago's lakefront and to whom the name "*Eastland*" conveyed little or nothing. For those with interest, patience, and, possibly, a legal background, there exists the labyrinth of Michigan and Illinois court dockets bearing on the case over the twenty-year period.

The murderous old steamer may be scrapped, but even to this day her ghost has a curious way of appearing. One morning in the Library of Congress, this author noticed a browning bound volume of the Chicago *Tribune* opened to July, 1915. Having a hunch why, he asked the rather elderly reader of the paper if he was checking on the *Eastland*.

"Yes," he replied. "A friend in Chicago thought he had a friend on it, and he wanted me to check for him."

CHAPTER 5. THE SPANISH FLU EPIDEMIC, 1918

This chapter is drawn wholly from *The Great Epidemic*, by A. A. Hoehling, published in 1961 by Little, Brown and Company, Boston. The author's initial research was based on interviews with physicians, nurses, and others who survived the Spanish influenza, upon the material in published medical tracts, and from direct consultations with the infectious-diseases division of the National Institutes of Health, Washington. *The Great Epidemic*, for those who might care to pursue this phenomenon in epidemiological annals, is available in many public and most medical libraries.

The author also wishes to thank several members of the American National Red Cross who aided measurably in various chapters of the present book in text, photographs, and general encouragement. They include Mr. George M. Elsey, president; Pete Upton, director of public relations; Rudolf A. Clemens, Jr., library; and Miss Caroline Smith, of the photo library.

CHAPTER 7. HURRICANE OVER NEW ENGLAND, 1938

The author wishes to thank especially these individuals for their aid in preparing this chapter: Miss Kathie Barry, *The Day*, New London, Connecticut; Lewis R. Greene, assistant to the publishers, *The Sun*, Westerly, Rhode Island, Henry Beetle Hough, editor, *Vineyard Gazette*; and Edwin A. Weigel, public affairs officer, National Weather Service.

Periodical material is vast. Listing but a sampling: *Atlantic* magazine of December, 1938, containing Frances Woodward's graphic description; *Memorable Hurricanes of the United States since 1883*, one of numerous background publications of N.O.A.A., National Oceanic and Atmospheric Administration, of which the Weather Bureau is a part; the *National Geographic* of April, 1939; New England Historical Events Association, Inc., which published *Photo Record of Hurricane and Flood, New England's Greatest Disaster,* New York, 1938; and *Yale Review*, Spring, 1939. Principal newspapers consulted were the Boston *Herald*, the Hartford *Courant*, the New Haven *Journal-Courier*, the Providence *Journal*, and the *World-Telegram* (New York). Books include:

Clowes, Ernest S. *The Hurricane of 1938 on Eastern Long Island.* Bridgehampton, N.Y.: Hampton Press, 1939.

Dunn, Gordon E., and Miller, B. *Atlantic Hurricanes.* Baton Rouge: Louisiana State University Press, 1964.

Federal Writers Project. *New England Hurricane.* Boston: Hale, Cushman and Flint, 1938.

Greene, Lewis R. *The Hurricane, September 21, 1938, Westerly, R.I., and Vicinity.* Westerly, R.I.: Utter Co., 1938.

Hawes, Richard K. *The Hurricane at Westport Harbor.* Fall River, Mass.: Privately printed, 1938.

Lafrentz, Olga L. *Letter to a Friend* (at Lincoln Memorial University, Harrogate, Tennessee). Privately printed, 1939.

CHAPTER 8. CIRCUS FIRE AT HARTFORD, CONNECTICUT, 1944

The author is especially grateful for the graphic eyewitness accounts and comments furnished him by Everett D. "Brub" Dow, then Hartford *Courant* reporter and now West Hartford town clerk, and Mrs. Everett (Dorothea) Felber, a resident of Chevy Chase, Maryland. The fact that her father was dying had brought her to Hartford that summer.

The author also wishes to thank Mrs. Jean H. Houtchens, Information Department, Ringling Museum of Art, Sarasota, Florida. Through her efforts an early draft of the chapter was reviewed by the retired bandmaster, Merle Evans, by Karl Wallenda, and by John Hurdle, the museum curator, for accuracy.

The author, who has covered many crime stories as a newspaper reporter, confesses to a suspicious nature. This inherent trait was further enhanced by his research for *Who Destroyed the* Hindenburg?, for *Women Who Spied* (New York: Dodd, Mead, 1967), and for other works involving crime, mystery, and intrigue such as his *The Week before Pearl Harbor* (New York: Norton, 1963). In other words, he is not fully satisfied of the accidental nature of the circus disaster, even though no evidence to the contrary has been unearthed.

Secondary research was accomplished through the files of the Hartford *Courant* (for which the author wrote when he was a student at Trinity College, Hartford) and the Hartford *Times.*

Emmett Kelly (who also has seen this chapter) published his life history in *Clown* (Englewood Cliffs, N.J.: Prentice-Hall, Inc., 1954).

Bradna, Fred. *The Big Top.* New York: Simon and Schuster, Inc., 1952.

Court, Alfred. *My Life with the Big Cats.* New York: Simon and Schuster, Inc., 1955.

Harlow, Alvin T. *The Ringlings.* New York: Messner, 1951.
Murray, Marion. *Circus.* New York: Appleton-Century-Crofts, Inc., 1956.
Plowden, Gene. *Those Amazing Ringlings and Their Circus.* Caldwell, Idaho: Caxton Publishers, 1967.

CHAPTER 9. EXPLOSION IN TEXAS CITY, 1947

The author is indebted to Brad Messer, editor of the Galveston *Daily News*, for making special research available, including photographs and a feature written on the twentieth anniversary of the explosion by Lawrence Lee, of the Associated Press.

Among others who assisted in the preparation of this chapter is Locke Mouton, now deputy chief of public affairs, Office of the Chief of Engineers, U.S. Army, who bears both the hurts and the memories of that night in Texas City; John G. Spano, manager of press relations and corporate public relations, the Monsanto Company, of St. Louis; and the public-relations staff of the U.S. Coast Guard, in Washington.

The writer is also grateful to the National Board of Fire Underwriters for granting permission to use a pamphlet, published in New York in 1947, "Texas City Disaster," and to reproduce the photographs therein. Other material:

Hearings, Texas City Disaster, U.S. House of Representatives, Judiciary Committee. Washington, D.C.: Government Printing Office, 1954.
Nation's Business, January, 1971. "Monsanto, Dealing with a Disaster."
Robinson, Donald B. *The Face of Disaster.* Garden City, N.Y.: Doubleday & Company, Inc., 1959.
U.S. Coast Guard, Board of Investigation, *Texas City Explosion, Galveston, 1947.*
Wheaton, Elizabeth. *Texas City Remembers.* San Antonio, Texas: Naylor Co., 1947.

CHAPTER 10. THANKSGIVING EVE TRAIN WRECK, 1950

Excepting the demimonde of ballad and folklore, the subject of train wrecks has been almost totally ignored in documented history. Although "Railroads" commands a generous card-indexing in most large libraries, the subdivisions are concerned with the development of routes and adjacent territories—i.e., the westward push of the iron horse in the last century—pure nostalgia aspects, or, at the other extreme, regulatory memoranda and rate structures by state and federal commissions.

This author encountered another facet, almost a phenomenon in disaster research. After an appreciable passage of time, the average survivor of a once-in-a-lifetime experience, irrespective of its catastrophic proportions, is only too anxious to talk about it. The author found, however, that no one living today who had walked away from Richmond Hill that Thanksgiving Eve had any inclination to reminisce (and those approached represented a more generous percentage than claimed by the average political polltaker).

One conclusion might be that even after twenty-two years the horror and stupid waste of that collision is still a repugnant memory. They do not feel, perhaps, that they were a part of significant history—as those aboard the *Lusitania* did when she was torpedoed in 1915 or those at Pearl Harbor the Sunday morning of the attack.

The most definitive and manifestly reliable reconstruction of the Richmond Hill wreck can be found in *Hearings*, Before a Subcommittee of the House Committee on Interstate and Foreign Commerce, 81st Congress (Washington, D.C.: U.S. Government Printing Office, 1951). This concise but complete report also contains the Interstate Commerce Commission findings, under the head "Ex Parte 176, December 18, 1950."

The subsequent reports of the Long Island Transit Authority would fill several volumes if bound together—and make for reading about as dreary as can be found anywhere, on any subject, with the conceivable exception of the so-called *Pentagon Papers* or the multipaged daily *Congressional Record*.

All of the New York papers, as might have been expected, covered the accident admirably, especially *The New York Times* and the *Daily News*.

For those interested in the history of the pioneering Long Island Rail Road, these two books in particular are suggested:

Seyfried, Vincent F. *The Long Island Railroad*. Garden City, N.Y.: Privately printed, 1961.
Smith, Mildred H. *Early History of the Long Island Railroad*. Uniondale, N.Y.: Salisbury Printers, 1958.

CHAPTER II. MIDAIR COLLISION, 1960

The bulk of the research for this chapter was done from the ten file cartons containing the results of the investigation conducted by what was then the Civil Aeronautics Board. This mass of testimony, including the interrogation of seventy-nine witnesses, flight recorder transcripts, diagrams, charts, and the mute evidence resulting from the reassembly, insofar as possible, of the shattered aircraft, was compiled after two principal hearings: the first in Brooklyn, three weeks after the accident, the second in Washington, June, 1961, at which time additional witnesses were subpoenaed and others recalled.

For making this material available, the author wishes to thank Ed Slattery, director of public affairs of the National Transportation Safety Board, who also served for many years in the same capacity with C.A.B., and Dorothy McKnight, in the accident inquiry section of this very large and manifestly important government entity, which in turn answers to the Department of Transportation.

The Air Transport Association of America made available fatality/passenger miles statistics, which are not only fluctuating but inviting of misinterpretation. In 1970 only two deaths were recorded by the United States scheduled airlines, a figure that jumped to 174 the very next year.

There are many yardsticks for measuring air safety or the lack thereof, including, as well, revenue aircraft flights and revenue plane miles. For example, there was a situation between 1968 and 1969 of somewhat decreasing revenue aircraft flights but increasing revenue plane miles—all of which perhaps can be made to add up to varying products.

Coincidentally, on assignment for *Argosy* magazine, the author researched and wrote the account of the Grand Canyon area collision in 1956 involving the same two airlines. In fact, at different times he worked in a public-relations capacity for both United and TWA, although he was not acquainted with any of the airline personnel involved in either of the two collisions.

The author further desires to express his appreciation to the Reverend S. Cangelosi, of St. Augustine's Church, Brooklyn; to Mrs. E. Ferrar Farrington, of New York City, the sister of Augustine

Ferrar; and to John G. More, a senior pilot with United Air Lines and longtime friend of the writer.

Captain More, who has handsomely survived the testing days of commercial air transport, has unintentionally penned the credo of today's senior pilot. "I enjoy my work probably more now than ever before because of the excellent type of product that I find I can now produce," he has written the author. "Sounds silly doesn't it, but it is quite true.

"There is a certain feeling of confidence that I know I have, and this extends over into the passenger compartment where those kind souls want to believe that I have it. . . ."

The passenger lists and additional eyewitness documentation have been cross-referenced among these principal newspapers: In Chicago, the *Tribune*; in Columbus, the *Evening Dispatch*; Kansas City, the *Star*; Los Angeles, the *Times*; New York, *The New York Times* and the *Daily News*.

Miller Field, on which the *Constellation* crashed, by happenstance was declared surplus in 1970 and handed over by the army to the General Services Administration. Its barracks and other dwelling facilities remain a public housing project. Rumors persist that the government wishes to swap the rather ample urban acreage for the famous old Willard Hotel, in Washington, D.C., also closed by its owners.

Across the Narrows from Staten Island, the rubble has long since been cleared from Sterling Place. The Pillar of Fire Church has never been rebuilt, as if in implied unwillingness to test again its inherent, wild portent. There remain spaces where certain tenements and stores were on December 15, 1960. Otherwise, Sterling Place is neither more nor less drab than it was a decade plus ago.

A postscript in the press in the spring of 1972 showed that the strain of instrument flight in congested areas is felt not by pilots alone. The newly formed American Academy of Air Control Medicine revealed some disturbing findings. For example, peptic or gastric ulcers were diagnosed in 36 of a group of 111 air traffic controllers who reported feeling ill during a one-year period. On a given day fourteen controllers at Chicago's large flight operations center, not far from O'Hare International, were off duty with ulcers. "When you are working with eighteen hundred to two thousand aircraft a day," said one controller, "and each of them may have a hundred to a hundred fifty people aboard, you are dealing with quite a few human lives."

The author also wishes to thank James A. Kennedy, Director, Public Relations, United Air Lines, for making available a long "memorandum" prepared by Charles F. McErlean, executive vice-president and chief operating officer of the company and presented in March, 1961, during the last minutes of the C.A.B. hearing. These are excerpts:

"The re-routing of 826 not only altered the time, distance, and course to Preston but, more importantly, superimposed upon the crew an additional burden of revising and adjusting in a critically short mileage span and time interval. On October 26, 1960, the New York Center had assured pilots that such last minute changes would not occur. In addition, traffic in this sector was not heavy, and no very good reason has been brought forth as to why a short-cut routing was given rather than allowing the standard routing, which permits a more appropriate interval of time for establishing a flight on Victor 123 prior to reaching Preston.

"It is significant that since the date of the accident the short-cut routing described has been discontinued."

"When 826 proceeded through the Preston intersection, the radar controllers did nothing. The facts are clear that 826 passed the Preston intersection *before* the New York Center radar controller advised the flight to contact Idlewild Approach Control and terminated Center radar service for the flight.

"When the radar controller at 1033:20 told 826 that he was terminating radar service it was a reassurance to the flight crew that their progress had been monitored on the radar scope up to that time and that there had been no deviation from the clearance given 826.

"Yet the fact is that at that precise moment 826 was already from eight to nine miles beyond Preston and the collision was no more than twelve to nineteen seconds away."

"While 826 was progressing as described, TWA 266 was being maneuvered by radar vectors directly into the path of the target moving up Victor 123 airway from the SW (part of UAL 826's amended route). La Guardia Approach Control radar controllers saw and continued to observe the moving target and warned TWA Flight 266 of the traffic on two occasions. No other effort was made by FAA personnel to determine what the traffic was or what facility was controlling it or to vector TWA 266 away from the traffic despite the fact that it is unusual for unidentified targets to appear in this area. . . ."

"It would not be possible for the United aircraft to have proceeded from one to three miles southwest of Preston at 1033:14 to the point of collision at 1033:32 to 1033:39. The distance is too great and the time interval too short. The physical facts make it apparent that 826 had already proceeded *past* the Preston intersection at the time the radar controller terminated radar service just seconds before the collision, but the controller did nothing. When 826 proceeded past its Preston clearance limit, it was an obvious deviation. Yet, the radar controller *who had not yet terminated radar service* made no effort to call and advise 826 of this fact . . . if the radar controller was performing his duties and maintaining radar separation and radar service, *why* was not a warning issued?"

"The facts of this record establish beyond any shadow of a doubt that Air Traffic Control in New York area had the capability of preventing the midair collision over Staten Island. To state it another way, on December 16, 1960, Air Traffic Control had the equipment, facilities and personnel which, if properly used, could have prevented the accident."

Note: The legal brief makes use of Greenwich mean or "Z" time. This has been translated back to Eastern Standard to avoid confusion.

CHAPTER 12. EARTHQUAKE IN ALASKA, 1964

The author received some excellent cooperation in the preparation of this chapter, especially from the staff of Senator Mike Gravel, of Alaska, including Dr. Douglas A. Jones, legislative assistant, who had served on President Johnson's special cabinet committee investigating the disaster, and Paula Slaymaker. Ed Naughton, now a member of the Alaska House of Representatives, happened to be calling on Senator Gravel late in 1971 when the author interviewed him.

He is again grateful to Ed Greene, who had assisted previously with the Texas City research, in making available material from the Office,

Chief of Engineers, including reports, photographs, and a Civil Defense film, "Though the Earth Be Moved."

Thanks also go to Brad Byers, National Academy of Sciences; and to James Landers and Mark Spaeth, U.S. Coast and Geodetic Survey.

The Saturday Evening Post carried a comprehensive article on the disaster later that year. Among the newspapers consulted were the Anchorage *Daily News* and the *San Francisco Chronicle*. Other material includes:

The Alaskan Earthquake. Office of Civil Defense, Office, Secretary of the Army, 1964.

Alaska's Good Friday Earthquake, A Preliminary Geologic Evaluation. U.S. Department of the Interior, 1964.

American Institute of Architects and Engineers Joint Council Report on the Restoration and Development of Alaska. Prepared under auspices of Federal Reconstruction and Development Planning Commission for Alaska, 1964.

Hulley, Clarence C. *Alaska, Past and Present.* Portland, Ore.: Binfords & Mort, 1970.

Impact of Earthquake of March 27, 1964 upon the Economy of Alaska. Office of Emergency Planning, Executive Office of the President, 1964.

Operation Helping Hand, the Armed Forces React to Earthquake Disaster. Headquarters Alaskan Command, U.S. Army, 1964.

Preliminary Report, Prince William Sound, Alaskan Earthquakes, March–April, 1964. Seismology Division, Coast & Geodetic Survey, 1964.

Response to Disaster, Federal Reconstruction and Development Planning Commission for Alaska (established by order of President Lyndon Johnson), 1964.

CHAPTER 13. BUFFALO CREEK, RAPID CITY, AGNES, 1972

No attempt was made—indeed time did not permit it—to research this chapter in depth. For that matter the vantage point of perspective was totally absent.

However, the author is indebted to the staffs of Representative Ken Hechler, of West Virginia (Buffalo Creek); Senator George McGovern, of South Dakota (Rapid City); and to the Executive Office of Emergency Preparedness for Rapid City and Agnes. Otherwise, he was dependent upon press reports, largely in the Washington *Post*, the Washington *Evening Star*, and the Kansas City *Star*.

Washington, D.C. was never "virtually isolated," as the NBC *Today Show* proclaimed one morning. The author, who lives in suburban Bethesda, Maryland, remembers changing towels at the west-exposure windows the night the heaviest rains came through and throwing them into the dryer in order to be ready for the next mopping. Otherwise, to most of the nation's Capitol, the downpour meant largely the tedium of commuting via slow detours. Although the Potomac River facade of the John F. Kennedy Center was submerged up to some twelve feet, no permanent damage was done or scars left. Wilkes-Barre, Scranton, and Elmira are another story.

Three general books on disasters not specifically listed in other chapters should be mentioned:

Banner, Hubert S. *Great Disasters of the World.* London: Hurst & Brackett, 1931.

Corbett, Edmund V. *Great True Stories of Tragedy & Disaster.* New York: Archer House, 1963.

Newton, Douglas. *Disaster, Disaster, Disaster.* New York: Franklin Watts, 1961.

Index

199